Women Wil

Women Willing to Fight
The Fighting Woman in Film

Edited by

Silke Andris and Ursula Frederick

CAMBRIDGE SCHOLARS PUBLISHING

Women Willing to Fight: The Fighting Woman in Film, edited by Silke Andris and Ursula Frederick

This book first published 2007 by

Cambridge Scholars Publishing

15 Angerton Gardens, Newcastle, NE5 2JA, UK

British Library Cataloguing in Publication Data
A catalogue record for this book is available from the British Library

TABLE OF CONTENTS

List of Illustrations vii
Acknowledgements viii

Chapter One 1
Why Women Willing to Fight?: An Introduction
Silke Andris and Ursula Frederick

Chapter Two..15
The Neomyth In Film: The Woman Warrior from Joan of Arc
to Ellen Ripley
Barbara Creed

Chapter Three..38
Just a Woman Among the Cyborgs: Sarah Connor in *Terminator 2:
Judgement Day*
Catherine Summerhayes

Chapter Four 55
Past, Present, Future: Finding Treasure in the Lives of Lara Croft
Ursula Frederick

Chapter Five..78
Violence, Duty and Choice: The Military Woman in Contemporary
Hollywood Cinema
Yvonne Tasker

Chapter Six..95
Million Dollar Baby: The Making and Unmaking of the Female Boxer's
Body
Silke Andris

Chapter Seven 112
Fighting to be Seen: Looking for Women in the West,
from *The Searchers* to *The Missing*
Martin Flanagan

Chapter Eight 128
Belles with Attitude: Genealogies of the New Hollywood
Wisecracking Action Heroine
Polona Petek

Chapter Nine 144
Zhang Ziyi, "Martial Arthouse" and the Transnational *Nuxia*
Leon Hunt

Chapter Ten 161
Superheroine: Women as Martial Artists in Early Twenty-First
Century Cinema
Catherine Driscoll

Bibliography 178
Filmography 189
Contributors 197
Index 200

LIST OF ILLUSTRATIONS*

One: *Women Willing to Fight* poster...1

Two: Milla Jovovich in *The Messenger: The Story of Jean of Arc* (1999)........15

Three: Sigourney Weaver in *Aliens* (1986)...29

Four: Linda Hamilton in *Terminator 2: Judgement Day* (1991)......................38

Five: Angelina Jolie in *Lara Croft Tomb Raider: The Cradle of Life* (2003)....55

Six: Demi Moore in *G.I. Jane* (1997) 78

Seven: Hilary Swank in *Million Dollar Baby* (2004)..95

Eight: Cate Blanchett in *The Missing* (2003)...112

Nine: Sandra Bullock in *Miss Congeniality 2: Armed and Fabulous* (2005)...128

Ten: Zangh Ziyi in *House of Flying Daggers* (2004) 144

Eleven: Uma Thurman and Gordon Li Jiahu in *Kill Bill: Vol. 2* (2004).........149

Twelve: Maggie Cheung in *Hero* (2002)...161

Thirteen: Halle Berry in *Catwoman* (2004) 167

* All images, besides Illustration One, are reproduced courtesy of The Kobal Collection. Illustration One was produced by The Centre for Cross-Cultural Research, The Australian National University.

ACKNOWLEDGEMENTS

There are several people we would like to thank for their support and encouragement throughout the development and completion of the *Women Willing to Fight* volume. First and foremost we are extremely grateful to the contributors, not only for their incisive work but their good-natured willingness to participate in this project and to remain steadfast and responsive at all times.

We would like to thank the Centre for Cross-Cultural Research, Australian National University, which helped us lay the foundation stone of this book by funding the "Women Willing to Fight" workshop in 2005. Thanks to all the participants and presenters of the workshop for their invaluable comments, theoretical insights and inspiration. We are grateful to Alison Macgregor, Carolyn Strange and Jill Julius Matthews who made important contributions to this event. We sincerely appreciate the Centre for Cross-Cultural Research, and its director Professor Howard Morphy, for support in numerous aspects of this publishing venture. Monique Skidmore deserves special mention for advising and guiding us through the unknown vagaries of publishing. We are also deeply indebted to Pip Deveson and Katie Hayne for helping to shape and finish this volume. Various forms of assistance were provided by John Carty, Suzanne Groves, Alison French, Maria-Suzette Fernandes-Dias, Jodi Parvey, Victoria Parkinson, Celia Vuckovic, Alan Wyburn and Karen Westmacott. Thanks are due to all the friends, family members and colleagues who have helped and encouraged us in publishing this book including Michael Andris, Jeanette Avins, Olwen Beazley, Roger Frederick and Karin Schneider Andris. Our appreciation is extended to the editorial staff at Cambridge Scholars Publishing, particularly Amanda Millar, for her support, patience, and encouragement throughout this project. We are grateful to Alison Walker at The Kobal Collection for her kind assistance with illustrative material.

CHAPTER ONE

WHY *WOMEN WILLING TO FIGHT?*: AN INTRODUCTION

SILKE ANDRIS AND URSULA FREDERICK

Figure One: *Women Willing to Fight* poster

Cinema, especially the action and adventure genre, has always been prone to sudden eruptions of physical violence and aggression. Yet rarely have we seen such an abundance of women spoiling for a fight than in the New Hollywood cinema. The 1980s and 1990s heralded the arrival of powerful muscular heroines the likes of Ellen Ripley (*Alien* quartet [1979, 1986, 1992, 1997]), Sarah Connor (*The Terminator* trilogy [1984, 1991, 2003]) and G.I. Jane (*G.I. Jane* [1997]). They set a new course for the representation of fighting women as strong in will, intellect and spirit as well as corporeal form. Together with more contemporary realisations such as Lara Croft (*Lara Croft: Tomb Raider* films [2001, 2003]), Gracie Hart (*Miss Congeniality* films [2000, 2005]), Maggie Gilkeson (*The Missing* [2003]), Maggie Fitzgerald (*Million Dollar Baby* [2004]) and the international success of the *nuxia*, the martial arts heroine appearing most notably in *Crouching Tiger, Hidden Dragon* (2000), *Hero* (2002) and *House of Flying Daggers* (2004), the woman willing to fight has become both a multi-faceted characterisation and definitive signature of late twentieth and early twenty-first century Hollywood cinema. This volume gathers together nine essays to analyse a representative sample of this contemporary lineage of well-recognised and popular characters.

The woman willing to fight is by no means a new film character.[1] Her antecedents have appeared in numerous guises since Kate Kelly brandished a gun in the first feature length film of the silent cinema, *The Story of the Kelly Gang* (1906).[2] Traces of warrior women and revolutionary figures of myth, archaeology, art, literature and early history are discernible in many of the representations of the fighting woman in film,[3] yet the figure at the centre of this volume eludes easy categorisation. It is not the purpose of this volume to imprison the woman willing to fight in a comfortable archetype. Our aim, rather, is to explore the diverse contemporary and globalised manifestations of the human, singular, female fighter who is physically willing to engage in her fight and in doing so contribute to the investigation of the fighting figure as a foci of film study.

These attributes—contemporary, human, singular, female who is willing to engage physically in her fight—function as an analytic lens through which the contributors can respond directly to the numerous cinematic representations in the New Hollywood era that portray women to be violent, aggressive and powerful, often militantly engaged in physical fights (and often victorious over their opponents) whilst contextualising their subjects in the wider history and recent development of the active heroine in film. They take this important figure as a guide for refocusing and refining ongoing discussions about the place of gender, action, violence, narrative and bodily spectacle in contemporary film. While the following set of essays expand, by analysis, our understanding of this figure, they also offer a series of intellectual engagements that move towards demarcating a place for her—in terms of origins, influences and meanings—within the context of contemporary cinema and society.

The Contemporary Female Fighter:
Genres and Transnational Flows

The Hollywood action and adventure genre has become an important vehicle for the representation of the fighting woman. Indeed, the increased inclusion of women in action roles has been a key in conceptualising how this particular "genre" has evolved in recent times. Some contributors discuss representations of the fighting woman in Western, sports, military, and martial arts films and demonstrate how the figure of the fighting woman is shaped by their distinctive narrative modes and conventions. Conversely, authors are also concerned with the question of how the woman willing to fight challenges generic traditions and form.

Martin Flanagan explores the representations of women, broadly, and fighting women, more specifically, in the genre of "The Western". In his discussion of *The Missing*—a reworking of John Ford's canonical *The Searchers* (1956)—Flanagan shows how the genre has traditionally established oppositional relationships between women and men leaving little or no place for the portrayal of the independent, active woman with ambition and agency. *The Missing,* argues Flanagan, while expanding the representation of women in Westerns by transcending some important gender dichotomies, simultaneously sets clear limits to an utterly radical reinvention of their role by carefully leaving some dichotomies intact.

Yvonne Tasker's focus is another male-dominated preserve: the military or war movie. Her analysis of *G.I. Jane* illustrates in detail what is required of an assertive woman in the combat genre. The emphasis on physical training, humiliation and testing of the female body demonstrates, according to Tasker, how the boot camp story of *G.I. Jane* makes physical struggle emblematic of sexual struggle, and further, how the transformative quality of a woman's body holds the key to her success and potential for gender equality. A similar reading is found in Silke Andris' exploration of the female experience of entering the so-called male domain of boxing.

The arena of the fighting woman is quite clearly delineated in certain spheres of the action and adventure cinema, such as Westerns, military and boxing films. Yet other female fighting characters may be found across the broad spectrum of Hollywood productions, including sci-fi, comedy and romance, in addition to films that may also be broadly classed as action and adventure films: martial arts, criminal/detective, thriller/mystery films. The prevalence of the fighting figure offers the opportunity to consider female characters within the context of a specific type of fighting, just as it demands a comparative and cross-culturally inclusive framework for discussion.

While this volume builds on the existing literature examining the fighting woman in action and adventure cinema it goes beyond the analysis of particular genres.[4] In this way, it explores the complexities ascribed by different narratives as alternative vehicles for the female fighting figure. Such an approach is necessary for considering New Hollywood films which are characteristically multi-generic or hybrid. Globalisation, coupled with innovations in technology such as CGI animation, has seen the emergence of films that defy the parameters of established genres, creating *genre-hybridity* across the cinematic landscape. Recent advances in the digital arts, with their renewed emphasis on visual style and form, have had further impact on the way the Hollywood film industry operates to create and distribute film and associated audiovisual material. Consequently, fighting women in film are *crossing over*; circulating around and within increasingly complex networks of global media. Leon Hunt and Catherine Driscoll, in their analyses of the "Martial Arthouse" of Hollywood/Asian crossover, explore the potential effects of a transnational cinema on Hollywood as a two-way flow. There is little doubt that Hollywood's global reach has provided opportunities of expanded scale for International talent and more obscure auteurs. Yet the flourish in *wuxia* (martial chivalry films) and other martial arts references is less indicative of a Hollywood turn towards cross-cultural filmmaking as it is a reflection of individual trans-Pacific connections. Both Driscoll and Hunt allude to the influence of particular film identities and industry players in forging the orientations of this alliance. Clearly, growth in the production and reception of Hollywood filmmaking has been advanced by new technologies of distribution and consumption.

The ongoing development in multi-media platforms, online environments and mobile devices, as well as home-info/entertainment systems has altered the viewer's experience of cultural forms. While partially shifting the cinematic event from the traditional movie theatre it has laid new ground for the accessibility, reception, and analysis of the fighting woman in film. This in turn has created enormous scope for the appreciation and reiteration of the fighting woman as heroine icon. Ursula Frederick points to the creative interactions that audience participation with such icons may yield. She observes that while retaining a celebrity poster-girl status, Lara Croft also operates with an "Everywoman"-like appeal. This belies singular readings of hyper-sexualised form precisely because of her conglomerate identity as multi-media text and her ambiguous conflation of "norms". Not only have developing technologies serviced existing demands for film production and consumption in different ways, new media has, according to Frederick, also challenged our expectations of cinema and reconfigured our understandings of nationality, gender, body and the self.

Through their collective focus on the contemporary female fighter, these essays, offer an important avenue for the analysis of particular genres, their traditions as well as their developments. They also contribute to an understanding of the broad spectrum of Hollywood productions, consumptions and transnational flows, including the strong presence and influence of martial arts fighters in the action cinema.

The Woman Willing to Fight as Human Being

Many of the action heroines of contemporary cinema are supernatural figures. The focus of this inquiry is the human female fighter. The exclusion of the supernatural fighter, we believe, illuminates the agency and ambitions of the woman who, more or less, chooses to fight. By contrast, the supernatural fighter is generally depicted as fighting to fulfil her destiny. Her fight is pre-determined and her ability to fight merely a means to a fated end. And while the viewer may often feel assured that the female heroine cannot lose, regardless of her mortal or supernatural status, the difference between them may be best described as a distinction in the way the fighter's motivational cause and power are acquired. The skills and "tricks" of the supernatural figure are characteristically passed on through a mystical transference of magical ability (*Elektra* [2005]), genetic manipulation, or procreative inheritance (*The Incredibles* [2004], *Aeon Flux* [2005]). Whether it is a gift or a curse, the superheroine's fight is rendered as an act of bestowal.

The flesh and blood woman in film that is willing to fight is marked with a signature difference. From the outset her fight is inflected with a different order of agency. The choice to fight is her *own*, even when it appears shaped by other characters, or a sense of manifest destiny. This depiction of agency has a powerful effect on the meanings one may attribute to the fight and the ways in which the parameters of the fight is circumscribed. It also raises the fundamental question of motivation—why does this woman fight? For whom or what is she fighting for?

The answers to these questions may be connected to her experience as a mortal being and it is often this very humanity that constitutes her cause. On the one hand, she is often fighting for the preservation of humankind or for what it means to be human (*Alien* [1979], *The Terminator* [1984], *Lara Croft: Tomb Raider* [2003]). On the other hand, her fight may be portrayed as emerging from personal motivations that come with being human (strong emotional feelings of love, revenge, maternal feelings or ambitions and dreams). The mortal fighter, however, unlike her supernatural counterpart, must operate within the

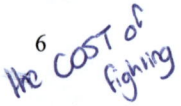

limitations and vulnerabilities of the human body. Barbara Creed shows how the death of the heroine is instrumental to the interpretation of her fight and her conceptualisation as saint and martyr. The fighter's mortality, Creed argues, enhances the magnitude of her challenge—it foregrounds the possibility and threat of death and has significance with regard to the choice, effect and outcome of her fight. The extent to which the death of the female fighter is aligned with failure and the way the success of the fight is measured is central to Silke Andris' discussion of the making and unmaking of a fighter's body in *Million Dollar Baby*. Andris asks what happens when a boxer's dream goes awry and the body seems to "fail" the heroine in the end? Thus, the fighter's mortality points to the magnitude of her fight.

While the greater emphasis in the volume is on the female fighter as a mortal human being, several of the papers explore the boundaries between the "real" and the "unreal" woman. They examine the inherent powers or potential of the body and the way it may be trained and transformed. In her analysis of *Terminator 2: Judgement Day* [1991] Catherine Summerhayes considers how the anxieties of posthumanism are played out—as human versus machine—through the characters of Sarah Connor and the Terminator, played by Arnold Schwarzenegger, and their respective transitions between being human and machine. Summerhayes uses the dynamic between these characters to draw attention to the way conventions are used to train and challenge the viewer in recognising particular (cross-over) performances of gender, cyborgs and humans. While Summerhayes study points out that Sarah Connor's humanity is instrumental in grounding the viewer's experience to the narrative force of the film, she also addresses the way the woman willing to fight is rapidly morphing in representational form. She is becoming anime, game avatar, replicant, cyber-heroine. Polygons, pixels, disembodied voices or transgenic beings—these are the future bodily manifestations of the woman who is traditionally portrayed as virgin, martyr, warrior or bitch. It is through this amalgam of competing manifestations—the nature of what she becomes and what she represents—that the female fighter becomes a contested site.

The Woman Willing to Fight as Singular Figure

Fighting in film has always been a gendered arena. The action film, according to Gallegher, "has historically been a 'male' genre, dealing with stories of male heroism, produced by male filmmakers for principally male audiences".[5] Prior to the 1980s, the majority of female characters in action films were limited to roles accompanying, or oppositional to, the leading action hero; appearing as the sidekick, comic foil or "evil" other. When women were central to the plot it was rarely as the sole and independent protagonist of the film. The

MARVEL

femme fatale and outlaw occasionally dominated the stage but the majority of fighting women were relegated to the background, as the buddy or support, or as part of a team. The singular female fighter began to emerge in 1970s and 1980s characters, such as the gun-toting "mama" of gangsta/blaxploitation (*Cleopatra Jones* [1973]) and the "final girl"/victim of the slasher/rape-revenge film (*I Spit on Your Grave* [1978]). By the early 1980s the fighting heroine with distinctly global gravitas had claimed centre screen. Thus despite their rich ancestry, in terms of sheer number and diversity of expression, these stand-out women are arguably a product of late twentieth century blockbuster production.

This singular fighter, has become a core protagonist through which the action narrative is played out. She holds the plot together, drives the narrative and shapes the fight's purpose and style with her own distinctive persona. The fight has become both personified in the singular fighter and individuated through her. The star persona status of the actress further supports this impression. Leon Hunt's attention to Zhang Ziyi illustrates the fighting female persona as it develops in conjunction with the rising stardom of a particular actor (currently favoured for her Asian-Hollywood action cross-over appeal). That certain celebrities are attuned to the reiterative powers of the female fighter within their own star persona and film careers demonstrates a degree of demand for such portrayals. Alongside Zhang Ziyi, there is a burgeoning group of award-winning actresses for whom the strong singular woman/fighting female character is easily identified. Included amongst these alumni are Jodie Foster, Angelina Jolie, Halle Berry, Geena Davis, Jamie Lee Curtis, Meryl Streep and most recently Charlize Theron and Hilary Swank. That star biographies may be so significantly shaped by the presence of the fighting woman is further suggestive of the growing presence and place cut out for, the fighting woman on screen. Frederick demonstrates in her essay how the audience may be complicit in the construction and demand for such (iconic) characters and the possibilities for subjective identification that they offer.

Being the centre of attention is to be at the core of the action, yet, paradoxically, the singularity of the female fighter tends to isolate her within the film's frame and narrative. She is often forced to assert herself in places that exclude other women and which, therefore, present her as an exception to the norm. That is, she displays exceptional behaviour often physically challenging the dominant (patriarchal) order. In other configurations of fighting her challenge is less about decimating the dominant order and more about securing a certain place or status within it. Demi Moore has performed all of these scenarios. Consider her portrayal of a corporate femme fatale in *Disclosure* (1994) with the role of female soldier in *G.I. Jane* or with the avenging, fallen angel in *Charlie's Angels: Full Throttle* (2003). In all three films she is an exceptional character, fighting alone and often choosing to do so.

However, as Polona Petek points out, a fighter's singularity does not necessarily mean that she must be solitary. She observes that Asian fighters are often seen to forge alliances with other women and men to improve their odds in combat. This doesn't detract from their core status, rather it keeps them *in* the fight and thus at the centre of the film. By comparison, Western female fighters are often represented alone, not easily accepting help or making friends. Petek proposes that this behaviour is both a reflection of Western individualism and symptomatic of her outlaw status and the failure of (male) colleagues to come to her aid.

The Fighter's Body: Transformation and the Embodied Fight in Female Form

The contemporary cinematic articulation of the energised, tough female figure centres on the body of the female performer. Traditionally, male action stars required a radical bodily transformation to act the part of the protagonist, whereas a women's central role was largely conveyed through make-up and costuming. The recent transformation of the female body into the exemplary body of the fighter has set the contemporary female fighter apart from her predecessors. In order to survive and, more importantly, to triumph over her opponents, the modern heroine does not only "speak up" but also trains her main instrument, her body, in combat techniques and martial arts.

Her empowerment intensifies as she masters fighting skills and the effective handling of fighting tools. The spectacle of physical exercise, such as training sequences and fights, indicate the fighter's readiness for physical confrontation and reveal her dedication to personal transformation and embodiment. In his discussion of the *wuxia* Leon Hunt alerts us to the fact that every fight is a form of practice since it helps to refine skills and psychologically prepare the fighter for the final confrontation with an opponent. Even in the absence of such preparatory spectacles, the fluidity of her movement and strategic manoeuvring imply a certain investment of time and training. This investment is clearly visible, after the action stops, in the contours of her sculpted fighter's body and in the marks of workout—wounds, muscle, scars—that her body bears. Thus, the body becomes both a weapon and a target. A circumstance which clearly spurs on the physical action and violence as well as propelling the narrative structure comprising fights, chases and explosions. In short, the fighter's body is the key element of the film's exceptional spectacle and narrative force.

The female fighter's body has appeared in film in a variety of forms donning a vast array of apparel, ranging in physique from the "musculine" tough to the androgynous,[6] and in costuming from the discreetly attired to the scantily-clad ultra-femme. Costuming alters the visual impact of the fighter's appearance, reinscribing or disguising shapes, revealing the tone and colours of muscle and skin and emphasising contours and gestures. Clothing can distract from the sincerity of the fighter's intentions (Petek), be used as a weapon (Driscoll), as defensive armour (Creed) or integrated with life-saving technological mechanisms (Frederick).

Uniform apparel, such as combat clothing, may be used to evoke either the culmination or the sublimation of an individual identity. Thus, costumes and with it the acquisition and handling of weapons are crucial markers for an analysis of a fighter's embodied transformation. These points are well exemplified in Petek's discussion of *Miss Congeniality* (2000) which promotes a particular notion of the body as an instrument to be moulded and shaped into something different or "other". The customised body makeover of Sandra Bullock's character—from tomboy to beauty queen—shows how costuming plays a significant role in signalling to the viewer this process of "becoming". The expression of the "other" through the "self" is akin to the alter egos of the superheroine, a point alluded to by Catherine Driscoll. The significance of the superheroine's costume, Driscoll explains in her account of the catsuit, lies in the ways the costume reflects the transformation of her body into a weapon, incorporating metal claws and pointed boots, as well as the fashioning of herself as a wounded body.

Like the props and setting, the protagonist's clothing may be influenced by the aims and codes of a particular genre to visibly link her to the iconography of that genre. The smoothing finish of the cling-wrap style bodysuit, for example, indicates the futuristic or technologically superior, in part because it adapts hard edges into vector-like graphics but also because it is linked to the lush, yet minimalist, style of cyborg or other science-fiction creatures (such as Pris, Trinity, Elektra, Aeon Flux, Leeloo to name a few).[7] Even with the repetition of such fashions, however, specific manifestations of styling become iconically embedded within a fighter's distinguishable character, particularly when it evokes their fighting attitude or is coupled with a particular gesture. Rather than fetishising the fighter's surface qualities, this emphasis on appearance demonstrates the extent to which a fighter's sensibility is encoded within their representation.

If we stop to consider the most memorable and monumental apparitions of these figures, we find ourselves returning, not surprisingly, to the well-circulated freeze-frames of climactic moments. It is in these stills, that the character is encapsulated and, significantly, it is her fighting persona that is conveyed. It is in the details of these representations that one finds the analytical clues to describe how fighting becomes embodied in a woman. Most obviously, these images present fighting as a female and (sometimes also) feminine activity—an emphasis that has initiated debate and controversy given that physical fighting is often seen as behaviour that is harmful and causes injury. Although fighting need not express violence, it is largely in the physical embodiment of challenge that the "fight" is construed. While the contributors to this volume mainly devote their attention to women who fight on physical terms, the emotional, psychological and spiritual states of being cannot be easily dislocated from the embodied encounters they engage in. That being said, the fighting woman may also be seen in the Norma Raes, Karen Silkwoods, Erin Brockovichs and Vera Drakes of film—women for whom the primacy of the fight is not expressed through the corporeal frame.[8] There is no exchange of fists, feet or weapons; these women use alternative routes to gain their goals, yet they seem equally willing to fight and may be motivated by a similar cause to their physically combative sisters. These women, although beyond the scope of this volume, deserve further scholarly attention. *Kill Bill   Scalpleye u. grave*

Death and injury are not the only consequences of the (physical) fight in film. The threat of injury, harm and death are often as disturbing as the physical attack or its outcome and can result in psychological harm. Some films present and explain the heroine's action as a result of extraordinary circumstances, adopting the rationale of self-defence—sometimes this motif is expanded to include the defence of the whole of humanity. Other films fold violent actions into the definition of a particular profession (soldier, boxer, police officer, tomb raider) and thus present it as a legitimate means to an end. The extraordinary lengths to which some films go to explain (away) the actions of the fighting women reveals the unease, horror and threat caused by her physical actions and violence. Entangled in the efforts to situate her actions and behaviour are complex socio-cultural and ideological processes which mark, at different times and in different social and cultural contexts, some actions and behaviours as violent and others as not, making violence an extremely expansive and interesting notion to work with.

Equally varied are the audience's responses to the actions of the fighting female. Some viewers might refuse to look, others enjoy violence and find it fascinating. Some dismiss it, shriek or laugh—violence causes visceral effects in the audience. Fighting, in its diversity of expression—Western showdowns, boxing fights, slapstick falls, acts of noir sadism, and balletic martial arts confrontations—necessarily elicit different responses and therefore demand different kinds of critical approaches to explicate and interpret the function, context and representational form of the physical behaviours displayed by the female fighter.

The Theatre of a Woman's Fight: Narrative and Spectacle

The display of practiced martial movement often deserves the label martial "art", qualifying the movement as especially skilled. The martial art fight scene tends not to be created through the postproduction editing together of a series of otherwise unconnected attacks and parries, rather, the actors, and sometimes stunt doubles, execute authentic attack and parry techniques from different martial art traditions (Aikido, Wing Chung, Hapkido, Tai Chi), which in their filmed form can extend to a great number of attacks and counter-attacks. These theatrical fights are highly stylised and although they look authentic they are not necessarily closer to "real" fights than those produced in postproduction. The cunning of the fight as spectacle is that "it begins and ends with its own artifice; as such, spectacle is simultaneously both display and on display".[9] The primary purpose of these theatrical fights sometimes ceases to be the immediate damaging or overpowering of an opponent and, instead, "becomes a highly stylised and choreographed performance conveying a narrative of conflict through 'representational movement".[10] In this way, spectacle becomes a narrative device.

This dimension of visual display is of course not limited to the spectacular display of the body but may also be seen in films where fighters might use weapons and other machinery. One prominent example is the so-called "technical thrills movies" which are laden with special effects. As Andrew Darley claims, "such films are, arguably, the principle emblem of the recent turn to image and form".[11] Technical thrills movies, martial arts and other action movies seem to award spectacular imagery and action equal status with respect to their narrative content and meaning. Most importantly, as Darley explains, "this does not mean that narrative content or ideological significance disappear in such films" but rather that this "dimension of visual display is now so distinctive that it requires recognition and analysis as a formal aesthetic element in its own right".[12] Hence, analyses of the spectacle of the fight—the fighting techniques, methods and tools as well as the ways the fight is presented—are important to an understanding of the meanings and motivations of the female fighter's actions.

The spectacle of the fighting female is a source of significant controversy amongst feminist and gender studies scholars. Laura Mulvey's postulation of a generic gender equation in classical film narratives constitutes the nexus of much of the feminist criticism. At the core of Mulvey's analysis lies the claim that representations of gender traditionally centre around binary oppositions of active/male and passive/female, encouraging a "male gaze" which leads to the eroticisation of the female star.[13] It juxtaposes, as Tasker explains, a peculiarly charged idea of a "male subject of power and agency" with a "female object of powerlessness and passivity" which, in turn, imposes clear limitations on the interpretation of visual display, especially the visual display of women in film.[14] Women are simplistically connected to eroticism, while men are fixed in the position of onlookers. The female, non-heterosexual and non-eroticising gazes and desires are, inevitably, unexplored and overlooked. Thus, as Tasker suggests, "what once may have provided an enabling critical concept, now seems almost completely disempowering in its effects, operating as a term which fixes and analysis within the restrictions of the very gendered system it seeks to question".[15]

This is not to deny that female fighters display their bodies, provocatively or otherwise. They are often depicted in various states of undress, exposing their well-conditioned musculature and physique. Their bodies become the core focus of the camera, turning them into objects of an appraising gaze. The resulting images have given rise to the "wholly justified objections of various groups—in recent years blacks, women, and gays, in particular—to the ways in which they find themselves stereotyped [and objectified] in the mass media".[16] Some, therefore, argue that the depictions of female fighters in film leave a lot to be desired in terms of encapsulating a feminist ideal. These contemporary representations, despite their ample configurations, are often seen as instances of (feminist) backlash, if not defeat.

Others are far more optimistic. They believe that the growing presence and popularity of the fighting women in film in recent years is a creative force that is mediating and generating a new cinematic form which is promoting transgressive and empowered visions of femininity. The wide scale diffusion of the female fighter across film genres and cultures is, they argue, testament to this phenomenon. It is perhaps no coincidence then that this transgressive figure is encoded with "rebellious", "lawless" and "revolutionary" traits and is thereby subject to the appeal of such qualities (*Aeon Flux, Run Lola Run* [1998], *The Messenger: The Story of Jean of Arc*). The female fighting figure is certainly presented as "outstanding" in her apparent rebelliousness, and the representations of her transgressive acts are often judged as signs of female liberation and empowerment. However, to take sides within these debates, or to position a particular female fighter within these debates is problematised by the figure's own fluidity or ambiguity. She (successfully and sometimes unsuccessfully) embodies paradoxical or contradictory extremes such that feminist, as well as post-feminist, notions of femininity and empowerment are displayed within a single persona.

Our woman willing to fight is therefore a valuable barometer of the ambivalence that marks the production, representation and circulation of femininity in our present socio-cultural climate. She is therefore not only inherently marked by her willingness to fight but also by the ways she herself spurs on a lively and at times heated battle over her meanings, readings and interpretations.

Notes

1. Steve Neale, "Action-Adventure as Hollywood Genre", for example lists a number of serial queens, two-reel westerns and early aviation films as belonging to a deep trajectory of warrior women representation. In *Action and Adventure Cinema,* ed. Yvonne Tasker (London: Routledge, 2004), 75. See also Tasker, *Spectacular Bodies: Gender, Genre, and the Action Cinema* (London and New York: Routledge, 1993), 1.
2. The image of Kate Kelly brandishing a gun is in fact one of the few surviving fragments of the *The Story of the Kelly Gang* (1906), the world's first feature length film.
3. From the numerous examples to draw, Amazons, martyrs and outlaws are amongst the most cited classes in film and televisual media. Mary Anne Doane argues that the femme fatale's emergence as a central figure around the time of the Industrial Revolution, is a clear indication of the extent of the fears and anxieties prompted by shifts in the understanding of sexual difference in the late nineteenth century." *Femmes Fatales: Feminism, Film Theory, Psychoanalysis.* (New York : Routledge, 1991), 1-2.
4. See for example: Yvonne Tasker, *Spectacular Bodies*, or Hilary Neroni, *The Violent Woman: Femininity, Narrative, and Violence in Contemporary American Cinema.* (Albany: State University of New York Press, 2005).
5. Mark Gallagher, "I Married Rambo: Spectacle and Melodrama in the Hollywood Action Film", in *Mythologies of Violence in Postmodern Media*, Christopher Sharett (ed.) (Detroit: Wayne State University Press, 1999), 199.
6. Tasker, *Spectacular Bodies.*
vii. Occuring in *Blade Runner*, 1982, *The Matrix* (1999), *Elektra* (2005), *Aeon Flux* (2005), *The Fifth Element* (1997) respectively.
viii. Occuring in *Norma Rae* (1979), *Silkwood* (1983), *Erin Brokovich* (2000), *Vera Drake* (2004) respectively.
9. Andrew Darley, *Visual Digital Culture: Surface Play and Spectacle in New Media Genres*, (London and New York: Routledge, 2000), 104.
10. Aaron Anderson, "Kinesthesia in Martial Arts Films: Action in Motion," *Jump Cut,* 42 (December 1998): 1-11. (reprinted online *Jump Cut*, No.48, winter 2006).
11. Darley, *Visual Digital Culture,* 102.
12. Ibid., 103.
13. Laura Mulvey, *Visual and Other Pleasures*, London: Macmillian, 1989.
14. Yvonne Tasker, *Spectacular Bodies,* 116.
15. Ibid., 115.
16. Richard Dyer, *The Matter of Images: Essays on Representation,* (London and New York: Routledge, 1993) 11. We have specifically set Hollywood as our site of production. This is in part due to the global reach of the texts it produces and because of the power of those texts as a barometer of mainstream sensibilities. It is disparaging then to note how few of the fighting protagonists from which we could draw are women of

colour, queer, transgender, or even non-American. The obvious exception is the marked influence of the Asian cinema.

CHAPTER TWO

THE NEOMYTH IN FILM:
THE WOMAN WARRIOR FROM JOAN OF ARC
TO ELLEN RIPLEY

BARBARA CREED

Figure Two: Milla Jovovich in *The Messenger: The Story of Jean of* Arc (1999)

There is a scene in Jean Luc Godard's 1962 masterpiece, *Vivre Sa Vie* that presents a daring comparison between two universal and mythical female figures—a Saint and a Prostitute. *Vivre Sa Vie/It's My Life: My Life to Live* (1962) tells the story, in twelve episodes, of Nana (Anna Karina), a Parisian wife and mother who wants to become an actor but instead drifts into prostitution. In episode three, Nana goes to the cinema to see Carl Dreyer's 1928 silent classic, *La Passion de Jeanne d'Arc*. The comparison between the two women might appear at first glance a little tenuous. What might a twentieth century prostitute have in common with an early fifteenth century saint?

Joan of Arc is heralded as the saviour of her country, a fighting woman and a fierce virgin who refused to compromise her beliefs in order to save her life. Nana is a pretty but otherwise unremarkable woman who saves no one and lives a life that some would regard as immoral. Critics have commented on the way both directors have recorded, in close-up, the faces, looks and private grief of the two women. Nana sits perfectly still, tears falling down her face as she looks up at Joan who also weeps silently, realising she is soon to die. Joan tells one of the clergy that her deliverance will be her death. Nana is herself drawn to the idea of death. In the first episode, she tells her estranged husband two things. "I exist too!" and "I want to die". This indeed is Nana's fate. In the final scene the pimps and gangsters she has defied shoot her in a street brawl. Because Nana is an ordinary woman, living an unexceptional life and earning her living as a prostitute, it does not follow that her life should not be viewed in heroic terms. Although she does not set out to defend her beliefs with her life, this is what happens. Nana is on an existential journey in which she, a lone figure, is trying to save her own soul.

Rarely if ever are these two characters, Joan of Arc and Nana, discussed in relation to the mythical journey of the female hero. Joan is viewed as a warrior and saint but not usually discussed in such terms. Yet, although very different from their male counterparts, both women in their own ways are heroes each undertaking the classic journey, in which each struggles against obstacles in the quest for self-identity. Joan and Nana each reject the roles society has carved out for them. They both set out on a journey, struggle against dominant stereotypes of female sexuality, and come into conflict with male power in their attempts to define their own identities. This analysis could equally apply to a range of female characters in the cinema, literature, myth and popular culture from Joan of Arc to Mata Hari, Nana, Madame Bovary, Thelma and Louise, Ellen Ripley and Sarah Connor. These women represent, respectively, a range of female roles including the conventional stereotypes of saint, prostitute, femme fatale, wife and mother. If we re-define all of these roles in term of the female hero, that is, the woman who undertakes a mythic journey in order to discover her identity, values and beliefs, then all could be seen, in varying degrees, as heroic.

There is another reason why Nana might have been drawn to the cinema that night to watch Joan of Arc. As well as identifying with her suffering, Nana may well have admired Joan, regarding her as a female hero to emulate. Nana herself wanted to be a film star—perhaps she wanted to star in roles such as Joan of Arc. Godard represents the cinema as a place where young modern women, adrift in the personal anonymity of the twentieth century, can go to identify with and worship their own female heroes. A contemporary form of myth-making, the cinema celebrates ancient mysteries in a modern way; particularly the ritual journey of the heroine and hero portrayed in larger-than-life images, flickering in the half-light in a communal place where strangers come together to embark upon a journey into the unknown, sharing similar fears and desires. This essay will explore the representation of female heroism in the cinema. It will set down a new structure—the neomyth—with which to analyse the journey of the heroine as a mythic quest. Finally, it will focus on an analysis of one form or transformation of the heroine—woman as warrior.

Woman as Hero

Why has so little been written on woman as hero or saviour figure in film?[1] Why is woman rarely seen as embarking on a journey of self-discovery, which, like the journey of the male hero, assumes mythic status? Why is her journey often minimalised, discussed mainly in relation to the tropes of melodrama, domesticity, madness, romance and sexuality? Why have feminist writers and critics spent so much time debating female heroism (as I am doing here) when male heroism is taken as an unproblematic category? The immediate and obvious answer is that in a phallocentric world, the heroic journey has become thoroughly masculinised. There are no formal narrative structures to use as a template for the mythic journey of the female hero. Consequently, discussion and analysis of hero myths have historically been produced in relation to the male. These narratives invariably draw upon masculinised spaces (exterior, outside domains), masculinised tests of courage (battle, combat), masculinised obstacles (the enemy as "other"), masculinised desire (for the femme fatale, forbidden woman), masculinised victories (saving the kingdom/preserving the status quo) and masculinised rewards (power, fame).

I am not arguing, however, that the female hero should be "masculinised" so that her journey becomes the same as the journey of the male hero. Nor am I arguing that when the heroine does take up arms, she becomes a pseudo-male. Rather, I am arguing that we need to define a completely new structure for the heroine's journey—not just the journey of the female action hero but of the hero in *all* of her manifestations. When woman decides to embark on a journey of discovery, which might involve the taking up of arms or occupation of traditionally masculinised spaces, she does so for reasons that can only be fully understood in relation to her traditional role as an "other" in a phallocentric world. While there should be room for areas of overlap with man's journey, the structure of woman's heroic journey needs to be one which draws, in the main, on feminised notions of space, courage, obstacles, desire, victory and outcomes. Freud argued that there is only one libido (and I agree) but this view must take into account that society attempts to regulate the various ways in which the libido speaks its fears and desires and this in turn affects its many forms of expression—for female and male hero alike.

Joseph Campbell's Monomyth

The classic work on this topic is Joseph Campbell's *The Hero with a Thousand Faces*. The cover states that this is "a brilliant examination, through ancient hero myths, of man's eternal struggle for identity".[2] Campbell described the journey of the mythological hero as cyclical and argued that it enjoyed universal applicability, that is, every hero myth to some degree followed a similar pattern which he described as "the monomyth". Drawing on Jungian and Freudian psychoanalytic theory, particularly the notion of the archetype, Campbell elaborated the structure of this journey as based on three key stages: *Departure*, *Initiation* and *Return*, each of which was divided into various sub-categories.

It is important to stress that Campbell's analysis focuses on *ancient* hero myths. He is primarily concerned with the past and its relevance, or lack of, to the present. In the Epilogue, in which he discusses "the hero today", Campbell laments the collapse of the "timeless universe of symbols". In the modern secular state, with its focus on scientific rationalism, "all of these mysteries have lost their force; their symbols no longer interest our psyche".[3] "Not the animal world, not the plant world, not the miracle of the spheres, but man himself is now the crucial mystery".[4] Man's journey is now one of individual self-discovery in which the existential forces of "personal despair" dominate the quest. Campbell would probably not agree that the cinema offers an alternative mythic space that celebrates ancient and modern mysteries in a new way. Although Campbell's analysis focuses on the past, his ideas, particularly the structure of the hero's journey as represented in the monomyth, has exerted a marked influence on popular Hollywood cinema through the writings of Christopher Vogler.[5]

Although Campbell refers to both male and female heroes (and the "hero" as male and female), his focus is predominantly on the male figure. Woman does not fit comfortably into the structures of the hero's mythic journey as set down by Campbell. He cites as instances of the hero's journey, the narratives of King Arthur, Buddha, and Odysseus; for the heroine's journey he cites the stories of an unnamed Arapaho girl from a North American tale and the unnamed princess from Grimm's fairy tale of *The Frog King*. The above cited male heroes are universal figures of heroic stature, all possessing proper names; the female heroes are unknown and unnamed figures whose stories share some elements in common with those of the male figures, but also cry out for a different set of terms or structures to provide us with a proper understanding of their journeys. In addition, the monomyth in several of its phases is gender specific. For instance under "Initiation" there are two phases, which refer specifically to gendered aspects of the hero's journey: "the Meeting with the Goddess" and "Woman as Temptress". In relation to the latter, the hero is called upon to resist the temptress and her many seductive offerings that are designed to lead him astray before he can continue his journey. He is the active, questing figure, whereas woman is positioned as an "obstacle" in his path, a trial or temptation to be overcome.[6]

Finally, the monomyth ignores the different faces of the female hero. In the section entitled "Transformations of the Hero", Campbell discusses the hero under a series of personae: the hero as warrior, the hero as lover, the hero as world redeemer, the hero as saint. All of his examples are of male heroes whom he selects from myths from around the world. These include Jesus, Buddha, Charlemagne, Krishna, the Irish warrior, Cuchulainn, and the Pueblo hero, Water Jar Boy. He does not discuss ancient female heroes such as Echo, Psyche, Demeter, Penthesilea, Antigone, Joan of Arc, Boedicea or Heloïse. This suggests that woman cannot be easily assimilated into Campbell's monomyth because it does not recogn ise that the female hero from earlier epochs might follow a different path from that of the male. Central to the heroine's journey from all eras are events associated with her generative or reproductive life (love, desire, the body, pregnancy, birth, motherhood) as well as her vocational life (saint, prostitute, wife, mother, boxer, soldier).

Some feminist writers have criticised narratives that focus on woman's sexuality as "reducing" woman to her body, but I believe that woman's physicality and sexuality, like man's, plays an essential part in her journey, influencing its direction and outcome. This is evident in the Joan of Arc narrative in which Joan proudly asserts her identity as a virgin in *Dishonoured* (1931), in which Dietrich in the role of Mata Hari defends her identity as a prostitute, and in *The Terminator* (1984) and *Terminator 2: Judgement Day* (1991) in which the heroine, Sarah Connor, courageously embraces her identity as a mother. Rather than dismissing the part played by the heroine's sexuality, it is more productive to define this as central to her quest. Such an approach means that we are compelled to reject the monomyth and formulate a separate, but related, mythic structure for the female hero.

The Neomyth

I have used the term "neomyth", or new myth, to describe the structure of the heroine's journey. Although this paper focuses on the cinema, the neomyth can equally be applied to the female hero of myth and legend, literature, popular culture and the arts. The neomyth is divided into three parts and consists of eight main structures that apply, in varying degrees, to all manifestations of the female hero in the cinema from the silent period to the present. The key paths in the heroine's narrative journey are: *Journey, Threshold,* and *Self-discovery.* The various paths/events do not necessarily occur in the order set down and of course may vary in terms of their importance from film to film. This structure is designed to focus on aspects of female heroism that might otherwise be ignored. Discussion of the neomyth also reveals that the female hero is different from the male in a number of key ways. The female hero is not necessarily a battlefield figure—particularly in the twentieth century. As well as warriors in the field such as Joan of Arc, Ellen Ripley and Xena, there are women who qualify as warriors because of their single-minded devotion to a cause; women who are prepared to sacrifice their lives in order to defend others, their personal beliefs and the course of action they have chosen. In this context female heroes, whose fight is almost always with the phallocentric order, include heroines as diverse as Thelma and Louise, Dian Fossey, Veronica Guerin and Vera Drake.

The Neomyth – Journey of the Female Hero

Part 1: The Journey
i.   The Call
ii.   The Cause
iii.   Obstacles

Part 2: The Threshold
iv.   The Paternal Symbolic Order
v.   The Threshold

Part 3: Self-discovery
vi.   Assertion of a New Identity
vii.   Female Hero as "Other"
viii.   Death & Rebirth

Part 1: The Journey

Stage i: The Call
"The Call" refers to an event that changes the status quo for the heroine. It may change her everyday life causing her to alter her usual circumstances (*Vivre Sa Vie* [1962], *Now Voyager* [1942], *Pretty Woman* [1990], *Kill Bill:, Vol.I* [2003]); or it may refer to a call to pursue a personal ambition (*The Red Shoes,* [1948], *My Brilliant Career* [1979], *A League of Their Own* [1992], *Girlfight*

[2000]); or it may refer to a call to arms in which the heroine must physically fight to save her life or the lives of others or the nation (*Joan of Arc* [1948] [1999], *Alien* [1979], *The Terminator* [1984]), or it may refer to a social or political or species injustice in which the heroine fights for a cause (*The German Sisters* [1981], *Vera Drake* [2004], *The Constant Gardener* [2005], *Gorillas in the Mist* [1988]).

Stage ii: The Cause
The heroine is called to fight for a cause for which she is prepared to place her life in danger or even to sacrifice her life. This is true of Joan of Arc, Ellen Ripley, Thelma and Louise, Mata Hari, Veronica Guerin and Vera Drake. She is also called to fight for love—as distinct from sexual desire. In contrast to the hero, love is more likely to play a central role in her journey. She may have to sacrifice her own personal life for that of her child or family (*Mildred Pierce* [1945], *Stella* [1990]); she may be forced to separate from her child (*The Old Maid* [1939]); or protect her unborn baby or child whether her own or a surrogate (*Chinatown* [1974], *Blue Velvet* [1986], *Terminator 2* [1991], *Aliens* [1986], *Kill Bill: Vol. 2* [2004]). In the love story, including "the woman's film", her emotions become an integral part of her quest. Sometimes this is because the loved one is not necessarily a socially acceptable figure, making her journey even more perilous (*Marnie* [1964], *November Moon* [1984], *Far From Heaven* [2002], *Mulholland Dr.* [2001]).

Stage iii: Obstacles
The heroine invariably encounters obstacles along the way—events that test her resolve, determination and courage. In contrast to the hero, the obstacles invariably put her into an antagonistic relationship with the male symbolic order. These obstacles may include emotional issues such as pressures or threats from an overbearing parent or partner, or a hostile protagonist (*Now Voyager*, *Rebecca* [1940], *The Burning Bed* [1984]); internal doubts which cause anxiety, hesitation and delay (*The Hours* [2002], *Portrait of a Lady* [1996], *The Piano* [1993]); institutional and legal obstacles (*Joan of Arc*, *Blonde Venus* [1932], *Blue Steel* [1990]); physical threats of violence (*Alien*, *The Terminator*, *Kill Bill. Vols 1 & 2*); or barriers created by the fact she is a woman (*Gilda* [1946], *Million Dollar Baby* [2004], *G.I. Jane* [1997]).

Part 2: The Threshold

Stage iv: The Paternal Symbolic Order
This passage takes two major forms: one is open conflict with the paternal symbolic order, the other is endorsement of the same order. Three different but

related female heroes emerge in terms of their relationship with the symbolic order: the anti-heroine, woman warrior and action heroine. In contrast to the hero's journey, the heroine's sex and gender are often central to this stage.

(a) Anti-Heroine:

In many films, the heroine comes into direct conflict with an authority figure (male or female) or institution (religious, legal) that represents the values of a patriarchal world. I have used the term "anti-heroine" to describe her.[7] Conflict with male authority is central to her struggle and in the end she almost always renounces phallocentric values. The heroine may refuse to adopt the proper feminine role in relation to dress, career, motherhood and procreation (*The Ballad of Little Jo* [1993], *My Brilliant Career*, *Blonde Venus*); or she may reject heterosexuality (*The Killing of Sister George* [1968], *Desert Hearts* [1985], *Boys Don't Cry* [1999]); or she may reject marriage and monogamy (*Mata Hari* [1931], *Vivre Sa Vie*, *Pretty Woman*). The femme fatale of film noir almost always comes into conflict with the paternal symbolic, testing the limits of the law. This conflict almost always leads to her death. The anti-heroine may also, but not necessarily, enter the category of the woman warrior or action heroine. The male anti-hero rarely falls into this category. Male protagonists often enter into conflict with a father figure, but almost always in order to take his place.

(b) Woman Warrior:

A significant number of anti-heroines also belong to the category of woman warriors. The woman warrior exhibits exceptional bravery and intelligence and is prepared to die for her beliefs. Although prepared to die, the women warrior is not necessarily a soldier or fighter.[8] Nor is she necessarily an expert with weapons or skilled at martial arts and other forms of combat. In the end, her battle is frequently with the dominant male order. She comes into direct conflict with male beliefs and values which she sees as inimical to her own ethical position. In the majority of instances (but not always) the warrior woman sacrifices her life rather than submit to a system in which she does not believe. Further, the woman warrior who sacrifices herself—does so not in the traditional sense—in order to protect the kingdom—but rather to make clear her total and complete opposition to the phallocentric values of the existing society. In many instances, her sacrifice guarantees her transformation from mortal woman to myth.

Women warriors in film include Joan of Arc, who clashed with Church and State; Mata Hari, who rejected male ideals of patriotism and war; Diane Fossey, who turned her back on anthropocentric values; Thelma and Louise, who rejected Patriarchy and the Law; Ellen Ripley, who refused to obey the wishes of Science and the Military; and Vera Drake, who opposed the laws of Church and State. It would appear that, while male heroism is defined in relation to preservation of the male symbolic order, female heroism is, in the majority of cases, oppositional. In many contexts, the male hero signifies fixity, the female fluidity. Unlike the classic male hero, she rejects the phallocentric, fixed nature of the world, preferring instead to question the meaning of patriarchal civilisation and its values. A key exception to this is the woman who fights for her country in time of war in order to defend its values and way of life. Films that explore war-time female heroism include *Carve Her Name with Pride* (1958), *Odette* (1950), *A Town Like Alice* (1956), *Plenty* (1985) and *Charlotte Gray* (2001). These heroines fill the role of woman warrior in that they are exceptionally courageous and are prepared to sacrifice their lives for their ideals.

From Joan of Arc to Ellen Ripley, the woman warrior frequently assumes the form of a female saviour figure whose journey through many films and genres over the twentieth century has assumed mythic status, despite the fact that it has rarely, if ever, been mapped. The woman warrior is a multi-faceted character who can signify many faces of female heroism. She can adopt a variety of roles including those of maiden, virgin, mother, prostitute, saint, spy, soldier and fighter. Despite her name, the woman warrior does not necessarily (but may) engage in physical violence. She may be, but is not necessarily, an action heroine. She is a warrior in the sense that she is the champion of a cause, one that she considers right and just.

(c) Action Heroine:

Unlike the woman warrior, the action heroine, as her name implies, is always skilled in physical combat and an expert with guns or heavy weaponry.[9] She often wears a uniform and is a member of the policeforce, the armed forces, or a secret agent or intelligence officer. Because of the increasing prominence of the action heroine in contemporary films, it is necessary to distinguish her from the woman warrior. The action heroine is closely related to the woman warrior, but her journey does not encompass the range of roles open to the woman warrior. Nor does she assume a mythic status as do many women warriors. In addition, the action heroine does not usually come into serious conflict with patriarchy; her struggle is more likely to be represented as a fight against crime and corruption or she might have embarked on revenge against a particular male as in the *Kill Bill* films. Here the action heroine and woman warrior differ—whereas the woman warrior almost always comes into opposition with male power and patriarchal culture, the action heroine, although also on a quest, usually supports the existing phallocentric social structures. Thus, the action heroine is not necessarily represented as an "other", that is, as a serious threat to patriarchy. In the context of this discussion, Charly Baltimore (Geena Davis) in

The Long Kiss Goodnight (1996), Clarice Starling (Jodie Foster) in *Silence of the Lambs* (1991), Sarah Connor (Linda Hamilton) in *The Terminator* and Megan Turner (Jamie Lee Curtis) in *Blue Steel* are all more accurately described as action heroines than warrior women. The two categories however are often inter-related. In the *Alien* films, the Ripley figure commences as an action heroine in the first of the series but by the third film, *Alien³* (1992) she moves into the role of woman warrior when she denounces the Military and sacrifices her life to save planet earth from a possible destruction by the aliens. Thus, Ripley is both action heroine and woman warrior .

Stage v: The Threshold
The female hero experiences a turning point in which her resolve becomes fixed on pursuing her new path of action. Once she overcomes the obstacles, inner or outer, that threaten her journey, she crosses the threshold and enters her new world fully. The nature of the crossing varies markedly from film to film. In some her entire journey is about the process of crossing the threshold (*Germany Pale Mother* [1980], *A Question of Silence* [1982], *Thelma and Louise, In the Cut* [2003]) while in other films she crosses the threshold with determination and ease (*Alien, Kill Bill: Vols 1 & 2, The Terminator*), becoming more fixed in her resolve as she continues on her journey. Crossing the threshold is closely related to a new awareness of her changing beliefs and identity.

Part 3: Self-discovery

Stage vi: Assertion of a New Identity
Central to the heroine's journey of self-discovery is her awareness of her new identity, which is in a state of fluidity and change. Such self-realisation is often closely related to Stage vi when the heroine comes into conflict with the values of the dominant patriarchal order. In some films she develops a new code of ethics in which she rejects the values of society (*Vera Drake, Thelma and Louise* [1991]) or tries to change the status quo in her battle against corruption (*Veronica Guerin* [1998]). In other films she learns to understand her changed sexual desires and asserts her right to enjoy, or experiment with, other forms of sex (*The Night Porter* [1974], *The Piano* [2003], *In The Cut, Romance* [1999]). In the rape-revenge film (*I Spit on Your Grave* [1978], *Lipstick* [1976], *Violated, Base-Moi* [2000]) she takes revenge for her own rape rather than fall back on the law or a male avenger. In rejecting the values of family and marriage, she asserts the right to a non-monogamous, independent lifestyle (almost all film noir, *Body Heat* [1981], *The Last Seduction* [1994], *Gilda, Mulholland Dr.* and television shows such as *Sex and the City*).

Stage vii: Female Hero as "Other"

After the heroine embarks on her journey, crosses the threshold and asserts her own beliefs, she is frequently represented as an "other"—that is, a woman who patriarchal society sees as a threat to its own stability. Society may "other" her as a heretic (*Joan of Arc* films), prostitute (*Dishonoured, Blonde Venus, Klute* [1971], *Pretty Woman*), criminal (*Thelma and Louise*), rebel (*My Brilliant Career, Adam's Rib* [1949]), lesbian (*The Fox* [1968], *The Children's Hour* [1961], *Monster* [2003], *Boys Don't Cry*) or a misguided deviant woman (*Far From Heaven*). For the heroine, becoming "other" is represented as central to her search for identity. Ironically, it is her new status as "other" (rebel/deviant/outsider) that also makes her appealing to her audience. Some films may represent her otherness as appealing or sympathetic without denigrating her outsider status (*Calamity Jane* [1953], *Girlfight* [2000]). Whereas the male hero is often a rebel or outsider, his outsider status is not usually denigrated to the same degree or in similar ways. The male outsider is rarely a prostitute, hysteric, careerist, or sexual siren. It is the female hero's journey, her becoming "other" , that clearly distinguishes her narrative from that of the male hero. This is why her portrayal is different from that of the male and why she should never be reduced to a "pseudo" male, even, or particularly when, she takes up arms.

Stage viii: Death & Rebirth

The heroine may experience an actual or symbolic death. The heroine of film noir (*Double Indemnity* [1944], *The Postman Always Rings Twice* [1946], *Lady from Shanghai* [1948], *Chinatown*), who deviates from the proper feminine role, almost always dies in the final scene. So too did the heroine of the woman's film who transgressed the proper feminine role (*Dark Victory* [1939], *Humoresque* [1946], *Beyond the Forest* [1949]). During the thirties, forties and fifties her death was required by the censorship code of the day. In contemporary films, women who step outside their proper roles still sometimes die (*Million Dollar Baby, Boys Don't Cry*). The woman warrior who comes into conflict with the patriarchal order frequently (but not always) dies. This is true of the *Joan of Arc* films, films that star woman as prostitute (*Dishonoured, Mata Hari, Camille* [1936], *Vivre Sa Vie*) and more recently *Thelma and Louise*, and the *Alien* quartet. However, death should not necessarily be seen as signifying failure—rather death in many films represents a symbolic act that reinforces the extreme action needed to highlight the corruption at the heart of the symbolic order. Death ushers in rebirth. Female protagonists such as Thelma and Louise are symbolically reborn at the moment of their death; the final freeze-frame that depicts the joyous faces of the rebel duo endows their images with an iconic larger-than-life quality. Ripley from the *Alien* quartet is perversely resurrected in the final of the series as a clone. In the majority of films, however, the heroine's death and rebirth form a symbolic function as she metamorphoses into a new being with a new identity. Having successfully embarked on the journey, she emerges at the end transformed by her experiences. Unlike the male hero, as defined by Joseph Campbell, the structure of "return and reintegration" into the community is not as relevant to all manifestations of the female hero, particularly the woman warrior. Because she often opposes the values of phallocentric values of patriarchal society, she does not always seek reintegration. Instead, she may face execution, seek death or remain an outsider.

Woman Warrior as Hero

Joan of Arc is the quintessential woman warrior. Soldier, virgin, prostitute, witch, heretic, hysteric, schizophrenic, saint, patriot—Joan has attracted a rich collection of appellations over the centuries. The myth of Joan of Arc is as strong as it was at the time of her execution in 1431 when she was charged with heresy and burnt at the stake. She was just nineteen years of age. Since its inception, the cinema has been irresistibly drawn to her story.[10] Because there are two detailed accounts of Joan's trial that have survived, the various films have been based on scripts that attempt to recreate the events and dialogue with some accuracy, although of course fictions prevails in many instances.

There have been over thirty films, fiction and documentaries, devoted to Joan's story. Eight were silent versions, which appeared between 1898 and 1928. The most important was Carl Dreyer's highly influential *La Passion de Jeanne d'Arc* of 1928. Renee Falconetti, in her one and only screen appearance, starred as Joan in what is still regarded as an incomparable performance. There have been over twenty sound versions, the most recent made in 1999. These were Christian Duguay's popular television miniseries, *Joan of Arc* (1999), and Luc Besson's *The Messenger: The Story of Joan of Arc* (1999). In the main, the numerous versions depict Joan in battle fighting courageously alongside her soldiers, as well as portraying her trial and execution. Ingrid Bergman won an Oscar for her portrayal of Joan in Victor Fleming's 1948 version. She played Joan again in 1954 for Roberto Rossellini in *Giovanna d'Arco al Rogo*. Otto Preminger's *Saint Joan* (1957), which starred Jean Seberg in her first role, was based on George Bernard Shaw's famous play. Conducting a national contest to find the right actress, Preminger auditioned over 3,000 young women for the role, finally selecting the unknown Jean Seberg. Robert Bresson's 1962 film of the trial, *Le Procès de Jeanne d'Arc/ Jean at the Stake*, ranks alongside Dreyer's film for its artistic power. Of all the women warriors in the history of the cinema, Joan's motives in taking up arms are well known. She wanted to free her country from English rule. To achieve this she had to drive out the English and bring the Dauphin, the uncrowned King, to Rheims for his coronation.

Joan of Arc as Archetypal Woman Warrior in Film

The Joan films emphasise the gendered nature of Joan's journey, struggle and death, emphasising what happens when the warrior is a woman. She threatens the male symbolic order in a variety of ways. Joan's androgynous looks and attire are particularly threatening. Joan claimed that her voices instructed her to wear men's attire, to take up arms and become a soldier. Although Joan did live and fight like a man, she made no attempt to disguise the fact that she was a woman. This is particularly evident in the name she chose for herself and always used—Jehanne la Pucelle, the Maid. As Warner explains, "Pucelle means 'virgin,' but in a special way, with distinct shades connoting youth, innocence and, paradoxically, nubility".[11] Despite this, the crowd demanded to see her body, before her burning, to assure itself that *La Pucelle* was a woman. When her critics attacked Joan for wearing male attire, her defenders, such as the Queen Mother, cited the many female saints who lived as men. These included Saints Margaret, Theodora, Perpetua, and Eugenia.[12] According to Warner, Joan's dress "protected Joan…against men, and it attacked men by aping their appearance in order to usurp their functions".[13]

It could be argued that by dressing in men's clothing Joan was a pseudo male and as such confirmed male power. If Joan had not insisted that she was *la Pucelle*, the Maid, this argument might hold. In reality, however, Joan was an androgynous figure who threatened male power because she made it very clear that a woman can fight like a man yet retain her female identity. This concept has been carried through to the *Alien* films in which Ripley fights like a man and wears masculine attire, yet reveals strong protective maternal feelings towards Newt, the orphaned girl she protects. Similarly, the heroine of *The Terminator* films is a mother and an heroic fighter who wears masculine attire and Veronica Guerin is both wife and mother and courageous fighter. This argument strikes at the heart of the patriarchal view that woman's maternal nature cancels out her potential for heroic action. To argue that these warriors are pseudo men is to endorse an essentialist view of gender based on a binaristic logic which defines men and women not as different but as opposites.

Critics have argued that many of the films about Joan appeal to the sadistic gaze of the male viewer who derives perverse pleasure from watching a woman suffering at the stake.[14] Carl Dreyer's film has been criticised for its intense emphasis on Joan's suffering. Rather than present scenes of her courage in battle or her power as a leader, Dreyer films her trial and execution. He adopts a stark, minimalist style with close attention to ordinary details such as the scene where

Joan's hair is shaved. The film consists mainly of close-ups of Falconetti's face filled with anguish, and the faces of the members of the Inquisition who are interrogatingher. It has been suggested that Dreyer's emphasis on her prolonged suffering (her tears, expressions of grief) opens up a space for the deployment of a masochistic identification on the part of the viewer, but Falconetti's controlled performance (she does not tremble, scream, or attempt to cry out) undercuts the possibility of interpreting her suffering as masochistic. The effect is to gender her suffering as female but because she endures it with the utmost bravery, her heroism assumes a specifically feminine identity. This in itself undermines patriarchal notions of bravery as a male virtue. Joan of Arc is not simply a warrior, she is a warrior woman. Strangely, feminist writers and critics have rarely discussed Joan of Arc as a female hero of the cinema.

Ellen Ripley as Woman Warrior

The story of Joan of Arc has exerted a profound influence on the cinema's representation of female heroism. The extent to which her qualities have influenced the cinematic ideal of the female heroine is most evident in the re-creation of Joan in the figure of Ellen Ripley, heroine of the four immensely popular *Alien* films (1979-1997) starring Sigourney Weaver as the woman warrior. Like Joan, Ripley has androgynous looks, cropped hair and wears male attire, including armour. Like Joan, Ripley at first fights for the phallocentric order. She is an ethical figure who performs heroic deeds, is betrayed, burnt alive and resurrected. Even the scenes of immolation are similar. As flames consume Joan, she clutches a cross to her bosom: as Ripley falls into the fiery furnace in *Alien*[3] (1992), she clutches the body of the alien baby to her breast as it emerges from her body. Amy Taubin has pointed to the Joan of Arc and Ripley parallels in the immolation scene. Taubin refers to it as "the Jeanne D'Arc scene" with its "fetishised close-ups" and Ripley's "ecstatic abandonment to the inevitable".[15] Joan of Arc and Ellen Ripley are archetypal woman warriors who exhibit extraordinary courage and personal integrity for a higher ideal: the former to save her nation, the latter to save planet Earth. In so doing both women come into conflict with representatives of the male symbolic order.

Figure Three: Sigourney Weaver in *Aliens* (1986)

Feminists have applauded Ripley as the first female hero to step outside the conventional role assigned to women in popular film.[16] Some have argued that while she is exemplary in many respects, she ultimately fails the test because she is a pseudo male. Ros Jennings argues that, in the final sequence of *Aliens*, Ripley is represented as a female sex object for the voyeuristic gaze of the male viewer and that this compromises her role as action hero.[17] Diana Dominguez argues that Ripley and Sarah Connor from the Terminator films, "eventually repudiate the feminine, becoming, in effect, sexless and less 'human' mirrors of male action heroes".[18] She concludes that Ripley is a parody of the male action hero because of the way the last two films (*Alien³* and *Alien Resurrection*) strip her of the femininity and humanity with which the first two (*Alien* and *Aliens*) had gradually endowed her. They do this "by giving her a shaved head in the third film, and making her an alien-human hybrid in the fourth".[19] "They are neither women nor men; they look suspiciously like women, but only display masculinised tendencies and behaviours".[20] Dominguez refers throughout her essay to a notion of "a true female action hero" and "true sexual difference"[21].

> Will the "real world" ever be ready for that seemingly unimaginable creature: a woman who can be nurturing, loving, sexual, vulnerable, and feminine, but also "kick-ass", able to overpower and kill the "bad guys", and save the world (or universe) —all at the same time? [22]

It is difficult to see why a "true female action hero" must embody the traditional feminine qualities of being "nurturing, loving, sexual, vulnerable and feminine"[23] as well as embody traditional male qualities of heroism, that is, kick-ass aggression and violence. Dominguez draws on an essentialist argument about what constitutes proper "womanhood" (and "manhood") which is itself problematic because it falls back on a binaristic view of what signifies masculinity and femininity. Nor does she demonstrate convincingly that Ripley does lose her humanity and femininity. The argument of *Alien Resurrection* is that Ripley, despite the fact that she is a clone or alien-human, is more ethical than her human counterparts. She remains as committed to principles of nurturance and salvation in her cloned state as she was, prior to her death, in human form. The desire to establish a "true female action hero" precludes the possibility that there may be many variations or faces of the female action hero and that such a concept retains its strength from the fact that it is fluid and variable. As Ripley says at the end of the series: "I'm a stranger here myself".

The *Alien* Quartet and the Neomyth

If we analyse Ripley's journey in relation to the stages of the neomyth, and across the four films, we can see that she is more appropriately described as a woman warrior. In all four films she is pitted against the symbolic order which assumes various faces: the Company/ Military/Government/Science. The aim of the latter is to capture the Alien Queen alive and return her to earth in order to study her deadly defence mechanisms. Ripley rejects this goal and attempts to destroy the Alien Queen rather than run the risk of the Alien and her brood taking over and destroying the earth. In so doing, Ripley opposes the symbolic order. She believes her mission is to save the planet, and to achieve this she is prepared to die. Given her mythic stature and her belief in a higher ideal than the State, she is, in the end, more appropriately described as a woman warrior. In the first film, *Alien*, Ripley fills the role of the classical action hero; drawing on her exceptional skills, she must destroy the monster single-handedly and pass through a series of tests before emerging victorious at the end. In *Aliens*, the second of the quartet, Ripley's mythic journey begins to assume a feminine structure. She finds an orphaned girl, Newt, and quickly becomes her protector and surrogate parent. To Ripley, Newt represents many things—a helpless child, an abandoned daughter, herself, the next generation. Newt symbolises for Ripley everything that she wants to protect, even if it means sacrificing her own life in the attempt. Just as Demeter descended into the underworld to search for her daughter, Persephone, Ripley also descends into the depths to find Newt.

The classical motif of *Aliens* prepares us for a new aspect of Ripley's mythic journey. Whereas Ripley might well be described as an action hero in the first two films, by *Alien³* she has come to occupy the position of a woman warrior. In the final scene, Ripley hurls herself into a fiery inferno in order to kill the infant alien growing inside her body. In so doing, she destroys the Company's plan to take the creature back to earth. As Taubin notes, "By choosing to hurl herself over the brink rather than bend to the will of the state, the hero guarantees her transformation from woman to myth".[24] In the final film, *Alien Resurrection*, Ripley, resurrected as a clone of herself, is now an "alien" of a different kind. Nonetheless, she retains her sense of identity and her inviolable ethical code. Like Joan of Arc, Demeter/Persephone and other classical heroes, Ellen Ripley is reborn. Part human, part alien, part cyborg—Ripley has crossed a series of dangerous thresholds, and transformed into a new being, "a stranger" to herself and to Earth. The final scene makes it very clear that—as we might have suspected all along—the true "alien" or monster of the quartet is woman herself.

Dishonoured: Prostitute as Warrior Woman

Mata Hari, the infamous WWI spy whose name became synonymous with that of a fatal temptress, seems an unlikely candidate for the title of woman warrior. Mata Hari has been the subject of films, novels, plays, biographies, anime series and video games. There have been at least four films about Mata

Hari, including Rex Ingram's *Mare Nostrum/ Our Sea* (1926), the 1932 version that starred Greta Garbo, and Curtis Harrington's *Mata Hari* of 1985. More recently, historians have argued that there is little, if any, evidence to suggest she was in fact guilty of spying for the Germans in WWI. During her trial Mata Hari is supposed to have said: "Harlot, yes—but traitor, never!" Mata Hari's capture and execution certainly improved the failing image of the French counter-espionage services for whom the war had not been going well. The name "Mata Hari" rapidly became synonymous with that of femme fatale, the fatal woman whose uses her sex to destroy men. Greta Garbo made her name even more famous in the 1931 film, *Mata Hari*. In the same year, Marlene Dietrich starred in Joseph von Sternberg's *Dishonoured*, based loosely on the life of Mata Hari.

Marlene Dietrich gives an astonishing and subversive interpretation of the legendary spy, Mata Hari. Because so little is known about the life of the actual woman, Margaretha Zelle, Sternberg and Dietrich have taken the freedom to construct or invent her life and character in terms of their own interests and desires—although they retain aspects of Mata Hari's own life such as the belief, popular at the time, that Mata Hari refused to be blindfolded when she faced the firing squad. Together they create Mata Hari as an intelligent, glamourous and courageous woman who, in the end, places herself in conscious opposition to the forces of militarism and nationalism. As with all seven of the films Sternberg and Dietrich made together, *Dishonoured's mise-en-scene* is filled with mystery—shadows, veils and drapes encase almost every scene.

Dietrich is Marie Kolverer (code name X27) who exchanges her life as a prostitute for that of a spy in the service of the Austrian Secret Service. Dietrich portrays Marie Kolverer/Mata Hari as a beautiful, mysterious woman. In the opening sequence, she says with an enigmatic smile: "I'm not afraid of life. Although I'm not afraid of death either". She easily seduces men in order to learn their secrets and flies bravely into enemy territory at night, where she continues her work, disguised as a maid. In the end, she challenges the power of the military establishment that has hired her in the first place. Throughout, she appears to be mocking the men who try to control her. Her disruptive presence is matched by the discordant music she plays on her piano. Although she appears to betray her own side (the Austrian-German alliance), because she values love over war, her deeper reason is her disgust with the forces of nationalism and militarism in general.

Before her execution, in the final hours in her cell, a priest asks her if he can grant her a final wish. She says: "Could you possibly help me die in a uniform of my own choosing?" "What would you call a uniform of your own choosing? She replies, "Any dress I wore when I served my countrymen instead of my country". Like Joan, Marie placed great emphasis on her clothing. Joan refused to relinquish her male attire for women's clothing because she regarded herself as a warrior who needed to dress in battle gear to fight effectively. Marie refused to relinquish her courtesan's dress because at the end of her life she would have no truck with military dress that she associated with male aggression and war. Thus she asserted the virtues of love and sex over those of hatred and death. In a sense, both women select clothing that threatens the values and beliefs of the male institutions that they have rejected. Joan is the virgin warrior, Marie the independent prostitute. Although each woman represents a mythic female stereotype that appears to be in complete opposition to the other, each is able to draw power from her image to undermine patriarchal values. In these two instance, the woman warrior is defined in relation to her appearance and sexuality, but this in no way undermines her power. On the contrary, woman's sexuality appears to be central to her role as a warrior and as such makes her an even more formidable opponent. The Sternberg/Dietrich portrait of Mata Hari challenges interpretations based on a binaristic logic that would interpret the Dietrich character as a conventional woman because of her dress and appearance.

Marie's journey of self-discovery is best understood in terms of the neomyth—woman's journey as hero through her encounter with the paternal symbolic, death and rebirth. This enables us to see that woman as prostitute can also be an heroic figure and that the journey of the woman warrior is very different from that of her male counterpart. Like other heroines, Marie is called to embark on a new journey; she is invited to change her life for a career as a spy. She says to her superior: "I've had an inglorious life. It may be my good fortune to have a glorious death". Dietrich's performance suggests that as a woman she is always one step ahead of the men she meets. This is emphasised in the exotic fancy-dress ball sequence. Dietrich appears in the black costume of a medieval Knight, complete with visor, cape and long boots. Clearly in charge, she flirts with the man with whom she later falls in love. He is symbolically dressed as a clown, limping along with the aid of crutches. Anonymous and unknowable, Dietrich exploits this aspect of woman, fully aware that man is perversely attracted to the femme fatale.

The stages of Dietrich's journey, the obstacles she must overcome, are mapped by the various outfits and costumes she wears: we see her dressed as a street prostitute, courtesan, knight, maid and femme fatale. She crosses the threshold when she realises she can no longer support the forces of nationalism and war, which she realises are part of the dominant male order. This realisation occurs after she falls in love with a man from the enemy side, but her love for him is not as significant as her realisation that nationalism and patriotism are destructive forces. Asserting her identity as a prostitute, Marie insists that she die as one, rather than in a soldier's uniform. Thus, Marie is represented as "other" in a double context; she is the "other" as prostitute and, in the end, the "other"/outsider of the male military order. For Marie, this realisation leads to the birth of a new sense of personal courage—one which the military commander who salutes her body, lying in the snow, understands full well.

In discussing the concept of female courage in relation to Marlene Dietrich's films, Haskell argues that the one thing that the men cannot forgive is "this alliance in Dietrich of death and the comic spirit".[25] Haskell refers to the final scene in *Dishonoured* where Dietrich faces the firing squad because, disgusted with war and militarism, she consciously betrays her own country in order to save her lover. An idealistic young member of the firing squad, drops his rifle, refusing to proceed. "No more butchery!" he shouts. Dietrich looks at him with a knowing smile. Haskell comments: "Marlene, as sure that there will be more butchery as she is that her own death will follow, merely applies fresh lipstick. This is the ultimate vision of beauty as courage and the ultimate victory of style (Dietrich's and Sternberg's) over content".[26] When Dietrich applies lipstick and adjusts stockings, she is demonstrating that feminine beauty and courage can stand up to male violence and aggression any day.

From a very different perspective, *Dishonoured* like the Alien and Joan of Arc films, demonstrates that there is such as thing as feminine courage. Women do not need to shed their feminine identity in order to qualify as warriors. Identity is not something that is determined by appearance. The woman warrior is a multi-faceted figure who may wear masculine or feminine attire—the key factor is whether or not she asserts her identity as fighting woman. The problem with definitions of bravery and courage as "male" is that these terms have become inflexible and one-dimensional. The notion of feminine bravery is fluid and flexible. The representation of the female hero in film offers us new ways of analysing what Rosi Braidotti sees as the fluid spaces between binaries.[27] The woman warrior is a multi-faceted concept; she can occupy the roles of soldier, virgin, saint, mother, wife and prostitute. Who cares if her hair is short or long, if she wears lipstick or carries a phallic gun? The female hero's dress and appearance does not function as a fixed signifier of either masculinity or femininity. The important thing is to analyse the *way* the film represents the heroine in relation to appearance, dress, actions, motivations and beliefs. The films discussed above are about woman in the process of becoming "other", that is, a female hero whose heroism is defined in relation to her "difference" as a woman. This difference does not constitute qualities that are fixed but fluid, transgressive and transformative.

Psychoanalytic theory argues that "in order to become autonomous, it is necessary that one cut the instinctual dyad of the mother and the child and that one become something other".[28] In order for woman to become autonomous it is equally necessary for her to cut the tie with the father, and the men in her life who represent the phallocentric extremes of the male symbolic. Each of the women discussed above—Joan, Ripley and Mata Hari—all refuse to recognise the power of the male symbolic order. In so doing, each becomes an abject other, a woman warrior—a source of both dread and fascination. In contrast to the male hero, the woman warrior sets out on a path that creates disunities and disjunctures within the symbolic order. In the very act of carrying out her heroic deeds the woman warrior abjects herself in a double movement. Ironically, this is also the source of her profound attraction. This perhaps is a key reason why Nana the prostitute in *Vivre Sa Vie* was so drawn to the story of Joan of Arc. Nana believed her only hope of salvation was to become an actor, to play the part of the woman warrior, to become an inspiration for other women following the mythic journey of the female hero in the ritualised spaces of the cinema.

Notes

1. The following are relevant: Rebecca Bell-Metereau, "Woman: The Other Alien in *Alien*," in *Woman World Walkers*, ed. Jane B. Weedman (Lubbock: Texas Tech Press, 1985); Carol Clover, *Men, Women and Chain Saws: Gender in the Modern Horror Film* (Princeton: Princeton University Press, 1992); Elizabeth Hills, "From 'Figurative Males' to Action Heroines: Further Thoughts on Active Women in the Cinema," *Screen* 40, no. 1. (Spring 1999): 38–51; Pay Kirkham and Janet Thumin, eds., *Me Jane: Masculinity, Movies and Women* (London: Lawrence & Wishart, 1995); Yvonne Tasker, *Working Girls: Gender and Sexuality in Popular Cinema* (London: Routledge,1998); Sherrie A. Inness, ed. *Action Chicks: New Images of Tough Women in Popular Culture* (New York: Palgrave Macmillan, 2004).
2. Joseph Campbell, *The Hero With A Thousand Faces* (London: Fontana Press, 1993 [1948]).
3. Ibid., 390.
4. Ibid., 391.
5. Christopher Vogler has drawn on Joseph Campbell's mythic structure to create a best-selling book, *The Writer's Journey*. Vogler's book has enjoyed great influence with Hollywood scriptwriters. Christopher Vogler, *The Writer's Journey: Mythic Structure for Storytellers and Screenwriters* (London: Pan Books, 1998).
6. In her study of filmic narrative Teresa de Lauretis has made a similar point. She argues that: 'the hero must be male, regardless of the text image, because the obstacle, whatever its personification is morphologically female" such as a cave or symbolic womb. Teresa de Lauretis, *Alice Doesn't: Feminism, Semiotics, Cinema* (Bloomington: Indiana University Press, 1984).
7. In *From Reverence to Rape*, Molly Haskell analysed the way in women's roles were almost always defined in relation to their sexuality. She did, however, draw attention to a handful of films, such as *Dishonoured*, that explored female heroism. Haskell defined "heroines that are motivated by fires of passion other than the sexual" as "anti-heroines" in that they do not enact female roles as defined by sexuality. She includes George

Bernard Shaw's Joan of Arc in this category. Haskell's notion of the "anti-heroine" is very relevant to this discussion. I have drawn up three categories in relation to Haskell's anti-heroine. Molly Haskell, *From Reverence to Rape: Treatment of Women in the Movies* (Middlesex, England: Penguin, 1979).

8. For a different approach, see Yvonne Tasker, "Women Warriors: Gender, sexuality and Hollywood's fighting heroines," in *Spectacular Bodies: Gender, Genre and the Action Cinema*, ed. Yvonne Tasker (London: Routledge, 1993), 14–34. I have drawn a distinction between the woman warrior and the action heroine. Tasker treats these two figures as one.

9. In an excellent article on the action heroine, Elizabeth Hills presents a discussion of the various positions presented by feminist theorists. She also calls for a "new mode of understanding" needed to analyse 'the changing representations of women in the action cinema". Hills proposes a model based on the writings of Gilles Deleuze and Felix Guattari and their notion of the "body without organs". Elisabeth Hills, "From 'Figurative Males' to Action Heroines: Further Thoughts on Active Women in the Cinema," *Screen* 40, no. 1 (Spring 1999): 38–51.

10. See Françoise Meltzer, "Jean of Arc in America" *Substance* 100, 31 no.1 (2003): 90–9. A discussion in which the author argues the continuing popularity of Joan, best described as a "cultural phenomenon", is the result of various often contradictory factors: a "nostalgia for certainty" in the postmodern era; Joan's appeal as a figure who blurs boundaries and signifies the collapse of clear categories "of subjectivity, gender, power, the historical Church"; the "passion and conviction" of her story.

11. Marina Warner, *Joan of Arc: The Image of Female Heroism* (New York: Vintage Books, 1981), 22.

12. Ibid., 23, 152.

13. Ibid., 155.

14. In 1996, Mark Rappaport directed *From the Journals of Jean Seberg* in which he explored the career of the actress as a means of critically investigating the nature of the Hollywood star machine and its misogynistic treatment of the female actor. He drew on Seberg's performance in *Saint Joan*, and those of Bergman and Falconetti, who also played Joan, in order to try and understand the industry's fascination with the virgin warrior. Mary Beth Hurt, narrates the film and tells us that the reason why so many films about Joan have been made is essentially misogynistic. The real reason "we are interested in Joan of Arc is the promise of the spectacle of a woman being burned at the stake ... It is horrifying and you want to see more". The other reason why so many films about Joan have been made is that Joan is such a powerful and heroic figure, a woman whose story continues to provide a source of inspiration for all viewers—particularly women. "I, Jean Seberg,'" *Film Quarterly* 55, no.4 (Fall 2001): 2–13.

15. Amy Taubin, "Invading Bodies: *Alien 3* and the Trilogy," *Sight & Sound* (July 1992): 10.

16. Hills, "From 'Figurative Males' to Action Heroines," 38–51.

17. Ros Jennings, "Desire and Design: Ripley Undressed," in *Immortal/Invisible: Lesbians and the Moving Image*, ed. Tamsin Wilton (London: Routledge, 1995), 197.

18. Diana Dominguez, "'It's Not So Easy Being Cast Iron Bitch': Sexual Difference and the Female Action Hero," *Reconstruction* 5, no.4 (Fall, 2005): 4.

19. Ibid.,18.
20. Ibid.,18.
21. Ibid., 8, 11, 13.
22. Ibid., 21–2.
23. Ibid., 21–2.
24. Taubin, "Invading Bodies," 10.
25. Haskell, *From Reverence to Rape*, 11.
26. Ibid., 110.
27. Rosi Bradiotti, *Nomadic Subjects: Embodiment and Sexual Difference in Contemporary Feminist Theory* (New York: Columbia University Press, 1994).
28. Julia Kristeva, quoted in Pierrette Daly, *Heroic Tropes, Gender and Intertext* (Detroit: Wayne State University Press, 1993), 147.

CHAPTER THREE

JUST A WOMAN AMONG THE CYBORGS: SARAH CONNOR IN *TERMINATOR 2: JUDGEMENT DAY*

CATHERINE SUMMERHAYES

Figure Four: Linda Hamilton in *Terminator 2: Judgement Day* (1991)

In this discussion, I explore the nature of a spectacular "woman willing to fight": Linda Hamilton's "Sarah Connor". I focus primarily on James Cameron's *Terminator 2: Judgement Day* (1991),[1] the second and most beautifully realised of the *Terminator* film trilogy, and suggest that the first film, Cameron's *The Terminator* (1984); and the third film, John Mostow's *Terminator 3: The Rise of the Machines* (2003), can best be understood as having the lesser status of prequel and sequel respectively to the provocative and disturbing story of *Terminator 2*.[2] My core questions about Sarah are as follows: Why is Sarah willing to fight? What is the importance, the significance of her fight? How does she fight? How does her code of fighting, her warriorship, effect our perceptions of gender stereotypes attached to women? What kind of woman is she, as we watch her journey throughout the three *Terminator* films?

In order to answer these questions, it is essential to read Sarah as a human woman who embodies multiple roles. Sarah is a tough, determined heroine who retains most of the agency available within the narrative whilst also negotiating the "feminine" traits of being the primary female in the stories of the other three strong characters, who are all male. She is mother to one hero, lover to another and once prey/now friend to a most powerful male protagonist—Arnold Schwarzenegger's cyborg character from another time, the Terminator. The exploration of Sarah's relationship with the other male (partly) human, or non-human, characters and their bodies is an interesting analytic lens for the exploration of Sarah Connor as one of the first and outstanding human woman warriors of the New Hollywood cinema.

Besides her gender, it is Sarah's humanness, in particular, that sets her apart from the other main characters, especially the cyborgs and time-travellers, of the *Terminator* films. For Sarah is the only main character who always exists in her own time-zone and who is the only human within this zone who does battle with "the Machines". Sarah is bound by the film's narrative to her own time and place, on earth, whilst other characters—time-travellers, cyborgs and androids—inhabit an ambiguous, albeit inglorious, realm in which they play out the battles that she has initiated. She is the woman who bears a child who can save humanity and it is she who decides to begin the fight against the inhuman world of the cyborgs, "the Machines".

The Story: "There is no fate but what we make ourselves"

The above quote appears originally in the first film of the trilogy. It is advice passed on to Sarah from the future, by her son John via her lover Kyle Reese (Michael Biehn); it is used almost as a mantra in *Terminator 2* and appears again on her "gravestone" in *Terminator 3*. The trilogy is about fighting against a seemingly inevitable apocalyptic future. The course the viewer is lead to follow in this conflict is through Sarah's own personal battle, from the time of the first film when she comes to realise a nuclear war will take place in the future, to the time when this mantra appears as her epitaph in the third film, over a grave which is empty of her body but full of the weapons she has stored away for when her son John needs them.

In *The Terminator*, the time-zones of Sarah's present life and a possible apocalyptic future are constantly juxtaposed. Sarah copes with two time-travellers. The first is *The Terminator* who is sent back from the year 2029 by "the Machines" in an effort to kill her. Their motive is to prevent Sarah from bearing her son John, who will one day become the resistant leader in the war of humans against the Machines. Then there is Kyle Reese, John's close comrade in this war, whom John sends back to 1984 to protect Sarah from the Terminator. Reese occupies a curious time-traveller position. He becomes Sarah's lover in 1984 and it is their son who later becomes his friend John Connor in 2029. Although Reese dies in 1984, it is this prior mission that sets up the human resistance which is played out in the future in the post-apocalyptic Los Angeles scenes of the first film. By the end of *The Terminator,* Sarah is convinced that there will be a nuclear war in which most of humanity will perish. This catastrophe is inevitable, unless the Machines are defeated in her time—and the possibility of their development is eliminated. In much the same way, the Machines believe that the only way they can win in the future is if John Connor is never born. By the end of the first film, in spite of her trials, a pregnant Sarah Connor survives.

Early on in *Terminator 2*, we see the young John Connor, as a juvenile delinquent. He is in foster care while Sarah is preparing for battle, even though she is living under the severe constraints of a high security facility for the "mentally disturbed" where she has been imprisoned because of her Cassandra-like warnings in the first film about the coming apocalypse. We are re-introduced to Sarah in this sequel by watching her restrained, imprisoned body being sexually assaulted by workers in this facility, and we also watch her in flash-back scenes re-living the powerful reasons why she has put her own body at risk. Even within the ruthlessly run asylum, Sarah bears the primary authority, courage and crucial agency in the film. In this sequence, we also see her body transformed from a soft curvy one to the lean, well-muscled body of the first woman who is fighting for earth.

Secondly the film fills in the story of how the creatures known as the Machines came to exist. They are beings that have been made by Skynet, a huge computer network that has both developed both self-awareness and autonomy. This film is set once again in Sarah's time-zone, the year is 1995. The nuclear apocalypse is envisaged only as waking dreams. A particular scene is repeated—an inferno engulfing a playground full of mothers and children and it becomes the visual motif of this film. This time, the Terminator (Arnold Schwarzenegger) returns from the future again; reprogrammed in the future by John (Edward Furlong) to protect Sarah and her son John who is now 11 years old. The Machines have also sent back another, more sophisticated Terminator version, known as T1000 (Robert Patrick), to kill John. The T1000 is a more powerful technology than the T800 model played by Arnold Schwarzenegger. The main weapon that T1000 has over the T800 is its ability to morph its body into the substance of other objects and people.

Terminator 2 is a fast action-packed film. In the end, Cyberdyne Systems, responsible for the development of Skynet, are blown up and the T1000 is destroyed in a fiery vat of molten steel. In an heroic act, the wounded T800 Terminator also destroys himself for the sake of humankind. Dramatically lowering himself into the same vat in order to destroy the final cyborg chip that can be used against humanity and resides in his internal circuitry. The final sequence is a night scene of a road rolling on, with Sarah's voice quietly saying:

> The unknown future rolls toward us. I face it for the first time with a sense of hope because of a machine, a Terminator, [who] can learn the value of a human life, maybe we can too.

Terminator 2 could easily have been the last film of this story. But in 2003, *Terminator 3: Rise of the Machines* was released. The time frame is unclear. At least ten years have lapsed but the nuclear war, which was supposed to have occurred in 1997, is yet to happen. Sarah is dead, John (Nick Stahl) is in his early twenties and is now the only hope for humanity. Once again, Schwarzenegger's Terminator (now a T101) travels back in time to protect John against the new cyborg sent back by the Machines: the Terminatrix T-X (Kristanna Loken). The T-X is encased in a tight body suit that shows off a very curvaceous slim fighting female body. She also can morph and the almost obsolete T101 is no match for her. Nevertheless, the fight goes on. This film sequel film is the weakest in the trilogy, sometimes lapsing almost into a parody of the second film. But once again, humanity prevails and the fight continues. By the end of this third film, another fighting woman steps into Sarah's boots: Kate Brewster, played by Claire Danes.

Why Sarah Fights

Sarah and the time-travelling Kyle Reese make love the one time and John Connor is conceived. This patrilineage appears strange because the unborn John is conceived by one of his own future age-mates, a colleague who "would do anything for him". It is not clear whether this manoeuvre is included in John's instructions to Reese or not. This conception is more of a time-travel twist than a major feature of the film's main narrative. This unusual relationship, of father and son between age peers, is less confronting if we accept simultaneous intergenerational superimpositions of lover, son and father as a woman's familial intimates.

Reese brings a message to Sarah from her son in the twenty-first century that she must fight so that John can exist. Overtly, this reason to fight locates her as one of the great iconic mother action figures, seen by Tasker "as either motivated by her maternal instincts or as taking over/inheriting her father's position".[3] I think that Tasker's theory, that this then cancels out a woman fighter's agency in favour of her relationship to men, is not the only conclusion to be drawn. In the *Terminator* films Sarah does not refer in any way to her father—she is the single woman, the single mother, without recourse to any kind of extended family. For example, while she is imprisoned in the earlier part of *Terminator 2*, the young John is living with foster parents who have no other relation to him. Her fight has its source in the "war business" of men and masculinised machines (she is dead by the time the "female" Terminatrix of the third film appears) but her motivation to fight is based on her singular understanding of the risks involved for human society and this understanding is informed by her own visions and experiences of humanity, in particular, her love for Reese and for her unborn son.

It is difficult not to include Sarah's mode of loving as one of her reasons to fight. This loving is also a two-way interaction rather than simply a submission to a masculine hegemony. I think it can be seen as a personal choice which is motivated as much or as little by gender-based (feminine) inclinations. The danger with gender analyses is that gender positions may be essentialised through their very articulation; the more androgynous nature of both female and male characters can be overlooked if we ignore the active interactions between characters of both genders. Such a gender-based reduction of possible motivations available to Sarah's status as a woman fighter can succumb to a basic sociobiological explanation for all activities undertaken by gendered beings.[4] Indeed such a reduction cancels out to a large extent the possibility for any human agency by either women or men.

Affection and loving are presented to be as much a part of Sarah's motivation as her rational reasons for fighting i.e. to save all humankind. These two aspects of her motivation are inseparable in Sarah's character. It is tempting to deconstruct all characters in this film in the context of idealised structures of gender. Sarah's formative fighting moments are framed more in conjunction with Reese than in the context of anything else. "On your feet soldier!" she yells at him as he is dying towards the end of the first film. And in *Terminator 2*, he appears to her in a vision, using these same words in order to rekindle her determination to fight after she has been humiliated and demoralised in the health facility for the mentally-disturbed.

The moments of care and admiration which Sarah and other characters share balance out the bitterness of war and the inhumanity of the Machines. This balancing act, in turn, displays the two major imperatives in this narrative and both are personified in Sarah Connor. They are first that the human race must survive, and second that the surviving "race" must be "human" in entirety. This is recapitulated in the positive image presented of humanity, through caring gestures shared and the fear of its loss in Sarah's apocalyptic visions in *Terminator 2*: visions of families in playgrounds who are incinerated in the nuclear explosion of 1997.

These threats to humanity are Sarah's particular nightmare: having gained self-awareness the military computer system Skynet launches nuclear missiles that all but eliminate humans from the Earth. Machines then take over and enslave the survivors. In 2029, humans begin to revolt under the leadership of her son John Connor. The simple answer to the question of why Sarah fights is not deeply disguised; it is explicit to the film's narrative. She has a moral imperative to fight at two levels: firstly to save her son and secondly, in consequence, to save the world. This second imperative is based firstly on an altruistic motivation that is associated with the parental ethics of both men and women. The figure of three billion is frequently used during *Terminator 2* to account for those killed during the nuclear holocaust. Sarah's cause is the lives of three billion people, for the world as we know it, for humanity in general. The question is not why would she fight but why she would not.

Sarah's significance to this battle, and what makes her stand out, is not so much that she is female but that she is human. But even Sarah's prescience lends her an extraordinary human faculty. What makes her unique in this battle concerns the fact that she is the only flesh and blood human that remains with in her own time-zone—with all a healthy human's capabilities for decision making and choice. In each of the three films, Sarah is identifiable as "one of us": she recognisably comes from a period within our society's time-zone; the various time-travellers and cyborg Terminators are as foreign and startling to her as they would be to us. With her as our guide, we are entering a particular vision of the future. The burden she carries is not only in saving us/the world, but in showing us how to adjust to life as it includes these strange, new beings and equally confronting concepts of time and space. We watch *Terminator* 2 from a human's point of view—our point of view is that of Sarah, the central character in the first two films. It is through Sarah's eyes that the audience encounters the Machines and grasps what threat the cyborgs pose to humanity.

Three definitions of cyborgs developed by Donna Haraway are useful for understanding how Sarah negotiates the cyborgs of the *Terminator* trilogy,[5] as well as informing her own position as the character, through whose eyes we read *Terminator 2*:

- A cyborg is a cybernetic organism, a hybrid of machine and organism, a creature of social reality as well as a creature of fiction. Social reality is lived social relations, our most important political construction...that changes what counts as women's experience in the late twentieth century...
- The cyborg is resolutely committed to partiality, irony, intimacy and perversity. It is oppositional, utopian, and completely without innocence...
- The main trouble with cyborgs, of course, is that they are the illegitimate offspring of militarism and patriarchal capitalism, not to mention state socialism. But illegitimate offspring are often exceedingly unfaithful to their origins. Their fathers, after all, are inessential.

These definitions are to some extent relevant to all three Terminators. These creatures were never human; they are cyborgs that can look and act like humans (they adopt human shape, or have human skin). The most developed character of these, however, Schwarzenegger's Terminator in *Terminator 2*, is generally perceived as cyborg primarily because of his individualised and powerful characterisation. This Terminator is curious about what it is to be human and uses John Connor as his guide, for example, asking him "why humans cry". However, we also see the Terminator as he "heals" himself, inflicting incisions on his body which look vividly like horrific human flesh wounds until we see the computer circuitry beneath. He is clearly both human and machine.

By the end of *Terminator 2*, the Terminator is capable of altruistic decision making, choosing to disappear into a vat of molten steel rather than remain a risk to humankind. It would be hard to trump this flamboyant gesture of altruism in any narrative as the Terminator is allowed dignity as he descends to his "death" because he is after all a cyborg: it is not a human body screaming in pain and fear that descends into the steel. His destruction is finally the demise of a machine with human emotions and ethics. This characterisation of the Terminator in *Terminator 2* strongly recalls Haraway's descriptions of a cyborg as "a creature of social reality as well as a creature of fiction"[6] and as "resolutely committed to partiality, irony, intimacy and perversity ... oppositional, utopian, and completely without innocence".[7] The fact that this Terminator goes from pursuing Sarah to helping her also recalls Haraway's description of cyborgs as "the illegitimate offspring of militarism and patriarchal capitalism" that "are often exceedingly unfaithful to their origins".[8] Such "unfaithfulness" is the core dilemma of cyborgs.

Early on in Forest Pyle's discussion of the cyborgs in both *Blade Runner* (1982) and *The Terminator*, Pyle comments that these two films "are unsettled and unsettling speculations on the borders that separate the human and the nonhuman".[9] Such "unsettling speculations" are certainly also played out in *Terminator 2*. In this film, we watch Schwarzenegger's character through Sarah's eyes as she wonders at the seeming humanity of this particularly heroic cyborg. She can perhaps be understood as speculating on the ways in which humans can learn from, use and perhaps even take machines into their bodies and yet retain a fundamental human agency—a concept that Pyle claims *The Terminator* describes as "the routing of technologica mastery into a rebellious subjectivity, a heroism capable of resistance and even self-sacrifice".[10]

In her essay on how computer technology is affecting literature, Kathleen Fitzpatrick speaks of textual representations which represent a view of humanism versus posthumanism and "the anxiety of obsolescence":

> The human contends with the posthuman, in the form of the cybernetic organism; humanism faces posthumanism, in which new forms of knowledge are privileged—these two challenges do not parse out discretely between those that imagine a threat to species and those that imagine a threat to knowledge, between ontological and epistemological anxieties.[11]

Fitzpatrick goes on to note that these two challenges are usually conflated in a single text "not only effacing the boundary between human and machine, but also for undermining humanist ideologies".[12] There is then also a metaphysical threat involved in the story of this trilogy: the fear that humankind as it is now might not only be obliterated but also made obsolete. It is this possible effacement of the difference between humans and machines which forms the core anxiety that drives Sarah Connor's battles with the Machines.

The Body of a Fighting Woman

What a woman's body can do and what it actually does is of significant interest in critical discourses of power, gender and identity. It is therefore not possible to discuss Sarah Connor without acknowledging at least some of the ramifications of how the female human body is represented in comparison to the bodies of male human and non-human characters in *Terminator 2*. As Sarah journeys from having a soft and rounded body in *The Terminator* to her finely honed hard and strong body in *Terminator 2*, she takes on relationships with four other adult main characters that are all male: her lover Reese, Schwarzenegger's "good" and "bad" terminators and the evil T1000. Yvonne Tasker's concept of "musculinity" in action films is a useful concept through which to read Sarah's body in relationship to those of the male characters:

> These films reinscribe, in different ways, the *female* body in terms of masculinity. It is for this reason that I want to introduce the term 'musculinity'. "Musculinity" indicates the extent to which a physical definition of masculinity

in terms of a developed musculature is not limited to the male body within representation. [13]

With this idea, Tasker makes space for a way in which to understand Sarah's body as the most "buffed" human body of all the main characters in the three films: the others may be "buffed" but they are not human. We do not need to describe her developed muscles and strength as masculine—this appearance and underlying strength is available to any gender inscribed body. Indeed, at the beginning of the twenty-first century, her female, strong, athletic body constitutes one of the norms in society, although at the time of making *Terminator 2* her body in this film would have been considered more androgenous than it would be today. Sarah has given birth to a child, but she does take on the mantle of a fighting woman to the extent that she denies herself and her child that conventional loving domestic relationship commonly associated with the feminine. And although she still possesses the distinctive hairstyle and smaller body of a woman, she also grows her muscles into the well defined "body armour" of a twentieth century fighting woman, as well as learning to use and accrue an armoury of heavy weaponry. In *Terminator* 2, we do not meet again the petite and pretty Sarah with the 70s-80s hair-style, whom we met in the first film. Rather, we are confronted with a Sarah who has rigorously developed the buffed, lean, strong body of a well-trained military fighter. The actress Linda Hamilton spent three months in military-style weapon training, and ate a severely fat-reduced diet to produce Sarah's new body.

This fighting Sarah emerges from the pretty young woman who works in a "hamburger joint" in the first film. Again to quote Pyle as he notes how *The Terminator* can be interpreted as a politically "progressive" film:

> Sarah Connor, who is not only the bearer of human potentia, the mother of humanity's savior, but the character that the film represents as achieving agency. [14]

This comment is also relevant for Sarah's depiction in *Terminator 2*. From the beginning of the first film, we see her as agile, full of stamina and deft in handling weapons, once she acknowledges to herself that she has to use them (when Reese is dying). She is also even then innovative and opportunistic in her fighting methods. In *Terminator 2*, we see her with a carefully crafted military fighter's body, as someone with extensive weapons training and as someone who is a strategic thinker. She is wounded several times in *Terminator 2* but although we watch the impact of these wounds, she never lets them keep her from fighting; in the same way in which the Terminators keep on going relentlessly, so does she.

A Woman Among the Cyborgs

There is one particular quality of *Terminator 2*'s cyborgs that is relevant to how we understand Sarah's body. This is the quality of morphing. The transformation of one image into another through digital morphing technologies creates the on-screen illusion of characters that can change their shapes, usually at will. The T1000, who remorselessly pursues Sarah and her son, is a shape-changer. His character can take on the shape of both animate and inanimate objects. He can also transform his parts of his body into other shapes, for example, a stiletto finger that threatens Sarah's body in the final fighting sequence in *Terminator 2*. Tasker discusses the T1000 as characterised in opposition to Schwarzenegger's bodybuilder's physique and also compares this shape changer with Sarah's more prosaic bodily shape-changing. She describes the T1000 as:

> typified by a lack of the bodily definition that is so important to the image of the bodybuilder. That the T1000 is a feminised monster is evident in this fluidity . . . Within the film Schwarzenegger's muscular solidity is played off against both the unstable qualities of the T1000 and the rather iconographically unstable figure of Linda Hamilton as Sarah Connor. [15]

This "feminine" fluidity is perhaps the most horrific aspects of *Terminator 2*, and recalls Barbara Creed's discussion of the uncanny gaze and the horror film. Creed maintains that the "uncanny sensation must be produced by the text itself, through the methods it adopts to uncover the uncanny".[16] The filmic text which is *Terminator 2* adopts the method of digital morphing to expose the horror of bodies that will not remain the same shape, bodies that epitomise the powers inherent in voluntary change and the uncertainty with which we try to understand them as reassuringly whole entities to which we can relate to with confidence. It is interesting to note that in the third film, such powers of shape-changing are embodied in the female form of T-X who is horror of the feminine personified.

Whilst morphing and issues of musculinity are newer and highly relevant ways for understanding the "action hero" bodies, both female and male, in *Terminator 2*, there are also other, more prosaic difficulties in representing coherent motivation for a character who is both a fighter and a woman. These difficulties arise mainly from our stereotypical preconceptions about what women and men can and should do: gender stereotypes. In her study of female "action heroes" in cinema, Marlo Edwards notes that:

> the violent woman necessarily presents a provocative challenge to traditional gender conventions. But given the regularity with which the active woman is coded as a sexually 'desirable' object … she can clearly also work to uphold

these conventions through her embodiment of resistance as erotic spectacle, commodity, nightmare, and fetish.[17]

While Sarah is not presented as a sexually desirable woman as she undertakes the battle shown in *Terminator 2*, she has had a lover in the previous film and he returns briefly to her in a vision even in *Terminator 2*—a film which focuses on her hardened fighter's body. It is also interesting to note that during this sequence with her lover in the second film, she is shown in a soft, silky slip and her well-defined muscles are softened and rounded. She is not represented as both desirable and as a fighter at the same time. Contrary to the heroes studied by Edwards, she must be one or the other. This imposes upon her character a much more stereotyped gender burden. She is less a freak of nature, a spectacle, as she is androgynous. To a certain extent, she is asexual within the films' narrative—with the exception that she is constantly placed in the position of requiring help from her male colleagues in order to achieve her ends and fulfil her mission of saving the world.

Every now and then in this film, there is a clanking contradiction in the way Sarah is represented which does, however, re-emphasise the female stereotypes at work. One of the most striking examples occurs in Sarah's fairly clumsy monologue when she rages against the character Dyson who is in the process of developing the software and hardware systems that will eventually become Skynet the computer template which will allow the Machines to become autonomous beings:

> You think you're so creative! You don't know what it's like to really create something. To create a life. To feel it growing inside you. All you know is how to create death and destruction...

This tirade is heavy handed and hammers home the overtly maternal reason for Sarah's fight—in case anyone had missed it earlier? Or perhaps in case we had been distracted by the flak jacket, SWAT style fatigues and weapons into thinking that Sarah had turned male on us? In fact this scene, with its wildly contradictory messages, to a certain degree "makes fun" of Sarah's warriorship, in its suggestion that she is merely dressing up, masquerading as a fighter who must be, by any "common sense" understanding, male. The boy John Connor is embarrassed by this outburst and cuts in on her, saying: "Mom, we need to be a little more constructive here, okay?" Roger Warren Beebe further suggests that this interruption by her son undermines Sarah's authority both as a woman and as a fighter. He notes that such "constant gestures of pathologisation in the film undermine Sarah's credibility as a centre of identification".[18] Whilst I agree that Sarah is undermined here, there is a definite continuation of a parental identification; and the pathology perhaps is rather her son's patriarchal, childish dismissal of his mother's role in his existence. And it is Sarah's tirade, combined with more calmly delivered explanations, which brings home to Dyson the mortal dangers of Skynet. In a literal sense then, this paradox of emotional display by this female warrior is a necessary part of the battle, suggesting that perhaps loving interactions, rather than or as well as, idiopathic hate, can justify the rage which lies behind war.

What is it like for Hamilton's characterisation of Sarah to have this Schwarzenegger-driven cyborg as her leading man? At first glance, he could be a hard act to follow. Sarah is inevitably the less spectacular in terms of special effects even though she is also an unusual character: a fighting woman. Secondly, this pairing can be understood also to suggest that this partnership of leading characters is a partnership of "freaks": two characters who "go against nature", or at least the nature of commonly accepted stereotypes of human male and female. Together, then, they are a confusing pair, and together they save the world. In these stories, is Sarah able to fight alone or with other women? No, and although her relationships with Reese, the Terminator and John Connor include their dependence on her, she, like them, is also inextricably dependant on them: for affection, information and motivation. No matter what ambiguities are represented in the relationships Sarah is shown to have with her "leading men", the continuing mantra, *"There is no fate but what we make ourselves"*, always imbues the very active character of Sarah's own agency. She is the bravest, the most aware and the most active and attractive character in *Terminator 2*—she survives to do her job no matter what the odds, no matter what powerful machines are against her. And she is always our major site for identification within the film. This position, together with her part in the film's action, keys her as the most significant, focal character in this film.

Time-Travellers and Simulacra

By now, most film viewers are literate enough in audiovisual viewing to accept without too much trouble the flashes forward and backwards in time that occur in *Terminator 2*. Chris Marker's *La Jetée* (1962) was one of the first films to introduce to us ways in which film can simultaneously represent ideas of cyclical and parallel time-zones; and although filmic time can still puzzle viewers, it is not as disturbing a concept as the monstrous thought that humans might not be the most dominant organism on Earth.

Sarah's colleagues and opponents in battle can be understood not only as masculine cyborgs but also as creatures that do not quite exist. They are time-travellers who therefore eschew the constraints of linear time. If we closely read these films' primary narrative, the Terminator and John Connor exist simultaneously in two spaces and times. The future is not fixed, nor is the past. Sarah then has a Herculean task of fighting with two characters who, we might reasonably say, may never, or do not, in fact exist. Following this line of reasoning then Sarah is fighting with "virtual" beings against a "virtual" situation: a heroic task that seems to be justified by a desperate belief in the worth of humanity as well as her own individual survival.

Understood from her and our point of view as we exist in linear time, Sarah's opponents and colleagues are simulations of what might be if the future is as she envisions it. Baudrillard's conceptualisation of simulation is worth noting here in this long quote from his essay "The Precession of Simulacra":

> By crossing into a space whose curvature is no longer that of the real, nor that of truth, the era of simulation is inaugurated by a liquidation of all referentials ... It is no longer a question of imitation, nor duplication, nor even parody. It is a question of substituting signs of the real for the real, that is to say of an operation of deterring every real process via its operational double, a programmatic, metastable, perfectly descriptive machine that offers all the signs of the real and short-circuits its entire vicissitudes. Never again will the real have the chance to produce itself.[19]

If the time-travelling Terminators and Kyle Reese are simulations then to some degree they can never really completely die, but they can be transformed rather into similar but different beings. Hence we know that the Terminators were made in a model of the future extrapolated from the films' "present", and although they can be destroyed in this present, they can also come back as a slightly different version, eg. Schwarzenegger's various Terminator incarnations throughout the trilogy. The character of Reese is a little more problematic in terms of thinking about him as a simulation, but in some ways he is even more uncanny because he is also to be understood as human. He is a human who dies in the present of the first film but we also see him as resurrected within the narrative presented in the film's model of the future, as well as in Sarah's dream.

In Baudrillard's terms, we are not simply watching the unfolding of events in these films, we are witnessing a struggle for and against an already modelled "future", and the main characters, except for Sarah, are creatures from that "maybe/as if model" of what might be. The message "*There is no fate but what we make ourselves*" passes through all three films and is an indication that the future is not necessarily fixed. If the future is not fixed, then where do the Terminators come from? They come from a modelled future. They can only exist within a particular conjunction of an embattled "present" and a time which might not happen. The films' narrative locks this subjunctive model of the future with the filmic "present" by a quite ephemeral device: that of the time-travelling cyborg Terminators, sent by the Machines from the future to destroy the present.

One of the dangers for Sarah is that these simulacra are treating her as if that is what she is too—a figment of an uncertain future. This threat recalls my earlier discussion of Fitzpatrick's "anxiety of obsolescence". Understood in this context, Sarah is not merely fighting for herself, her son and those three billion other people, she is also, and very importantly, fighting for a concept of reality, time and space, that allows our comfortable, everyday notions of the real world to exist.

The "Ghost in the Machine"

I now want to look a little more closely at what Sarah's own alliance and battle with cyborgs may mean for our understanding of her role as a fighting woman in this trilogy of films. In *Blade Runner*, cyborg characters are called "replicants". The terrifying aspect of these cyborgs is that they do not always know what they are. They possess memories which they think are true but which can all too easily be proven to belong to someone else. This anxiety over identity is an innately human trait and our current anxious understanding of human memory over time is pre-visioned by Scott's confused replicants. Another film that has been analysed by other writers for the nature of the cyborg in Japanese anime films is Mamoru Oshii's *The Ghost in the Shell* (1995), which, to quote Christopher Bolton, is: "a visually evocative film that explores the boundary between information, human, and machine".[20]

This film's central character is Major Motoku Kusanagi. The major has an enormous, buxom and almost ungainly exoskeleton which encases the neural ghost of her own human agency, the brain matter that by the end of the film ends up in the body of a girl child. Although this film essentialises even more than the *Terminator* films what it is to be human, it is finally the will of the human part, the ghost of Kusanagi, that wants to be completely unified with a virtual system—her erstwhile enemy, the software system called "The Puppet Master". This recalls Haraway's following claim: "Pre-cybernetic machines could be haunted; there was always the spectre of the ghost in the machine".[21] Oshii's film seems to suggest that such ghosts of the human can also exist within cyborgs, android cybernetic systems—a theme borne out in Sarah's musings on the Terminator being a good "father" to her son.

These creatures envisioned in films as cyborgs do not yet exist and probably never will. They are fantastic simulations, extrapolations from various models of current technologies, copies of what has never existed: simulacra. And humans have imagined them. This creative act by human authors allows an exploration of what humanity is and might become.

Sarah is an embodied human "ghost" among the various machines of *Terminator 2*, who saves her son's ghostly future and who loves another ghost from another time. It is possible then to read *Terminator 2* as a tale of a woman who comes to terms with the unsettling space simultaneously occupied by humans, cyborgs and machines. She works with and against masculine militaristic cyborgs and she negotiates her own status as a woman who is also a ruthless fighting "machine" for a cause determined by the very substantial ghost of her own humanity. In the sense that she assumes a body armour of muscular development and masters current fighting technologies; she is inescapably cyborg herself, as perhaps are all those who work closely with machines. [22]

Sarah Connor: The First Human Fighter for Earth

Summarising my exploration of the questions posed at the beginning of the chapter it is important to note that Sarah is the only primary human character who figures in all three films and who can fully realise what will be lost: she is an adult who stays still in time and whose life spans almost to the time of the first predicted nuclear holocaust. She is the powerful still centre of a world in chaos, a world of time-travellers—"still" in the sense that she remains in her own time and fights her battles single-mindedly. She never waivers. We can identify with her emotions and even with the ways in which she fights. Sarah is human just like us and we see and hear the story from her point of view. She has been told that she can save humanity. She is also the active mother of another "redeemer" of humankind—she fights for her son, although she also has the power to reject or take up this responsibility. She has had her "annunciation" and makes her choice.

The character of Sarah Connor as it emerges through this trilogy of films is that of a highly successful woman in current terms. Her fighting body in *Terminator 2* can now be contextualised as the lean, healthy and desirably strong body of a female athlete. She manages to have a lover, a son, an eventually cooperative and subservient, male cyborg colleague with the muscles of a Mr Universe, and a capability for ruthless, strategic thinking—and she goes a long way towards "saving the world". This is literally a fantastic representation of woman. Sarah's character can certainly be read as an affirmation of women's ability to bear very well the burdens of living that are usually stereotyped as masculine responsibilities. Her story also offers hope for a successful resolution of humanity's "anxiety of obsolescence" in the face of the cybernetic technologies which humans are now developing and using. Although gothic and often violent, the adventures of Sarah Connor, especially through the narrative of *Terminator 2*, are the adventures of a very human "action hero" who knows how to use technology rather than be ruled by it. She might well agree with Haraway's famous judgement: "Though both are bound in the spiral dance, I would rather be a cyborg than a goddess". [23] So why does

Sarah fight? She fights for her son; and for a kind of humanity that is "un-machine-like", that is compassionate, loyal and all the characteristics that are recognisable to us the audience as being "human". She fights using all the powers and strengths of a woman and some that she hijacks from the realm of the masculine/"masculine". It is through her eyes only that we read the story of how it is to be human in a world of cyborgs and other machines.

Notes

1. Hereafter this film is referred to as *Terminator 2*.
2. While there are discussions to be had on the female Terminatrix of the third film, this character only came into being after Sarah had died. So I am going to side-step this character in order to concentrate on Sarah herself and the masculine world which is her battleground in the first two films.
3. Tasker cited in Marlo Edwards, "The Blonde with the Guns: 'Barb Wire' and the 'Implausible' Female Action Hero", *Journal of Popular Film and Television* 32, no. 1 (2004): 2.
4. Haraway's argument with Catherine MacKinnon is relevant here. She claims that MacKinnon's "totalizing" feminism produces ". . . what Western patriarchy itself never succeeded in doing—feminists' consciousness of the non-existence of women, except as precuts of men's desire." Donna Haraway, "A Cyborg Manifesto: Science, Technology, and Socialist-Feminism in the Late Twentieth Century," in *Simians, Cyborgs and Women: The Reinvention of Nature* (New York: Routledge, 1991), 158.
5. Donna Haraway, "A Cyborg Manifesto", 149–51.
6. Ibid., 149.
7. Ibid., 151.
8. Ibid., 151.
9. Forest Pyle, "Making Cyborgs, Making Humans, Of Terminators and Blade Runners." in *Film Theory Goes to the Movies,* ed. Jim Collins, Hilary Radner and Ava Preacher Collins (New York and London: Routledge, 1993), 227.
10. Ibid., 232.
11. Kathleen Fitzpatrick, "The Exhaustion of Literature: Novels, Computers, and the Threat of Obsolescence", *Contemporary Literature* 43, no.3 (2002): 518–29.
12. Ibid., 2.
13. Yvonne Tasker, *Spectacular Bodies. Gender, Genre and the Action Cinema* (London and New York: Routledge, 1993), 3.
14. Pyle, "Making Cyborgs, Making Humans", 233.
15. Tasker, *Spectacular Bodies*, 83.
16. Barbara Creed, *Phallic Panic. Film, Horror and the Primal Uncanny* (Melbourne: Melbourne University Press, 2005), 27.
17. Marlo Edwards, (2004).
18. Roger Warren Beebe, "After Arnold," in *Meta-Morphing: Visual Transformation and the Culture of Quick-Change*, ed. Vivian Sobchack (Minneapolis and London: University of Minnesota Press, 2000), 162.

19. Jean Baudrillard, *Simulacra and Simulation*, tr. Sheila Faria Glaser (Ann Arbor: The University of Michigan Press, 1994), 2.

20. Christopher A. Bolton, "From Wooden Cyborgs to Celluloid Souls: Mechanical Bodies in Anime and Japanese Puppet Theater", *Positions* 10, no.3 (2002): 730.

21. Haraway, "A Cyborg Manifesto", 152.

22. In her dealings with cyborgs and other time-travellers, Sarah shows the same kind of consciousness that Sherry Turkle describes in her study of children's (whom she calls 'cyborg children') understanding of computer games: "the cyborg consciousness that characterises to-day's children: a tendency to see computer systems as 'sort of' alive..." "Cyborg Babies and Cy-Dough-Plasm: Ideas about Life in the Culture of Simulation." in *Cyborg Babies: From Technosex to Technotots,* ed. Robbie Davis-Floyd and Joseph Dumit (New York: Routledge, 1998).

23. Haraway, "A Cyborg Manifesto", 181.

CHAPTER FOUR

PAST, PRESENT, FUTURE:
FINDING TREASURE IN THE LIVES OF LARA CROFT

URSULA FREDERICK

Figure Five: Angelina Jolie in *Lara Croft Tomb Raider: The Cradle of Life* (2003)

In the first moments of *Lara Croft: Tomb Raider* (2001), Lara Croft is introduced to us through her eyes. She stares directly, confidently into the gaze of the viewer. A woman who fills the frame. For an instant she remains silent and still, and then our perspective unexpectedly turns. Her full figure is revealed, suspended from a rope, "standing" upside down. Descending with a leap, Lara proceeds into the chambers of an ancient Egyptian sanctuary. She moves through the space in fits and starts; springing acrobatically and running across the stony floor, then pausing, looking, skirting columns with stealth as she makes her way towards the prize. Following Lara's line of sight the object of pursuit appears, at a suitably reified distance. It is raised on a plinth and gloriously bathed in the ray-of-heaven light that so-becomes an artefact of its stature. Before Lara can reach it, a moving mass of techno-savvy steel crashes into her path. The action is on! They fight, she wins, the reward is hers.

Soon after the gunsmoke settles it becomes clear that the entire scene is a simulacrum. Lara's battle was a training exercise—an exhausting bit of fun. Her monstrous opponent is really a robot named Simon, harmless unless otherwise customised to kill. The booty is a microchip formatted to fit Simon's hard-drive and play Lara's favourite tunes. Even the Egyptian antechamber is just a spare room redecorated to fulfil Lara's particular penchant for archaeological practice, a unique method Mark Rose describes as "excavating with bullets".[1]

As a scaled down simulation of the feature narrative that follows, this opening scene goes a long way towards establishing the gameplan of the Tomb Raider film, and its sequel *Lara Croft Tomb Raider: The Cradle of Life* (2003). The aesthetic direction, plot formula, and the symbolic devices that it encodes draws attention to many of the propositions about Lara Croft that I set out to explore in this chapter. Through this sequence the viewer becomes attuned to the protagonist as a convergence of dualisms, a chaos of temporal cues, and a wealth of allusions to the form and nature of the past. The ideas of multiplicity, replication and "replay" are central to the communication of the films' leading figure and her narrative quest: the parallel resolutions of personally imbued and universally meaningful past and future. It is from this very start that the premise of the film and the figure unfolds: Lara Croft is both subject and object in a game of intrigue, an archaeologist in pursuit of the past in a fight to save the future. Her battle is with time.

Many Versions, Many Lives

From the "woman-on-top" of the opening frame to the Pandora/Universal Mother dynamic of the sequel's name Lara Croft is a complex configuration of various historical, classical, mythical and contemporary literary allusions.[2] Often described as "part" something or someone else Lara has drawn parallels with Tank Girl, Indiana Jones, James Bond, Trinity, Dirty Harry, Barb Wire and even Jessica Rabbit. Beyond film, her character exposes links to Amazon warriors, contemporary cyber-heroines and various manifestations of the female heroine and Goddess archetypes. It is in fact this very in-between-ness of identities that is the source of her popular appeal and which situates her in an uneasy critical conundrum. As a character composed of many pasts it is hardly surprising to see how Lara may engender alternative futures. A point to which I will return towards the end of the chapter.

The difficulty in locating Lara Croft firmly in one camp of critical discourse or another may well reflect the unresolved tensions between different strands of feminist debate and popular media's perceived position as a communicative vehicle of a particular dominant agenda. Since she first emerged there has been considerable conjecture about Lara's "place". Some want to claim her, some revile her and many still ask, as Helen Kennedy framed the question, "is Lara Croft a Feminist Icon or a Cyberbimbo?"[3] For those who herald her as an emanicipatory figure she is imagined as a vehicle for the redistribution of strength and power, out of male dominion and into feminine form. Others contest that she is a virtual pornstar unequivocally condemned as an empty shell designed, pure and simple, to feed and fuel male desire.[4] Like her various cross-media versions, even Lara's popularity is best described as being in a state of flux. Rather than occupying any secure position in the hearts and minds of fans Lara's transformative nature has spilled into fan discourse, their opinions and interest wavering as frequently as she is rewritten.[5]

Perhaps such divergent perspectives are to be expected given Lara's vanguard appearance, rarely have formative figures been met without some consternation. Indeed it is this same groundbreaking status that makes her difficult to dismiss. As the first female character to drive a videogame's plot—to be the protagonist to be played—Lara's emergence signalled a revolution in gaming. Linked with this, and a series of other "firsts",[6] Lara's presence may be strongly aligned with a notion of exception. Her singularity, as exception, is recapitulated in a number of ways. Lara's solo appearance and achievements have been aligned with that of Western individualism—a supermodel celebrity amongst a growing pantheon of "femme fatales digitales".[7] Black sees her as an anomaly of technological success akin to Fritz Lang's female android Maria. She is the artificial woman, engineered to overcome "woman's" inherent adherence to nature and its resistance to technologisation.[8]

For many members of the gaming community it is precisely those traits which make Lara so outstanding—her spirit of adventure, her independence, intelligence, her humour, her virtual presence—which were lost in her translation to the big screen.[9] Similarly, much of Lara's "original" appeal appears to have bypassed film scholars, critics and fans for whom she is merely one amongst many "action babes",[10] the female equivalent of Indiana Jones,[11] or the poor conversion of a videogame heroine.[12] Yet, with the exception of cursory comparisons to Indiana, there has been little exploration of Lara's position within the archaeology adventure film. How does Lara stand up as an archaeologist and as a fighter within the context of this tradition? And what may she contribute to a reading of its films?

Who is Lara Croft?

The film figure played by Angelina Jolie is part of a broader network of manifestations of Lara Croft. Unlike the majority of characters that have migrated one way or another across different media, Lara exists in a more interactive matrix. A nomadic, almost slippery entity passing through, across and between textual arenas, she is repeatedly reshaped and rendered in altered states and reconfigured forms. At times the boundaries between these texts elide distinction thus making it impossible to extract a purely distinct film version. Moreover, there is a case for suggesting that these different representations operate, to some extent, recursively. The *Tomb Raider* (hereafter *TR*) games, as some scholars have argued, model existing Hollywood traditions with regard to representation, narration, aesthetics and script.[13] The *TR* films, meanwhile, clearly reference the game within specific narrative sequences, structure, sets, costumes, action moves and in the orientation of viewpoints. The repetitive logic of gaming is only mildly discernable, in the way Lara is continually immersed in subterranean circumstances, a position which reiterates both the game scenarios of *TR* and the essential archaeology motif of the underground.

In summary terms the *TR* films present Lady Lara Croft as a professional young woman of independent means. She is both a product and rebel of upper class English society, enjoying the privileges that her family title and estate has bestowed upon her and the freedom to ignore its conventions. Lara is an archaeologist whom, like her deceased father, is well recognised as a specialist in her field. And it is as a direct consequence of her professional activities that her identity as a fighter is revealed. It is in the context of her cinematic avatar that Lara's identity as an archaeologist assumes greatest emphasis. Unlike the "heiress", "independent adventurer" and "writer" personas that dominate the video game and its backstory, Lara's professional standing as an internationally renowned expert is central to both films. Press reports suggest that Paramount and Angelina Jolie went to some effort to dispel Lara's "raider" reputation, an attribute that would certainly tarnish any professional merit.[14] One outcome of this emphasis on profession is that Lara is immediately located within an established repertoire of action-adventure films referred to here, for the sake of my argument, as the cinema of archaeology.[15] This subgenre is replete with its own set of representational devices and formulaic conventions, some of which it shares with other film types like the "swashbuckler" and "fortune-hunter".[16] Through these archaeological associations, the viewer is inserted into a familiar terrain of recognisable signs and scenarios made most famous through the antics of Indiana Jones.[17] Though the *TR* films broadly conform to the motifs and melodramatic mode of this archaeological cinema, I suggest that Lara's presence represents a unique intervention within it.

Tomb Raider as Archaeology Adventure Cinema

I invoke Lara's profession because it is central to her identity as a woman willing to fight. Archaeology frames her personal world and it conveys the past-as-future danger and dilemma that stimulates her drive. O'Day observes that the "action babe" is motivated by a desire to do her job well.[18] Importantly, I would add in the case of Lara, profession is used to define the heroine's purpose and contest. This aura of specialisation and duty to work removes the stain of bloodlust, greed, vengeance, or emotionally-crazed violence, which might otherwise fuel a character's will to fight. More specifically, the lens of the archaeological cinema offers another perspective on Lara Croft's ambiguity and her transgressive impact and appeal. Four motifs of the archaeological cinema are explored to this effect. They are the artefact, the subterranean, time-travel, and the earth disturbed.

The express purpose of the archaeological metaphor in the *TR* cycle is to create a narrative context and motivating force for Lara's quest. The archaeological frame is useful in providing the value-laden objects and exotic locations required of the literary medieval romance format that the film adopts.[19] Furthermore, the domain of the classics (myth, history and archaeology), as a symbol of the past, is where we may find links to the cause and meaning for Lara's fight. In both films the disruption of the past and the secrets that it stores creates a chain of reaction that ultimately threatens human existence and the future of the world. *Lara Croft: Tomb Raider*'s plot is driven by Lara's search to find and realign the two halves of the legendary Triangle of Light. This mysterious artefact symbolises the temporal order of the universe. At the precise moment of planetary alignment this key, inserted into its companion device, holds the power to bestow its bearer with the ability to alter history and control time. The film's sequel, *Lara Croft Tomb Raider: Cradle of Life* opens with Lara's underwater discovery of a golden orb housed in the sunken Lunar Temple of Alexander the Great. The orb, or "eye", is a globe which maps the location of a fabled chest, the notorious Pandora's Box. The pestilence it contains may be used as a weapon against the world.

The Earth Disturbed

The notion of a world under threat is commonplace within the action-adventure genre and a consistent trope of popular archaeology films. Significantly, a causal relationship between world endangerment and archaeological disturbance is a hallmark of the type. Consider the dark clouds passing over and the cuts to lightening that intercede Indy's break into the chamber of the Ark (*Raiders of the Lost Ark* [1981]) or the sandstorm that forms as Evelyn opens the Book of the Dead (*The Mummy* 1999). If it does not unleash disorder, the archaeological act is always, at least, coincident with it. In *The Lair of the White Worm* (1988) the floor mosaic of a Mercia-aged temple is uncovered, in a modern-day farmyard, just as the cult of the serpent deity Dionine is ritually reactivated. The disruption of the earth that results from excavation—and the moral doubt cast on the act of discovery—is coded in foreboding visual cues: pestilence swarm, the earth opens up, and dust storms sweep through. Natural elements arise to aesthetic excess and cosmic display: torrential rain, fire, wind, crumbling stone. It is as if the ground which is spoiled speaks back in protest. Thus the forces of nature become both a warning and barrier that each of the protagonists, and their cohorts, must overcome if they and humankind are to be saved. With such spectacular moments of revelation the audience is left without doubt that a course of action has been set.

In *Cradle of Life*, the transgression of ground occurs early, thereby establishing the archaeologist's purpose (to retrieve) and provoking the narrative (the pursuit) that follows. The earthquake that opens the film precipitates Lara's action and signals the impending upset. The first strands of dialogue reinforce nature's prescience and squarely locates the danger within the protagonist's fold:

> Lara: Something wrong?
> Gus: First Alexander doesn't record the temple's location, then God wipes it from the earth with a volcano, now even the currents change. Lara, maybe this temple is not meant to be found.
> Lara: Everything lost is meant to be found...

Representations of earth and ground are inextricably tied to the empowered object that it is believed to contain. Since the all-powerful artefact represents cosmic balance the space it occupies is, by consequence, a kind of hallow ground. The sanctity of this space is conveyed in static imagery—such as warnings encoded in glyphs—as well as in active form. Booby-trapped chambers create suspense and reiterate the message: some places should remain undisturbed. There are dramatic consequences for those who walk there and who do not belong. Whomever ruptures this spatial order is either pre-destined to own the object and/or its sacrilegious despoiler. The archaeologist by association, is rendered, momentarily, in uncertain terms. It is here, at the pointy end of professional practice, that the archaeologist's act is called into question and the inherent ambiguity of their role revealed. It is in the symbolic effects of their ransacking and raiding "discoveries", that the politics of archaeology and ethics of cross-cultural engagement are played out in disguise. Tapping into well-worn images of uncontrollable power when the feminine is unleashed,[20] the cataclysmic events that follow archaeological discovery seem all the more loaded when it is a woman who does the unveiling. *TR* reworks Lara's role along these lines, albeit to a limited degree. On the one hand, she acknowledges the idea of sacred space and assumes a respect for maintaining its existence. She acknowledges what she is doing, which effectively supplants the "tomb raider" cast with more honourable ambitions. Lara's recognition of other cultural custom and laws is rare in the repertoire of archaeology films.[21] And it is an almost self-reflexive nod to the subgenre's often racist and colonialist imperatives. On the other hand, there is no doubt that she will proceed. Before entering the cradle of life Lara's apology to the African tribal elder, "Now I am sorry if I have to disturb your Gods" is immediately followed with a declaration of intent "but I will do it if I must".

The danger of disruption reveals, furthermore, the uncertainty that the pursuit of the past may bring. Discovery does indeed threaten accepted knowledge and can change the "world as we know it", revealing new answers to debated questions and upsetting long-regarded historical "truths". This is the power, both disruptive and regenerative, that the archaeological pursuit produces. The knowledge inherent in significant discoveries comes at a cost. Information is lost at the same time information is found. The archaeological process which produces information, also destroys. Thus, an archaeological site, once uncovered or excavated, may become lost information and can never be "restored".

The Artefact as Empowered Object

If unveiling the past is associated with emergent danger then that same threat may be posed by the very object or site disclosed. A consistent format of the mummy film, for instance, is that the desecration of the corpse, through its discovery, initiates an evil awakening (for example, *Talos the Mummy* [1998], *Blood from the Mummy's Tomb* [1971], *The Awakening* [1980]). In other archaeology narratives "the relic" at the heart of the quest has multiple identifications, commonly oppositional in nature. Construed as a missing link in the chain of knowledge the empowered object both threatens *and* promises to unseat the prevailing understanding of the past. Most importantly, the object vacillates between being a talisman for good or an object of evil. The devices Lara pursues contain a dormant power that are more or less beholden to the will of the individual that wields it. To ensure that neither the time-piece nor the chest falls into the wrong hands Lara must first find these objects herself. In both cases, therefore, Lara is confronted with the forces of time and the challenges set by the materialisation of a mythic past in the present. In a daisy-chain of clue seeking events, each film's narrative evolves in a chase across exotic landscapes as one artefact leads to another.

While the fetish object or long-lost treasure is a prevalent motif of quest narratives, such artefacts carry a specific salience in archaeology-adventure films. The object often represents a lifelong pursuit, the climactic discovery resulting from scholarly endeavour. It also aligns the protagonist's purpose with a degree of faith: a resolute belief in the existence of evidence that had otherwise not been there. Thus, the artefact embodies the tensions that reside between belief and knowledge, evidence and doubt. Initially, the object's worth is assigned through its material substance, as a unique jewel of the ancient past. Out of its original context it exists alongside other antiquities: no more than a pretty fragment or a pricey collectable, with no inherent power to bestow. It remains symbolically neutral in this passive out-of-place state. Yet once its background is uncovered, its story brought to life, the object's value is found in its intangible magic rather than its market price. Once "discovered", "understood" or "decoded" in this way, the object is activated as a living presence and becomes an instrumental force in the narrative arc. This is exemplified when the Book of the Dead (*The Mummy*) or the Key of Solomon (*The Librarian II: Return to King Solomon's Mines* [2006]) are brought to life through ritual invocation. From this point it becomes a kind of time-bomb that must be managed until it is returned to rest. In *TR* this fight against time is made explicit in the "counting down" to the planetary alignment ticking away in the Medieaval clock. Hence, it is when the (dead) past is made (living) present that the object becomes a problem faced as well as a solution to be attained. Thus, the earth invaded and the object out of place signify a temporal and spatial order that has been ruptured. Once the normality of this order (time and space)—as contained and preserved—is disturbed it threatens the future.

Time-travel

What is clear from the roles afforded the archaeological site and artefact, is that the past constitutes spatio-temporal order within the narrative of the archaeology film. The ability to operate across different dimensions of this order simulaenously, by "unlocking" (understanding) the secrets of the past, gives popular archaeology its metaphoric power to time-travel. This is a motif which is clearly illustrated in *Stargate* (1994), where the amulet and the stargate act as a portal between past and future as well as parallel worlds. *Stargate*, and the more recent *Timeline* (2003), are reasonably sophisticated renditions of the archaeology/time-travel fantasy "to witness in person the ancient events and phenomena we study today…".[22] The journeys of teleportation are routinely pictured as both perilous and desirable. Pivotal moments in the plot centre on the fear that one may "get stuck" or that the course of future events may become corrupted. Archaeology conceptualised as time-travel transgresses the linear arrangement of time and space to challenge and alter accepted histories and "truths". In the cinema of archaeology such ventures are the source of imbalance, an overturning of order to chaos. Once again, the tension of the archaeological character is that s(he) manages this order ambiguously, initiating its imbalance as well as its restoration. *Timeline* registers this anxiety—as a conflict between the ways of the past and the life of the future—through the relationships of its characters. The senior archaeologist Professor E.A. Johnston (Billy Connolly) and his colleagues Kate (Frances O'Connor) and Marek (Gerard Butler) possess a passion for the past that his son Chris (Paul Walker), the film's protagonist, does not share. Suspecting his son's love interest in Kate, the professor warns, "You and Kate are from different worlds…Trust me, if its between archaeology and you, you'll lose". This rift in "time", and personality, is reiterated further when Chris attempts to woo Kate, who is diligently digging a tunnel late into the night. "So are you going to follow in your father's footsteps?" she asks Chris, who replies "I'm not all that interested in the past", and the courting goes downhill from here. Recounting this rejection to Marek, Chris says "I don't understand you guys, you all live in the past…none of you archaeologists look to the future". These differences in direction—one looking forward the other back—distances Chris from the rest of the team, his father's surrogate brood. This discord is set against a war, 600 years ago. The experience of time-travel first illuminates these conflicts then ultimately unifies and resolves the two. The tunnel which Kate is excavating when Chris' feelings are voiced (and subsequently deflected) is the physical entrypoint into the other conflict and time, the Medieval world of Castlegard, France. Once again this positions the past as a threat and the archaeological fabric as the conduit between times and *other* worlds. As the custodian, keeper and translator of the past, the archaeologist mediates this threat on behalf of the future.

Subterranean Settings

From ice caves and stone chambers, to jungle caverns and underwater ruins, the subterranean setting is prevalent within archaeology films. The spatial metaphors of under and inner depict alternative sides to the normative surfaces of the exterior world. These subsurface contexts are the archaeologist's terrain, and it is in such environments that Lara's dominance prevails. The world of the past is depicted as a place of inhospitable strangeness. It appears as a mildly gothic image of the underworld; dank, dark and replete with contorted forms. It is a place that evokes mystery and fear and where the unexpected may easily occur. Notably, the pivotal moments and memorable spectacles of the archaeology film occur within this sphere: in hidden chambers, tombs and temples. Both *TR* films open and end within the realm of the subterranean. This image of the world is of a place inverted, inside out, upside down.[23]

It is difficult to ignore Natalie Zemon-Davis' reading of disorder in exploring this image of the earth upturned. Zemon-Davis' analyses of early modern European literary, artistic and performative texts suggests that the source of disruption is often aligned to the figure of a powerful active female— a process she termed "the woman-on-top".[24] Namely, that the woman out of her place was used to denote contemporary and spiritual disorder—a potent image of inversion denoting a world turned upside down. Zemon-Davis' critics are uncomfortable with the notion that a woman in power is read as inversion and disarray.[25] Yet what we may take from her reading, with regard to Lara, is the transgressive potential of a woman who will not be ruled and whose strength is so openly on display. Notably, Lara frequently appears in the film as comfortably suspended upside down. Plunging from skyscrapers, swinging on the bungee, entering the Cradle of Life, and even poised for attack. This framing—the inversion of Lara in the viewer's gaze—re-evaluates the association of female dominance with disarray. It urges the question, what might it mean to be seen as a woman-on-top and a woman inverted, in a world already upside down?

Ambiguity and Archetype

The four motifs, the artefact, the subterranean, time-travel, and the earth disturbed, show Lara's will to fight is shaped by conjoining fragments of the popular archaeological discourse. This context situates the nature of the fight as fundamentally a battle with and against the forces of time. The ultimate outcome of this fight is similarly framed as a temporal imperative: restoring the past in order to ensure the future. These motifs also communicate the archaeological cinema as ripe in archetypal contradictions. This is evident in the inherent duality of the artefact: as dead/alive, dazzling surface/embedded power, creative/destructive, good/evil. Similarly, above-ground and below-ground, past and future all exist in the frame of the present. There is a strong theme of ambiguity in the popular rendering of archaeological motifs. The archaeologist, by association, embodies this theme and its air of transgression.

The integration of these central motifs demonstrates the *TR* cycle's adherence to popular archaeology film convention. Yet they also exhibit factors that place her outside of the formula, shedding new light on Lara's existing aura of ambivalence and boundary transgression. Thus despite the derision of some gaming fans, Lara retains her mantle, as a revolutionary first, even here in the well-established "age-old" tropes of the archaeology cinema. For in many ways Lara Croft represents a radical departure from the cliché of the archaeologist hero, his female support, or the female archaeologist as background model. She is a far cry from the macho cowboy or the damsel in distress: stereotypes which enshrine an outmoded gender division, thereby operating on romantic nostalgia for a lost era.[26] By contrast Lara is a thoroughly forward-oriented figure. Evidence of this is construed in subtle character details. As suggested, for instance, in a comparison of musical preference between Lara and her contemporary Kate (*Timeline*). While "excavating", Lara's predilection is for techno mix the latter is accompanied by what sounds suspiciously like Patsy Cline.

By envisioning the context within which Lara performs her profession and her fight, I return to the air of ambiguity with which she is so strongly identified. I take the position that this ambiguity, which I prefer to read as a plurality or multivalence, is central to her construction as a fighting woman. What I set out to discuss is how her characterisation—as a fighter and as an archaeologist—is central to her configuration as a symbolic representation of the woman warrior and to some extent a goddess and originary figure. This plurality is established through a convergence of oppositions and is in keeping with the many faces of legendary women, and men for that matter, from whom she draws aspects of her identity and purpose. It is in the context of an archaeological appreciation—where the linearity of the temporal continuum becomes more fragmented and layered—that this virtual collapsing of identities is apparent.

Archaeology is well-suited as a framework for communicating Lara Croft as a warrior woman and Goddess archetype for three primary reasons. First, it is a means of accessing the past within the present: by drawing lines of connection between myth, tradition and history and thereby figuratively awakening legendary metanarratives for the present world. The discourse and visual language of archaeology serves as the perfect platform for the performance of woman as warrior-goddess precisely because the discipline forefronts the power of the past within the present through a process of "story"-telling. Allusions to archetypal figures are easily communicated through its reference to the ancient past. Secondly, it is a type of cinema replete with motifs of a dual or contradictory nature. The expression of goddess and woman warrior identities, are also commonly construed as an ambivalent or equivocal character.[27]

In addition to the discussion of motifs already raised, the ambivalence of the archaeologist is conveyed through the concept of the double life, assigned to superhero(ine)s, and the alterego or the evil twin. It is a template predicated upon the primary roles that the archaeologist undertakes: fieldworker, scholar, lab technician. Dirk Pitt (*Sahara* [2005]), for instance, does the work of a maritime historian/archaeologist, salvage expert and materials conservationist. As with Pitt, these identities are often conflated into the one encyclopedia-brained "supercapable" character. Yet the different scenarios and skills that the archaeologist performs can sometimes jar, as if they are a contradiction in terms. Indiana Jones is both a shy stiff-suited professor and a bold rugged outdoorsman. His turf is the library and the cave. Egyptologist Daniel Jackson (*Stargate*) is at once brilliant and incompetent. And then there are those characters which undergo a more sinister Jeckyll/Hyde transition, like that of Angus Flint (*The Lair of the White Worm* [1988]) who is converted (by a poisonous bite) to become a member of the cult whose ruins he uncovered. Finally, there is the cinema of archaeology's most iconic figure—the mummy— a convergence of opposites that supports what Eric Wilson calls the maintenance of the organic in inorganic form.[28]

I suggest that this conflation of roles—harmony of contradictions and the overall aura of ambivalence that such dualities support—allows space for multiple complex identities to emerge and for the viewer to "realistically" entertain. First, it allows us to suspend disbelief about what the protagonist may or may not reasonably do. The mortality of Lara Croft is made believable (if barely) by virtue of the absurd breadth of her interests and skills, (and because she reiterates a well established model). Secondly, it introduces the tension of internal dilemma or inconsistency at the core of the archaeological character and their associates. Lest we forget the title of the film, Lara raids tombs, even if it is presumed to be for a good cause! Lara's associates reinforce the potential for the line between good and evil to be blurred. Her cohort, Terry Sheridan is an ex-Royal Navy commander turned traitor while the "evil" conspirator bio-terrorist Jonathon Rice also earned a nobel prize. If Terry can imagine Lara's latent dark side: "We are two of a kind … a pair, opposite sides of the same coin", Rice attempts to tease it out:

> Think of what I'm offering you, the chance to find out how it all began. Life, Lara, how it all began. Don't tell me you're not tempted…Take us to the cradle of life, it's your destiny to see what's inside.

If Lara's counterpart Terry can come good, might Lara also turn bad? Though the viewer is unlikely to truly entertain that position, the idea/possibility still operates as a source of play.

This multivalence of Lara, her shape-shifting potential, is no accident, it is intentionally inferred. It is signalled visually through a series of costume changes, attitudes and styles. Gone is the one-type-fits-all, feature-length safari garb comprising earthy tones and natural fibres. It is an unfortunate aesthetic, in its resemblance to the colonial adventurer but it is modelled frequently all the same: Rick O'Connell (Brendan Fraser), Flynn Carsen (Noah Wyle) and Dirk Pitt (Matthew McConaughey), Allan Quatermain (Richard Chamberlain, Patrick Swayze), Matthew Corbeck (Charlton Heston) and Indiana Jones (Harrison Ford). In the first film, Lara's wardrobe incorporates attire for any occasion, from her trademark combat-sportswear look (skimpy shorts, t-shirt, boots and gunbelt) to flowing nightwear, motorcycle leathers, and saffron sari. A range of apparel supports a range of identities and moods. *Cradle of Life* costumes comprise more elaborately site-specific clothing. Like the blizzard-wear fashion (with snow-inspired collar) she adopts for her visit to Siberia. Or the gold satin jacket complete with embroidered Chinese dragon emblazoned on her back for her excursion into hinterland China. Loose-fit (for Lara) Asiatic styled tops carry her through Shanghai and Hong Kong, while in Africa she reverts to classic khaki. In this way her appearance is chameleonic cosmopolitan; attuned to fit her local environment with the iconicity of a designer ethnic touch.

Beyond the corporeal body Lara's shape-shifting identity is delineated through a vast array of armoury, Bond-like gadgets, and machinic props at her disposal. Her mastery of these instruments impresses upon us her adaptability and technical prowess. While the bodily integration of tracking devices and transmittors produces a cyberheroine feel. Such chameleonic displays are complementary to the varied socio-cultural settings that Lara occupies with ease: from the domestic sphere of her own aristocratic estate, the auction houses of the hoipolloi, the jungles and Buddhist monasteries of SE Asia, the boat houses of Hong Kong, to the native communities of remote Africa and the Arctic. As well as offering "eye candy", these shifts in appearance are structurally significant. They synthesise Lara with the plot, propelling it forward as narrative and display. And in alluding to different aspects of character they operate a parallel quest: to amplify and unveil, by gradation, the mystique of Lara Croft. This search is more elusive: the more that Lara is known the less she is boxed in. However, the mutability of her character makes it difficult to assign her any single course of personal development. Internal transformations are largely kept hidden, change is only observed in the surface qualities of her person: her clothes, attitude and skin. The spectacle of fashion and styling work like misguided clues directing us towards but never revealing Lara's inner life. It may well be because there is no single Lara to be discovered, just a series of maps and keys. Or it may be as Lara suggests, at the end of *Cradle of Life*, that "some things are not meant to be found".

Fighting (for) Time

In looking at Lara as a fighter and an archaeologist I have drawn parallels with other characters and films, as exemplars of the mythos of archaeology. By discussing Lara Croft within the same context I explore concurrently the representation of archaeology and of fighting as an accepted and necessary feature of the genre, though neither generally attributed to women. The "fight" is significant to archaeology adventure films for two reasons. First, the pursuit and the fight are essentially conflated into a chain of challenge, which drives and interrupts the narrative, thereby creating the "ups and downs" pace of action. Overcoming obstacles, acquiring objects and reading the past (deciphering code) are acts enmeshed with swordplay, knife rumbles and gunbattle. The protagonist is perpetrator of both violence and the invasive disruption of time and space. It is this tension—which mirrors the conventional opposition between good and evil—which structures the plot. And it is its resolution—through battle—which culminates in the film's conclusion. Lara's position as the fulcrum of this ambiguous act places her not only at but *as* the convergence of this classic dichotomy. A position which leads her to be read as a contemporary manifestation of good and evil, goddess and monsterous-feminine.[29] Along this line, the fight for and against time that Lara imbues may be read as the provocation and restitution of balance. Upsetting convention, disturbing norms and breaking new ground are exactly the kinds of empowering gestures that contemporary warrior heroines might bring.

Lara's prominence within the gaming and archaeology arenas, both perceived and represented as masculine spaces, is in and of itself transgressive. In the context of gaming Kennedy argues: "By being there she disturbs the natural symbolism of masculine culture".[30] In the *TR* films Lara is not the only woman left standing, she is the only woman. And in the context of archaeological cinema this alone makes her unique.

Returning to the metaphor of a world turned upside down is significant to the image of the warrior woman goddess archetypes in so far as her dualistic nature is considered to constitute balance. Alluding to her own divine duality Lara demonstrates her knowledge of this mythic ideal, when recounting the "history" of the legendary Pandora's Box to MI6:

> Lara: How do you think life began? Shooting star? Primordial ooze? In 2300BC an Egyptian Pharaoah found a place that he named the *Cradle of Life* where we life began. And there he found a box the box which brought life to earth. The Pharoah opened the box but all that was left inside was the "ramunti", or anti-life the plague which came as the companion to Life.
> MI6: Companion?
> Lara: Nature is about balance, all the world comes in pairs, yin and yang, right and wrong, men and women, what's pleasure without pain?…Alexander felt that the box was too powerful to be trusted to any man so he returned it to its home in the Cradle of Life and it has never been seen since.

Conceptualised as an ancient deity, the Goddess, encodes a principle of complementarity where balanced oppositions coexist to establish and promote a dynamic essence of life. She represents to "become" by fulfilling the "wholeness" of being. She appears as a singularity of self yet she is connected to all life. The Goddess figure also commonly possesses a dual aspect, comprising complementary feminine and masculine principles, light and dark, summer winter, creation destruction, benevolance and rage.[31] She is in command of her body and the various instinctive, intuitive and sensual powers it may convey. Other versions of the Goddess reflect aspects of a monsterous-feminine.[32] In comprehending nature's dynamic wholeness as an amalgam of complementary principles, it follows that if the harmonious integrity of this being is split a destructive power is unleashed. The mythic figure of the Goddess Monster has served as a source for other female characters in film and it is possible to read this balanced composite of "opposites" within the various identity expressions of Lara Croft. As noted, Lara's appearance serves to communicate her as an embodied conjunction of difference. She wears the uniform of the imperialist adventurer and the ethnic other. She replicates the image of the mythic past and the cyberheroine future. And importantly, the two assets by which Lara is most frequently identified, and critiqued, are her big breasts and her big guns. A highly loaded set of pairs signifying the conventional principles of the feminine and the phallus. In the *TR* films they are regularly contrived in partnership with one another; her arms outstretched, guns elevated, shooting considerably higher than the hip. It is Lara's trademark fighting posture, which effectively disarms the dominance of either and through a doubling act reissues the power of both.

There is a well-established pattern in representations of the warrior and goddess archetypes as inherently fluid figures, or capricious character, freed from the binaristic logic of Cartesian dualism by virtue of being neither one nor the other but both and beyond the sum of the parts. Lara's earlier antecedents, in this regard, comprise female warriors, goddess figures and superheroines. Thus it is through her ability to harmonise duality and apply different sides of her self that she may be read as an expression of both the Goddess/monster and woman warrior figure. In her complicity with the dualities of nature and ability to control time she is able to upturn in the act of preserving world order. Lara achieves this balance through the immediacy of fighting, but the more symbolic weapon in this fight is her choice. The battle operates on two levels, it is a race against time to save the world and it reflects a personal contest that takes place within. The ambivalence of the archaeologist, the artefact and discovery itself, in conjunction with the duality of mythic figures, allude to Lara's identity as potentially both good and evil. While the viewer is in little doubt that she will make the right decision, Lara's choice is a pivotal instrument in winning her fight. A fight that determines the future. This is most clear in *Cradle of Life*, where Lara recasts the mistakes of Pandora (the past) to create Hope (a better future).

The mixed messages and responses that Lara Croft, the character, evokes only seem to substantiate this notion of duality within her. As Mikula succinctly observes, she "is everything that is bad about representations of women in culture, and everything good".[33] What I have suggested is that this ambiguity draws upon archetypal configurations of the Goddess/monster and warrior woman figures and that the construction of Lara's identity as a fighter and archaeologist is central to this. Allusions to Lara's antecedent figures are akin to the fetish of the film's discovery: once removed from a place in the past the artefact is rendered as a path to the future.

The inherent ambiguities of her character coupled with the camp humour and connotation of the carnivalesque lend Lara a "playability" made all the more apparent through her association with video game culture. It is this playability that posits Lara as a site of subjective becoming and belonging, as an object of desire. This may well boil down to wanting to be her, with her, or both but it is the multivalent message that Lara's lives offer. For some fans she represents the escapist pleasures of popular archaeology, a way into other worlds. Based on her multiple texts and the varied responses there is no doubt that Lara is an "object" of our gaze and a fantasy character to be played. Further still Lara embodies such traits as a convergence of attitudes, rather than as a strictly dichotomous divide. Rather than lean one way or another in a false dichotomy of conventional "norms" Lara occupies both poles of the gender, class, and even arguably, cultural divide and every position in between. I suggest that this convergence of traits past/future, organic/technological, creative/destructive, sexually available/forbidden, active/passive amongst others communicates a range of subjective positions with which the viewer may choose to identify.

To Control the Past, is to Control the Future

In Spielberg's seminal treatment of the "genre", Indiana Jones attempts to dispel the myth of the archaeological endeavour:

> Forget any ideas you've got about lost cities, exotic travel, and digging up the world. We do not follow maps to buried treasure.[34]

Indy encapsulates, in word and image, the popular conception of what archaeology is presumed to be: an escape from the mundane present, both in the adventurous pursuit and in the "riches" to be found. Framed within this metaphor Lara represents both the archaeologist leading the discovery and the illusory object being pursued. It is this very kind of ambiguity that underpins the Lara Croft character and her discourse.[35]

It has been suggested that the medium of film has fixed her game avatar's fluidity. I argue the contrary, that the cinema of archaeology grounds her ambiguous presence and its multivalent function. Yet as critics, scholars and fans debate Lara's value, it is worth proposing that she is nothing more, or less, than a jewel of speculative fiction: a convergence in time and "place where writers, artists, and readers gather to speculate about the past, the present and the future".[36] The archaeological metaphor is central to Lara's configuration as a professional and a fighter. Her ambiguities and transgressive presence serve to reinforce her position as contemporary heroine and goddess-like figure. While Lara's fighting and archaeological personas are instrumental in communicating mythic identities of "universal" appeal, and positing her as source of projective potential. The extent/index to which Lara's latent possibilities may be realised lie outside the cinematic frame.

In addition to the commercial spin-offs that have reproduced the Lara Croft character into a marketable commodity[37] she has inspired a wealth of "independent" versions. These include a range of artistic engagements, performative renditions and "unauthorised" products.[38] Perhaps the most startling creations are the reenactments of Lara's identity through the bodies of her fans. Fans and "cosplayers" dress up and pose in her familiar clothes.[39] They photograph themselves performing as Lara Croft and share them in various online environments. In the more creative compositions other images are borrowed and digitally manipulated to create whole narrative scenes which the fan-as-Lara inhabits. A large proportion of these images not only place the fan in the body of Lara but in the imagined fantasy settings of her fighter/archaeologist profession. However the authors/artists view this process—as embodiments of Lara's identity, or as reformatting Lara to fit their own—they are a powerful index of Lara's transformative potential. These artistic fan fictions render Lara in all her ambiguity as myth and as a site to project their own fantasy lives and futures. Thus the archetypes of the warrior woman and metaphor of archaeology become tools for new readings and identifications and, potentially self-discovery. Timeline gives voice to this projective potential encoded in the archaeologist's time-traveller ego:

> It's not just about the rocks and the rubble ... its about these people, who were they? What were there stories? It helps us to understand where we come from, or where we're going ... You make your own history.

Such imaginative reversionings of Lara's selves (and Lara as self) provide a tangential insight into the question of the viewer's subjective identification and female fighter's agency. They also offer perspective on a consistent critique of the fighting female "formulation", as too often defined by or in relation to men. Not only is the heroine's strength seen to derived from male characters, who "are always lurking, either as potential lovers, as controlling father figures or bosses, as potential threats, or sometimes all three at once",[40] but she is also predominately produced and directed by men. Critics and scholars of Lara Croft feel a need to point out that she—her gaming avatar at least—was created by a man (Toby Gard) for a teen male audience.[41] At the same time, there exists a degree of resentment over Angelina Jolie's corporeal intervention into Lara's polygon frame. Diane Carr likens such fetishised emphases on Lara's construction as "a leering over Dr Frankenstein's shoulder".[42] Surely, it is precisely in these kind of fan fictions that Lara's reconfigured body reasserts her origins of play. As inhabitations and manipulations of the authorised version they are in keeping with the idea—and the myth—of Lara Croft as a revolutionary, and as a transgressive interventionist form. Further still they resonate with Lara's own characterisation as a repeat and a copy of mythic warrior and goddess archetypes.

Despite her iconic singular presence Lara Croft should not be read in isolation. A point served by the ambiguity of the texts within which she is represented. Moreover, she embodies the myth of the warrior goddess, not as a depiction of any one entity but as a series of selves that channel ambiguity and flux into perpetually morphing versions. Using her multiplicity to serve their own ends, Lara's fans and cosplayers tap into the tradition of the woman-on-top, and the critical use of the carnival by women; and they draw attention to another archetype, the empty cipher of the universal "Everywoman".[43]

We may read the multiple images of Lara's identity as lenses reflecting different, sometimes contradictory, aspects of an integrated whole. We might also consider these representations, like each of Lara's integrated selves, as another "playable" version. Each of which casts a different light, and if read intertextually, suggests a more complex configuration. A configuration which, nonetheless, avoids any single definitive interpretation. Opinions continue to diverge on whether Lara is a vision of female liberation or one of exploitation. Many suggest that her value lies in being all at once. Perhaps a constructive way of thinking through what Lara offers, as an image of archaeologist and iconic female fighter, is not to mistake her for any particular treasure—but to imagine her as a key and a guide that may eventually lead us to it.

Notes

1. Mark Rose, "Excavating with Bullets (review)," *Archaeology,* June 14, 2001. http://www.archaeology.org/online/reviews/tombraider/movie.html
2. The title "Cradle of Life" may be read as a twofold allegory. The "cradle" is in the first instance, a direct reference to the Pandora's Box of Greek mythology and explicitly communicated in the film. The recasting of Lara as *both* Pandora and Hope, in the closing climax, is an example of Lara's characterisation as a convergence of apparently opposing traits, ie as threat and salvation. A secondary allusion of the title may be found in the association of the "cradle of life", in human evolutionary terms, with both Africa

(where the scene is set) and the notion of the African/Mitrochrondrial Eve—popularly presumed to be the "mother" of all humankind.

3. Helen W. Kennedy, "Lara Croft: Feminist Icon or Cyberbimbo," *Game Studies* vol 2 issue 2, December (2002).

4. Two examples are Germaine Greer, cited in Maja Mikula, and Kurt Lancaster, "Lara Croft: The Ultimate Young Adventure Girl or the unending media desire for models, sex, and fantasy," *Performing Arts Journal*, 78 (2004): 87–97.

5. The degree to which fans clearly discern Lara's difference: within particular media (eg film vs videogame), as compared to other characters (eg Lara vs Buffy or Indiana Jones), and within 'herself', (eg game avatar *TombRaider v1* vs *TombRaider v2*); and importantly between realities, shows a markedly media-savvy consciousness, which belies some scholars, and to some extent obviates any distinction between scholarly and fan readings.

6. For instance, Lara Croft is the first non-human model to be listed by a professional modelling agency and, arguably, "the world's first computer-generated star". Daniel Black, "The Silicone Chick: Lara Croft and Sexy Technology," *Metro Magazine*, no.127/8 (2001): 76. Kurt Lancaster lists a number of Lara's other accomplishments as evidence of her "star personality" in "Lara Croft: The Ultimate," 87. And just as *Tomb Raider* departs from the traditional game play format, Lara Croft is recognisably unique in popular stereotypes of archaeologists.

7. Black, Lancaster and Verena Kuni, for example, see Lara Croft as a digital supermodel or celebrity of computer technology. Verena Kuni "Cyborg configurations as formations of (self-)creation in the fantasy space of technological creation: Old and new mythologies of <artificial humans>," in *Mythical Bodies I*, http://www.medienkunstnetz.de/themes/cyborg_bodies/mythical_bodies_I/. Black, "The Silicone Chick"; Lancaster "Lara Croft: The Ultimate".

8. Schleiner refers to Lara as an automaton. Black argues that Lara's position "at the intersection of woman and machine" is a reversal of "a dominant gendering of technology as masculine". Black, "The Silicone Chick", 77-8. For an examination of *Metropolis* and Maria within the broader context of android creation and representation see Eric Wilson's engaging study of *The Melancholy Android: On the Psychology of Sacred Machines*, (Albany: State University of New York Press, 2006).

9. Fantone for one suggests that the film lacks the temporality and other features of the game and that "the ambiguous characteristics associated with Lara's gender identity were changed into a more stereotypical gender role" Laura Fantone, "Final fantasies: Virtual Women's Bodies," *Feminist Theory* 4, no.1 (2003): 66.

10. Marc O'Day coined the term "action babe cinema" to describe contemporary action heroines like Lara. "Beauty in Motion: Gender, Spectacle and Action Babe Cinema," in *Action and Adventure Cinema*, ed. Yvonne Tasker, 201–18. (London and New York: Routledge, 2004). As noted in text, other film characters (female and male) are employed by scholars and critics in attempts to describe Lara. Tank Girl is a favoured comparison.

11. Many scholars, critics and fans situate Lara through comparison to Indiana Jones. Such "equivalences" often dismissively ignore Lara's difference. Andrew Ko sums it up in his assertion that "Lara Croft is no Indiana Jones" Andrew Ko, "And then I saw her face… *Lara Croft: Tomb Raider*," *Metro Magazine*, 129/139 (2001): 215. Archaeologist

Cornelius Holtorf suggests representations of female characters like Lara Croft "are essentially male characters in female disguises". *From Stonehenge to Las Vegas: Archaeology as Popular Culture*, (Walnut Creek, CA: Altamira Press, 2005), 42.

12. For Geoff King and Tanya Krywinska the cinematic Lara represents a lost opportunity to incorporate game-logic into film, "Introduction," in *Screenplay: cinema/videogames/interfaces*, (eds) King and Krzywinska (London and New York: Wallflower Press, 2002), 18. Interestingly Margrit Grieb finds a stronger parallel between the game version of *Tomb Raider* and Lara Croft and Tom Tykwer's film Run Lola Run. "Run Lara Run," in *Screenplay: cinema/videogames/interfaces*, (eds) King and Krzywinska (London and New York: Wallflower Press, 2002), 157–70. See also Dianne Carr and Fantone's "Final fantasies" for critical accounts of their own playing practice and discussion of the film(s). Carr, "Playing with Lara," in *ScreenPlay: cinema/videogames/interfaces*, ed. Geoff King and Tanya Krzywinska, 171–180. London: Wallflower, 2002.

13. The connection between Tomb Raider as third-person adventure games and the cinema is discussed by Derek Alexander Burrill, "Out of the Box: Performance, Drama and Interactive Software." *Modern Drama*, 48, no. 3 (2005): 492–512. Astrid Deuber-Mankowsky, *Lara Croft: Cyber Heroine,* tr. Dominic Bonfiglio. Minneapolis, MN: University of Minnesota Press, 2005). Saige Walton specifically examines the Tomb Raider Chronicles alongside the "cinema of attractions" tradition. Saige Walton, "Showcasing the Spectacular," *Metro Magazine* 134, (2002): 234–9.

14. With some degree of irony Angelina Jolie is reported to have said "Lara is not a looter…and she would probably shoot you for saying so" cited in Alexandra A. Seno, Lights, Camera - Tourists! AsiaWeek.com 27 no. 8, March 2, 2001 http://www.asiaweek.com/asiaweek/magazine/nations/0,8782,100229,00.html

15. By a cinema of archaeology I refer to popular media or fictionalised accounts of archaeology; films which significantly employ archaeological method, motif or metaphor. By this I do not mean non-fiction documentaries or film which are intended as renactments or as a process of data recording, such as those summarised by Thomas Beale and Paul Healy "Archaeological Films: The Past as Present," *American Anthropologist*, New Series 77, no. 4 (1975): 889–897. In the sense that I coin the term this may also include many of the treasure seeker style films like *Sahara* (2005), *National Treasure* (2004), *The Librarian: Quest for the Spear* (2004) (TV), *The Librarian II: Return to King Solomon's Mines* (2006), for instance. Although they are not labelled as archaeologists, referred to instead as marine salvage experts, historians and librarians, they are essentially engaged in archaeological pursuits and I would argue reflect different aspects of the archaeological profession.

16. Steve Neale, "Action Adventure as Hollywood Genre," in *Action and Adventure Cinema,* ed. Yvonne Tasker (London: Routledge, 2004), 75.

17. To varying degrees a poetics of archaeology, to employ Michael Shanks' term, is employed within the Indiana Jones cycle ([1981], [1984], [1989]) as well as a number of other feature films including such hits as *The Mummy* (1999), *The Mummy Returns* (2001), and sci-fi successes *Stargate* (1994) and *The Fifth Element* (1997) and a number of lesser known films *Talos the Mummy* (1998), *The Lair of the White Worm* (1998), *The Awakening* (1980).

18. Marc O'Day, "Beauty in Motion".

19. Thomas Sobchack, cited in Steve Neale, "Action-Adventure as Hollywood Genre", 74.

20. The threat/fear/dangers represented of "feminine" power unleashed runs through a variety of texts, from the biblical Eve, the *Wonder Woman* comics, to Hammer films (perhaps epitomised in *She*), is well documented, and aligned with Creed's analysis of the monstrous-feminine.

21. In contrast, cultural beliefs and rites are often used in a dubious manner, to assert the trope of "dark magic" or play on fears of the exotic other. Jane Eva Baxter discusses the problematic way in which indigenous people are represented or lacking in popular archaeology films. Jane Eva Baxter, "Popular Images and Popular Stereotypes: Images of Archaeologists in Popular and Documentary Film," *The SAA Archaeological Record*, September (2002):17.

22. James R. Mathieu uses this fantasy for espousing the benefits of experimental archaeology. "Time Travel, Trebuchets, and Atlatls," *science & archaeology* 45, no.3: 6-7.

23. Although it appears in disarray, the viewer's entry and departure from this film and image of the world is clearly signalled and the narrative is thereby contained. A parallel may be drawn to Bakhtin, for whom the disorder of the carnivalesque is viewed as a time out of life when dominant ("normal") rules are suspended. Mikhail Bakhtin, *Rabelais and His World*, tr. Hélène Iswolsky (Bloomington: Indiana University Press, 1984).

24. Natalie Zemon-Davis, "Women on Top," in *Society and Culture in Early Modern France*. (Stanford: Stanford University Press, 1975), 124–151.

25 In critiquing Davis, Kate Chedgzoy reiterates the historical evidence for women using carnival discourse to serve their own ends. Impudent Women: Carnival and gender in early modern culture.
http://www.arts.gla.ac.uk/SESLI/STELLA/COMET/glasgrev/issue1/chefgz.htm

26. While the macho cowboy is a stereotype recognised by the discipline as part of its own mythos (see for example Holtorf, *From Stonehenge to Las Vegas,* or Thomas F. King, "Preservation and Rescue", *Journal of Field Archaeology* 8, no.4 [Winter 1981]: 505–9. I would add, that the dirty rigorous work of archaeological practice ensures, that the damsel-in-distress is not. While Jane Eva Baxter, "Popular Images and Popular Stereotypes",16, suggests that "female characters in archaeology films are never extracted from their role as an object of sexual desire even when engaging in 'archaeological pursuits'", I would argue that this may also be said for the men, consider the casting of "sex symbols" like Harrison Ford, Matthew McConaughey, Brendan Fraser, etc.

27. Mother, huntress, virgin, monster, martyr and guide: there are many configurations of the goddess or warrior woman. Lucy Grig provides a case for the cult of female martyrs in Late Antiquity, citing the saint Agnes, the heroine Thecla, and others. In reference to the North African martyrs Perpetua and Felicitas she demonstrates an early example in text and oral traditions of the performative power of spectacle. Nor is the hypersexualised appearance of heroines and Goddess iconography especially new. Saint Agnes' story of martyrdom is an explicit account whereby "the body is sexualised and exposed, but at the same time sacralized and forbidden to us". See Grig, *Making Martyrs in Late Antiquity*.

(London: Duckworth, 2004). In a similar combination of sexy and sacred Marianne Maaskant-Kleibrink summarises the transcendental powers and changing depiction of nymphs, with regard to nudity and dress. She argues that the iconography of nymphs was directed at creating a "special type of 'blessed' and seductive female" as a "fantasy female and seductress...not belonging to the 'normal' world and thus being conducive to religious thoughts about an afterlife" are in later Roman art compared to angels. "Nymphomania," in *Sexual Asymmetry: Studies in Ancient Society,* ed. Josine Block and Peter Mason (Amsterdam: J.C.Gleiben, 1987), 285.

28. Wilson, The Melancholy Android, 34. The mummy motif is a good example of how the archaeology cinema crosses a range of genres, including comedy, horror and sci-fi. In addition to those already mentioned mummy films include: *Abbott and Costello Meet the Mummy* (1955), *The Mummy* (1932), *The Mummy/Terror of the Mummy* (1959), *The Mummy Lives* (1993), *The Mummy's Shroud* (1967), *Wrestling Women vs. the Aztec Mummy/Las Luchadoras Contra La Momia* (1964), *Ancient Evil: Scream of the Mummy* (2000), *Attack of the Mayan Mummy* (1963).

29 Schleiner makes reference to her cyberstatus by suggesting she "is the monstrous offspring of science". "Does Lara Croft Wear Fake Polygons? Gender Analysis of the '3rd Person Shooter/adventure Game with Female Heroine' and Gender Role Subversion in the Game Patch", *Leonardo/The International Society for the Arts, Sciences and Technology* 34, no. 3 (2000): 221–6.

30. Kennedy, "Lara Croft: Feminist Icon".

31. Jane Caputi, *Goddesses and Monsters: Women, Myth, Power, and Popular Culture* (Madison,WN: Popular Press, 2004).

32. In ancient mythology, modern psychology and popular iconography, the goddess or warrior woman archetypes are often/commonly reiterated as the monstrous feminine. Barbara Creed, *The Monstrous Feminine: Film, Feminism, Psychoanalysis.* (London and New York: Routledge, 1993). The warrior goddess Athena (Roman Minerva) is noted for her androgynous conflation of attributes traditionally associated with women and men. According to Pomeroy the Mother goddess is featured in Minoan Crete and examples in later Greek myth include Ge, Rhea, Hera, Demeter and Cybele. The monstrous Harpies or Sirens devour men. Also, Neumann describes the "Great Mother" as both nurturer and devouring. Cited in Sarah B. Pomeroy, *Goddesses, Whores, Wives and Slaves: Women in Classical Antiquity.* (New York: Schocken Books, 1976), 1-15. See also Claudia Hart and Claudia Herbst, who also argue that she is not "new" and further "nor truly 'woman.' Instead, inspired by the male-dominated technological and militaristic culture of our era, a culture emanating from the monastic culture of the Middle Ages". "Virtual Sex: The Female Body in Digital Art" *Bad Subjects,* #72, (February 2005) http://bad.eserver.org/issues/2005/72/hartherbst.html

33. Maja Mikula, "Gender and Videogames: the political valency of Lara Croft," *Continuum: Journal of Media & Cultural Studies* 17, no. 1, (2003): 79–80.

34. *Indiana Jones and the Last Crusade* (1989).

35. In many respects one may argue that this is the conventional critical reading, as the tagline of Deuber-Mankowsky's book, *Lara Croft: Cyber Heroine,* makes clear "Avatar of girl power or sexual plaything? The ambiguity of being Lara." Though it must be said that it is used more in the context of the game than the movie.

36. Mitra C. Emad, "Reading Wonder Woman's Body: Mythologies of Gender and Nation," *The Journal of Popular Culture* 39 no.6 (2006): 956.

37. As well as the film merchandise produced around her and other popular characters (including Indiana Jones), Lara Croft's massive celebrity has made her a popular pinup for other consumer products from softdrinks to magazines.

38. Examples include the work of videoartist Peggy Awesh, musicians Die Ärtze, and U2. Anne Marie Schleiner has discussed the development of "unauthorised" plugins and patches. "Does Lara Croft Wear Fake Polygons?"; See also Allyson D. Polsky, "Skins, Patches, and Plug-ins: Becoming Woman in the New Gaming Culture", *Genders* 34 (2001). http://www.genders.org/g34/g34_polsky.html

39. See Planet Lara, http://www.planetlara.com for example. There are numerous other websites incorporating such images. See Lancaster, "Lara Croft: The Ultimate", for a different interpretation to mine.

40. Mary Magoulick, "Frustrating Female Heroism: Mixed Messages in *Xena*, *Nikita*, and *Buffy*," *The Journal of Popular Culture* 39, no. 5 (2006): 742.

41. As noted Lara's character lies in a man's shadow, in terms of both Indiana Jones and her father Lord Croft. The latter relationship is emphasised by the casting of real-life daughter and father, Angelina Jolie and Jon Voight.

42. Diane Carr, "Playing with Lara," 174.

43. See Mikula "Gender and Videogames"; Kennedy, "Lara Croft: Feminist Icon,"; Carr "Playing with Lara,"; and Schleiner, "Does Lara Croft Wear Fake Polygons?" for similar conclusions.

CHAPTER FIVE

VIOLENCE, DUTY AND CHOICE: THE MILITARY WOMAN IN CONTEMPORARY HOLLYWOOD CINEMA

YVONNE TASKER

Figure Six: Demi Moore in *G.I. Jane* (1997)

Asked to consider military women willing to fight in contemporary Hollywood cinema, we might expect to find any number of competing images of the female soldier. She is undoubtedly a sign of modernity after all and a highly visible figure in the US media more generally, featuring in television (from movies to reality programming), magazine and print journalism. She has also long served as a sign of imagined gender integration in science-fiction cinema (*Aliens* [1986], *Starship Troopers* [1997]) and television (the *Star Trek* franchise, *Stargate SG-1* [1997–]). By the same token, Hollywood cinema of recent years seems to have reconciled itself to the commercial potential of the fighting woman.[1] With the commercial success of a cycle of semi-humourous, explicitly eroticised images of female violence, from *Charlie's Angels* (2000) to *Kill Bill* (2003, 2004), US cinema has seemingly set aside its longstanding reluctance to cast women as credible protagonists in action/adventure/fantasy scenarios.

Yet despite the visibility of military women in the media and the cinematic showcasing of (typically eroticised) fighting women more generally, the most recent Hollywood film to be centred on a military woman remains the 1997 release *G.I. Jane*. If the high profile of Demi Moore's military performance in that film, together with the previous year's *Courage Under Fire* (1996) starring another A-list performer in Meg Ryan, suggested an emergent space for women at the centre of genres of war and combat, ultimately this was not to be the case. Even as supporting characters military women are relatively rare in contemporary Hollywood cinema, with films such as *Basic* (2003), in which both Connie Nielson and Roselyn Sanchez play tough, remaining very much the exception.[2] Thus my starting point for this chapter is a contradictory cinematic absence within a context of wider media visibility for the military woman.

In this distinctive context of visibility and silence, I aim here to offer a feminist analysis of the terms in which the military woman is both present in and absent from the Hollywood cinema. I focus primarily on *G.I. Jane*, not only as the most recent Hollywood film to centre on a military woman, but also since it is in many ways paradigmatic in its explicit celebration of and anxious mediations around white female masculinity. In offering the spectacle of an A-list female star body rendered as a (relative) mass of muscle, *G.I. Jane* seemed to suggest both the potential and the requirement for female bodies to transform in order to achieve success within a martial context. My analysis also seeks to think through what has become clearer in retrospect—that is, the film's atypicality in terms of its distinctive accommodation to the demands of gendered discourse. Here I focus on the centrality of bodily spectacle and physical transformation, issues widely discussed within the popular media's response to *G.I. Jane*. The final section of this chapter shifts to a discussion of more recent films, focusing on *The General's Daughter* (1999) in particular. Here I aim to consider Hollywood's military woman as she appears in supporting roles, with the aim of teasing out other aspects of her status as a figure associated with conflict and violence. Throughout I explore the figuring of military women in terms of a rhetoric of choice—with all the complex political resonance of that term—set against other languages commonly associated with military narratives, for example those of duty, force or violence.

"Failure is not an option": Duty and "Choice" in *G.I. Jane*

In many ways the cinematic absence of military women is not that surprising; a superb icon, the US military woman poses considerable problems when it comes to narrative. Put simply the military woman is a troubling figure, especially so within a generic economy of violence that trades in female fetishism; that is, the action heroine as "sexy tough". As we will see, the perceived need to provide a convincing back story and/or character motivation for military women (that is, to *explain* them), as well as the need to reconcile Hollywood femininity with military masculinity, frequently threatens to destabilise the whole project. Hence, I will argue, the importance of Demi Moore's physical transformation as a defining source of both spectacle and anxiety within *G.I. Jane* (is she strong enough to get the job done; is she rendered lesbian by her strength; is she still sexy?). Yet even as Moore's developing physique seeks to picture her as a credible military woman who is both willing and able to fight, the film's tortuous plotline of duplicity on behalf of military leaders and politicians unfolds primarily as a reflection of (and on) a widespread reluctance to accept combat roles for US female military personnel. That is, *G.I. Jane* fantasised a combat role for the US military woman when no such role was available to her (or required of her) in actuality. This fantasy of narrative possibility is in turn limited by and intricately linked with the film's fantasy of a combat-ready (female) body. Thus Moore's muscled-up body seeks to lend credibility to her character's claims to combat status while speaking to and even confirming deep-seated anxieties as to the masculinising consequences of physical endeavour on the part of women. The film is, to this extent, haunted by the troubling spectre of female masculinity.

I am quite aware that *G.I. Jane's* narrative functions primarily to establish a premise, a basis from which to stage spectacular action and scenes of masculine bonding. Nonetheless I wish to offer here some thoughts on the narrative context which the film provides for its defining promotional image of Moore/Jordan as a shaven headed soldier. *G.I. Jane* stages a scenario of conflict between an ambitious but relatively junior female naval officer, a successful and experienced female politician, resistant military men and conservative male politicians/military leaders. Whilst this may suggest a narrative which straightforwardly opposes female and male characters, the latter representing tradition under siege and the former a group that seeks or even demands admission, this is far from the case. The narrative unfolds as follows. Under pressure from an influential female senator, Lillian DeHaven (Anne Bancroft), the male military leadership agrees to a test case to assess women's combat capabilities. With full integration as the prize, they select CRT, the navy SEALS training programme, as the most arduous and physically demanding within the services. It is clear that they wish the test case to prove the correctness of combat exclusions, and that they have no expectation that a woman might successfully complete the course. The media savvy DeHaven agrees to their terms but insists that she must approve the test cases, vetting files to ensure an appropriately media-friendly (that is, feminine) candidate is located. Ironically, Jordan develops precisely the sort of body that DeHaven seeks to exclude: emerging triumphant from the most difficult part of the training to confront DeHaven over her duplicity, Jordan is shaven headed, muscular in her development and with a face that bears traces of physical violence readable as abuse and/or duty. She is a powerful woman legible as both subject and potential source of violence. When it becomes apparent that DeHaven had no more expectation of a woman's success than the male military leadership, we understand that the character most obviously associated with feminism is simply an unreliable establishment figure, a generation removed from determined, ambitious young women such as Jordan.[3]

Thus we have the improbable scenario of Lieutenant Jordan O'Neil's induction into an elite combat unit via the combined forces of naval leaders opposed in principle to her presence in even a limited combat role. In the context of Hollywood action cinema this scenario serves to inscribe Jordan as an underdog. Just as the male military leaders expect her to fail, generic conventions suggest that she will succeed, overcome seemingly impossible odds and force her adversaries to eat their words. However, it is only DeHaven, her female adversary, caught backtracking in an attempt to avoid unpopular base closures in her home state of Texas, whom Jordan ultimately confronts face to face. Appropriately enough in this battle of images and rhetoric, Jordan threatens to talk direct to the cameras, using the media as leverage against her influential former mentor. Through this gesture—the mobilisation of her appearance and presence as a weapon—the film suggests that Jordan is quite aware of her iconic status, and of the troubling potential of her female masculinity.

Moreover, whilst institutionally powerful men and women are certainly significant players within the film, Jordan/Moore's physical transformation and determination works primarily to convince her fellow soldiers of her worth, including those supervising the gruelling SEAL training. The Command Master Chief (Vigo Mortensen) who oversees the group's training endeavours to demonstrate Jordan's disruptive presence to the male trainees. Later he will privately confide in an instructor his view that "she's not the problem, we [i.e. military men] are". Whoever best embodies it, there remains a problem which Jordan's presence calls attention to. It is the direct hostility of these men, whose high status role Jordan's presence undermines, which is most vividly portrayed and most decidedly overcome in the film. On a field exercise designed to test evasion and survival skills, Jordan's failure to command the authority of all her peers results in their capture and brutal treatment. During these scenes of capture it is through her sheer ability to take punishment and humiliation, emerging triumphant if bloodied, that Jordan secures the support of her men. Becoming part of the group is an exercise in masochism, an effacement of self that produces a coherent soldiering identity in which individuals are subsumed within the unit. During the final stages of their training the group are called on to go operational, providing the opportunity for Jordan to prove her capability, and her leadership potential under fire. The wider political questions to do with military women and combat exclusions are thus both addressed (via the achievements of the protagonist) and left unresolved amidst the celebratory conclusion of Jordan's graduation and acceptance into the unit.

When it comes to the US military, women's *willingness* to fight is not of course the primary issue. Indeed, we might speculate that Hollywood avoids narratives centred on military women in combat precisely because of the politically contested nature of the subject. *G.I. Jane* is certainly at pains to avoid an association with feminism, which is it seems widely conceived of as a restrictive political agenda incompatible with commercial entertainment.[4] Since feminism is also historically associated with pacifism and with a critique of the military, it seems doubly out of place within a film of this kind. Nonetheless, *G.I. Jane* undoubtedly deals with a feminist issue—that of equal opportunity based on ability rather than gender. That it does so in what I can only describe as a postfeminist mode is telling. That is, the film formulates not so much a narrative response to the issues with which it grapples as a striking visual spectacle of the exceptional military woman. Ironically, both its narrative and central star transformation suggest some of the anxieties which a conservative media culture associates with feminism: that women will become masculinised by their desire to succeed in male spaces; that women will enter male spaces and in the process change them. A lament for tradition on the part of some was seen to accompany the entry of women to the military academies in the 1970s and militarised colleges VMI and the Citadel in the mid-1990s.[5]

In response to this contested context, *G.I. Jane* separates off two distinct areas of conflict for its protagonist. On the one hand we have the machinations of politicians and senior officers who dictate whether Jordan will have the opportunity to train and fight; in this arena Jordan has limited abilities to affect the outcome. On the other hand, the resistance and scepticism of fellow servicemen represents a source of conflict that Jordan can and does overcome through her background in intelligence and her efforts during the training and in combat. As I have already indicated, Jordan's physical transformation is central to the film's staging of much wider debates concerning the place of women in the US military. I focus more directly on the film's visualisation of Jordan's body as ready-for-combat in the next section. Here however, I turn to a discernible tension within *G.I. Jane* between a language of *choice* and of *duty*.

G.I. Jane's promotional tag line, "Failure is not an option", suggests a gritty military tale in which soldiers gut it out against the odds. Yet while failure may not be an option, it is a very real presence. The training section of the film is punctuated by the sounds of the bell as a succession of cadets choose to give up. The first day will not end until one of the volunteers has made that choice. There is no shame in quitting they are told, in a fashion that makes the undesirability of such a choice quite plain. Although there are no immediate life or death consequences, excepting the film's brief combat coda, clearly failure is not an option for Jordan; we understand that she is challenging herself (mentally, physically) as well as the military establishment. Since genre plays such an important role in guiding expectations here, it is worth considering the nuanced fashion in which generic conventions developed in large part through films of and about WWII, films, that is, centred on citizen-soldiers, play themselves out in more recent films centred on a professionalised military force made up of volunteers.

WWII combat films, as Jeanine Basinger shows in her comprehensive study of the genre, work to draw together diverse ethnic/religious groups and physical/character types, in the process underlining the strength of the US as a diverse nation.[6] In the wartime context each soldier must do his (or occasionally her) best, in part at least because it is their duty to do so. The training camp film serves as a distinct setting for (primarily, though not exclusively) male rites of passage, a prelude to the challenges of combat.[7] *G.I. Jane* also uses this familiar structure as the core group emerge, cohere and mature, proving their ability and status as elite soldiers in the final scenes of combat. Jordan is the sole female in her crew which also features a sole African-American male and white guys of varying ethnicities. Although African-American women are a disproportionate presence within military ranks, none are visible in this film which introduces the audience to only one other military woman, a blonde medic named Blondell. *G.I. Jane*'s presentation of a high achieving white woman seeking first-class citizenship through military service is in line with Hollywood's racial hierarchies more generally; thus the film's construction of an analogy between the experience of white women and African-American men erases women of colour.

In WWII movies personal challenge serves to give emotional intensity and dramatic resonance to a more abstract sense of duty or patriotism. Young male soldiers may be attempting to live up to their father's reputation for instance, or seeking to overcome their fears. In similar fashion personal challenge and ambition serves to give meaning to the difficulties faced by a professional, volunteer force in more recent training-oriented war films.[8] Alongside individual challenges, recruits must also learn the importance of teamwork, of setting aside personal desires and ambitions for the good of the unit if necessary. In those narratives that seek to discipline and harness aggressive masculinity, this also involves learning to accept authority. In this process a crucial generic figure is the stern disciplinarian who shapes recruits into an aggressive fighting force; resented but ultimately respected such paternal/patriarchal figures recur in numerous military films.[9] In *G.I. Jane* this role is taken on by Master Chief Urgayle whose antipathy towards Jordan is evident. Figured as a brutal yet cultured man, Urgayle is a figure of male authority to whom all must submit; he claims control over every aspect of their lives and demands obedience. Torturing the troops in order to toughen them, Urgayle ultimately comes to accept Jordan after she first faces him down and then saves him under fire during the Libyan combat scenes. The final, wordless encounter between the two follows Jordan's discovery of a medal and a collection of D.H. Lawrence's verse left by Urgayle in her locker. Here the official business of graduation is matched by a private induction into the military elite; brutality and hostility are replaced by respect and poetry.

At key points within *G.I. Jane*'s narrative of exclusion and incorporation Jordon mobilises a language of choice. Thus, for instance, she first requests and then demands the *choice* to accept or reject "gender norming", a practice whereby allowances are made for her in terms of the threshold standards she must meet ("I think I should have the choice", she asserts). Pushing aside the steps mandated as "female aid" on an assault course, Jordan makes herself into a step for the men in her crew, helping them up only to be left behind. When confronted with a charge of conduct unbecoming and the possibility that she must undergo the harsh training once more, Jordan responds with disbelief. Moderating her anger in formal terms she tersely tells the C.O. that "I would not choose to repeat the training". Later in the film, Jordan confronts DeHaven again insisting she should have the right to choose: "I wanted the choice. That's how it's supposed to be".

Choice is a term consistently foregrounded within postfeminist rhetoric, where it connects with a consumer led individualism that proposes women's ability to shape their body, identity and life trajectory through appropriate choices (that is, purchases).[10] Yet, as I've already implied, choice is a concept oddly dissonant within the military context of *G.I. Jane*'s narrative. Time and again combat and training movies demonstrate that choice, and the individualism which the term implies, is entirely inappropriate within a military context. Following rules without question, uniformity, teamwork and selfless heroism are the masculine military values aspired to within the genre. Indeed this message is clearly enacted within *G.I. Jane* when Cortez (David Vadim) chooses not to follow Jordan's orders. Jordan herself has reluctantly taken charge, her seniority stemming from date of enlistment. These are the rules and no exceptions are to be made. In choosing not to accept military hierarchies since they are here personified by a military woman, Cortez gets the whole group captured. The consequences of such poor judgement are prefigured earlier when the same soldier fails to assist Jordan in an attempt to discredit her. That this judgement is noted and punished by Urgayle holds out the possibility of equitable treatment. That is, Urgayle's commitment to military codes is seen, in this instance, to overcome his misogyny.

The film as a whole yokes the concept of choice to issues of fairness and opportunity. This is perhaps most explicit in the staging of an open comparison between Jordan's experience and that of African-American servicemen during WWII. It is McCool (Morris Chestnut), the only African-American in Jordan's crew, who initiates this comparison, speaking of the ignorant prejudice encountered by his grandfather in his quest to serve his nation in a combat role. It is also McCool who is most willing to give Jordan a chance from the beginning, pronouncing that "if she pulls her own weight I got no problem with it". The terms of this comparison are of equality of opportunity, competion without prejudice. Ultimately the military is presented as *both* a site of prejudice (hostility towards women) and as an honourable, rule-bound institution with the potential for equality. In this context we might note that military service has historically provided a route to citizenship within the US. It has also functioned to underline the hierarchies of gender, race and class that organise US society, with hard fought battles against racial and gendered segregation. During WWII the military service of African-Americans, amongst others, provided a platform for those seeking a more equitable society. The same year, 1948, saw President Truman's Executive Order ending racial segregation of the military and requiring equality of treatment and opportunity, and the passage of the Women's Armed Services Act through Congress, ensuring the permanent establishment of the women's services. Both developments were framed in terms of equality of opportunity and an acknowledgement of past service, although the US military's need for personnel (and the logistical difficulties of segregation) are crucial factors.

The language of service and citizenship provides one discursive context for Jordan's demands in *G.I. Jane*. Yet Jordan herself openly speaks not of nation, duty or rights, but of a desire for operational experience in order to secure promotion; before commencing SEAL training she attempts to reassure her lover Royce that the program is "just a career opportunity". Jordan explicitly desires career advancement then, whilst her male peers—to the extent that their motivation is discussed at all—are more often presented as thrill seekers, whooping and cheering in a charged male environment. It is Jordan's femaleness that requires an explanation of course. Yet in naming the connection between operational experience, medals, money and promotion, the film's dialogue makes explicit something of the structural issues at stake in Jordan's attempt to gain entrance to the SEAL unit. Cynthia Enloe writes of the limits typically placed on female recruitment, noting a perception that while many nations' military forces depend on their labour, "women should not deprive men of the chance to serve in those posts held most precious to masculinity-seeking men".[11] *G.I. Jane* centres precisely on such a disruptive endeavour. If anything, the distinction mentioned above between professional and citizen-soldiers is heightened in the film since the opportunity to attempt the CRT course is explicitly presented as a privilege. It may seem odd to think of such a punishing experience as one of privilege; after all, the cadets are pushed to their limits, starved, sleep deprived, humiliated and tortured by their trainers. Yet the CRT is a trial, a rite of passage, firmly associated with elite soldiering and male masculinity. Early on the very difficulty of getting onto the program is openly seen to generate hostility towards Jordan who is perceived as having unfair privilege due to her gender.

As I have explored elsewhere in relation to *Courage Under Fire*, the perception that military men will not trust, follow or obey military women underpins the antipathy of some commentators towards an extension of combat roles irrespective of gender.[12] In presenting male resentment of and hostility towards women as a fact that must be dealt with, such perspectives reinforce misogyny in the guise of pragmatism. Within the fictional narrative of films such as *G.I. Jane* (and to an extent, *Courage Under Fire*) good military men are eventually seen to be willing to serve alongside an exceptional military woman. That is, they *choose* to accept Jordan on the grounds of her particular qualities, rather than necessarily being *required* to do so on principal. Jordan is resented, tolerated and finally accepted; as to whether other women might have a right to serve in combat units (elite or otherwise) the film reserves judgement. Of course this tension is to some extent an inbuilt element of *G.I. Jane*'s narrative since Jordan's very presence involves questioning the rules, challenging tradition even as she indicates her willingness to abide by those rules and traditions. In this context we might note how Demi Moore's superior star status within Hollywood hierarchies works to limit the extent to which her performance suggests an inappropriate or presumptive act. That Moore's celebrity was firmly linked to her shape-shifting, as Linda Ruth Williams terms it, is not insignificant. It is to the centrality of the body in *G.I. Jane*'s visualisation of the military woman that I now turn.

"G.I. Jane": Muscles, Masculinity and the Military Woman

In *G.I. Jane* as with wider media discourses to do with military women, resentful men express a view that women are somehow unfairly advantaged in the service of an inappropriate doctrine. *G.I. Jane* has Jordan rejecting dual standards, wearing standard issue clothes and moving into the male barracks. She stakes her claim for inclusion in the elite force on the basis of exceptional achievement rather than dual standards. In the process she challenges male privilege, but in no way subverts the terms of militarised masculinity. Since Jordan is presented as seeking career advancement within a military establishment defined in masculine terms, she must also (choose to) accept the terms in which advancement is accessed. Thus, as Linda Ruth Williams notes, Jordan's first battle is with "her own body"; her second with "fellow countrymen of a different gender over the issue of her body", a process in which "the spectre of feminine physical unreliability [is] pitched against the certainty of muscular prowess".[13] In this section I focus more directly on these questions of gender and embodiment.

G.I. Jane focuses on a military woman who is not only willing to fight, but eager to do so in order to secure career advancement and opportunity, as well as to secure a space within an elite masculine military group. Her ultimate acceptance into the group and her triumph through training and combat points to Jordan's contradictory status as both a test case, as somehow representative of all military women, and as atypical, or, more precisely I would argue, exceptional. The media generated nickname "G.I. Jane" suggests the former, while the secretary of the navy's exasperated allusion to Joan of Arc, by contrast, situates Jordan as an exceptional female warrior (albeit one associated with martyrdom and victimisation). The picture of an elite masculine military unit which incorporates a sole, exceptional, masculine military woman is rather different from the full integration speculated on, albeit briefly, in the conspiratorial scenes that set the narrative in motion. Indeed the film consistently emphasises Jordan's exceptional status, most obviously through her position as the sole female on the CRT program, but also through the evident contrast between her developed physique/shaven head and the more conventionally feminine appearance of the other (relatively few) military women that we encounter during the course of the film.[14] The staging of Jordan's rite of passage as a form of extreme makeover, in which she is transformed from a disciplined female body to a more evidently built muscular mass, from the glamourous feminine associations of long hair to a shaven head, seems telling with respect to her claims to combat status.

Male disgust at the female body is a marked feature of the hostility Jordan encounters during the CRT training. Some of the male cadets grumble loudly in the mess, one commenting with revulsion that the "average" female body is "a quarter fat", whilst another predicts that a "split-tail" has no chance of success at making it through the program. If, as seems to be the case, the female body signifies a malevolent threat to men and masculinity, it is interesting to note that *G.I. Jane* simultaneously flaunts and disguises Jordan's sexed body.[15] Thus the film features numerous fetishistic shots of Jordan working out, images which serve to underline the hard work she is putting into her transformation whilst offering the muscular female body as pleasurable spectacle. Yet this transformation also serves as a form of disguise, a strategy to deemphasise Jordan's femaleness and thus to facilitate the credibility of her integration into the group. When Jordan moves into the male barracks, one cadet responds hysterically at the sight of tampons in her possession; his fear and loathing is clearly framed as excessive, no serious threat. Even so, it is later revealed in the course of a medical examination that Jordan's periods have stopped; this, we are informed is normal for a female athlete, resulting from a drop in body fat. Her body is being reformed, de-emphasising reproductive capacities and emphasising physical strength and the capability for violence.

Jordan's transformation is both physical—she works out to "overcome" her body's female qualities—and gendered, a fact expressed most succinctly in the sequence which has her shave her own head in an effort to fit in. The recruit's shaven head symbolises uniformity as the group will be cast together into a new unit, a new identity.[16] Moore's iconic image here literalises what I referred to earlier as the film's staging of familiar contemporary debates concerning combat exclusions and the place of women in a modern military. Jordan's trip to the barber shop immediately follows her confrontation with the base commander in which she demands equity of treatment; her shaven head makes visible her desire to assimilate, to fit in with those around her. This gesture in turn allows Jordan to initiate a new level of proximity to the men with whom she both works and competes by moving into their barracks. Rejecting the isolation of gendered segregation precisely as she begins to appear less (conventionally) feminine, Jordan both asserts her right to be there (in the barracks, on the program) and effectively acknowledges the need for her to transform her appearance in order to secure her goal.

Jordan's transformation is both visually striking, even spectacular, and performs important narrative work in producing a credible combat ready female body. The process is also somewhat at odds with Hollywood femininity, a discursive space within which even minor gender transgressions are typically met with a retributive narrative logic. Jordan's body/appearance stands in for her wider disruptive presence here. In this context the film interrogates her physical capabilities, as well as pointing to persistent anxieties as to the military woman's gendered and sexual identity. Building on contemporary debates, *G.I.*

Jane ponders whether a woman can physically handle the demands of soldiering. Even with the (hyper)visible work on her body, Jordan is seen to be physically weaker than many of her male peers although she outlasts them. In compensation the film emphasises her intelligence capabilities and her fighting spirit, the latter encapsulated in her challenge to Master Chief Urgayle to "Suck my dick!" Jordan's refusal to be quelled and her assertion of her masculinity bring the unit round to her cause; her male peers delightedly chant the phrase in support.

Jordan is selected as a test subject for the trial in part since she embodies a media-friendly version of the female soldier: classy, high achieving, an athlete yet resolutely female. She is expressly told on her arrival that the object of the exercise is not to "change [her] sex", an observation that turns on a complex institutional history through which branches of the military have sought to ensure the femininity of servicewomen. Military rituals, uniforms and so forth are intended to ensure uniformity whilst maintaining, even policing sexual difference. Unsurprisingly Jordan's transformation into a very different image of the female soldier brings with it implications of mannishness and, subsequently, lesbianism. With her every move subject to illicit inspection from the military and the press, Jordan makes the "mistake" of spending leisure time with other women. DeHaven's office exploits the opportunity provided by photographs of Jordan within a female group on the beach to suggest a lesbian connection that puts her whole career in jeopardy.[17] In the process this section of the film serves to remind us that women cannot be relied on and that women together spell danger. Of course *G.I. Jane* establishes Jordan's heterosexuality early on. DeHaven openly quizzes her on the topic; their interview is followed by a scene featuring Jordan and her lover Royce. Shot as they bathe together, the scene initially suggests romance and sexual intimacy. Yet Royce's inability to deal with the situation or to comprehend why Jordan would want to spend time with what he terms "cock swinging commandos" produces a rupture in their relationship. Royce's incomprehension positions him somewhere between the openly hostile male soldiers competing to become SEALs and the Washington military men who attempt to engineer the program's failure. Jordan's desire for operational experience means an almost aggressive distance from intimacy/domesticity, but also from Washington where she has made her career to date. Over the phone she tells Royce, in Moore's distinctive guttural tones, "The more everybody fucks with me, the more I want to gut it out. So don't you expect me back any time soon". The phrasing suggests a departure from both decorum and, potentially, from the heterosexuality that Royce secures. Royce is ultimately brought round to her cause, providing her with evidence of DeHaven's duplicity. A marginal figure in some respects, Royce also plays a crucial role in attesting to Jordan's continued desirability.

Moore/Jordan's transformation is perhaps the most marked instance of recent Hollywood configurations of the military woman. The woman's capacity for violence is expressed through muscle, scars and other markers of female masculinity. As we have seen, this visualisation of the military woman, so dependent on Moore's star persona, has not been replicated. In this context it is perhaps productive to briefly consider more representative instances of contemporary Hollywood action bodies. Consider Carrie-Anne Moss in *The Matrix* (1999) and its sequels (both 2003) or Uma Thurman in *Kill Bill*. These female bodies are taut and toned; muscles are defined but not significantly developed. We are asked to treat both as credible fighters and as exceptional women, but in overtly fantastic narrative settings. There may be plenty of male hostility towards women in these films, yet scepticism as to women's capacity for violence has nowhere near the narrative significance accorded to it in *G.I. Jane*. After a career lull, Moore too would reinvent herself as a surgically made over (villainous) action body in *Charlie's Angles: Full Throttle* (2003). Media coverage emphasised the star's sexy (aging) body, marvelling at her capacity to physically reinvent herself.

Choice and Force: (Sexual) Violence and the Military Woman in Hollywood Cinema

In contrast to the sexualised capability of violent women of fantasy, Hollywood cinema seems to suggest that the military woman's choice places her in danger. This danger stems more from her fellow soldiers than from the sorts of national enemy typically seen in war and combat films. Thus in *Courage Under Fire*, it is her men's betrayal, rather than Iraqi gunfire, which leads to Karen Walden's death. In *G.I. Jane* Jordan undergoes physical punishment, as do her male peers, but the threat of rape is intended to reveal her continued (feminine) weakness, her penetrability. Some commentators have indeed opposed a combat role for women in terms of their vulnerability to rape by enemy combatants, a possibility that Urgayle openly uses against Jordan in *G.I. Jane*. Here the language of choice and opportunity is starkly opposed to force and (male) violence. Both Urgayle's assault ("her presence makes us all vulnerable") and O'Neil's spirited fight back are staged for the benefit of the watching male group. The former repels the group, the latter binding even previously hostile men in support of Jordan.

I have argued that *G.I. Jane* deploys a postfeminist language of choice, one that suggests gender equity is already achieved and that an individual woman's choice fuels the narrative. Clearly the film also confronts the limits of choice, in part by drawing out the incongruity of the concept in a regimented environment such as the military. A more explicitly feminist terminology of choice permeates debates on rape and sexual violence, experiences which form an ongoing backdrop to debates about, and representations of, military women in the US. As Susan Jeffords writes, the situation is more complex than a rhetorical desire to protect US womanhood might suggest: "While ostensibly concerned about 'protecting' women from the potential of being raped by the 'opposing forces' during combat, they are judging actual rape that occurs by men in their own military as one of the consequences of service".[18] Ironically, Hollywood cinema, to the extent that it deals with military women at all, seems more preoccupied with the danger that female soldiers face from resentful male peers than from enemy soldiers.

In this context we can productively consider a very different narrative of military women, *The General's Daughter*, a film that revolves around the investigation of the title character's rape and murder. The narrative commences when the spread-eagled, naked body of Captain Elizabeth Campbell is discovered by a remote vehicle in an urban warfare training site; she has been strangled. Although the crime scene suggests rape, this is soon revealed as a staged effect. The investigations of hero Brenner (John Travolta) and "rape investigator" Sara Sunhill (Madeleine Stowe) reveal that while Campbell was not raped at Fort Hadley, she had been attacked seven years before during her time as a cadet at West Point, a crime her military father asked her to keep silent about. As the story emerges it becomes clear that Campbell's rape by several of her male classmates was conceived as a response to her success, a punishment. Her intelligence, her achievements and her femaleness produce a deep, visceral hatred that is channelled into sexual violence as a strategy for keeping (military) women in their place. This scenario may imply a feminist analysis of rape as power is at least implicit within *The General's Daughter*, yet the ambivalence about military women registered in the film, as in the wider culture, makes this more problematic. Brenner's investigations reveal not only Campbell's victimisation but a perverse response to her experience; seeking revenge and recognition from her father she systematically seduces the senior male officers at the base he commands. Grainy video images of Campbell as arrogant dominatrix suggest a sexualised play with the gendered hierarchies proposed by military culture. In contrast to Jordan's assimilation via a sort of androgyny, Campbell asserts her disruptive female presence through sexual power.

Though *The General's Daughter* could arguably be read as an exposé of sexual violence against military women, following in the wake of sexual scandals such as Tailhook and revelations of seemingly systematic bullying/abuse at the Air Force Academy for instance, like *G.I. Jane,* the film does not significantly undermine or question military masculinity. Masculine military culture is seen to treat Campbell brutally; that her father requires her to keep her rape a secret reinforces the potential critique of patriarchal authority put into play here. Yet Campbell's strategy of seduction rather than assimilation suggests once more the disruptive or even corrupting consequences of women's entry into masculine, male spaces. Her choices make a mockery of military (and paternal) authority, as they are clearly intended to do. Though very different, both *The General's Daughter* and *G.I. Jane* typify Hollywood narratives centring on military women in that the primary area of conflict is insistently that between a sole, high-achieving military woman and a hostile male military. The fact that this struggle tends to become *the* primary story is significant in generic terms. Crudely, narratives involving military women cannot simply follow the generic conventions of the male military. Instead these conventions must be adapted, shifted to register the insistent figuring of the military woman as an outsider within.[19]

In this context we can reflect on the different incarnations of the military woman in contemporary Hollywood, noting the varying gendered stereotypes that work to situate her as a problematic presence. Though the epithet "G.I. Jane" suggests an everywoman quality, in this film and more broadly, Hollywood's military women are either exceptional high-achievers or unreliable victims; rarely, that is, are military women cast as average soldiers. The two military women featured in Steven Bochco's short-lived Iraq-based series *Over There* (2005) follow this pattern with one hyper-capable and one unstable female (feminine) soldier in the unit. In terms of the bodily discourses foregrounded in this essay, we could also describe Hollywood's construction of military women as on one hand mannish, physically capable figures, on the other feminised victims of rape. That *G.I. Jane* portrays the torture and simulated rape of its mannish female soldier suggests that these two gendered types inform each other in a rather more complex fashion. The militarised hard body identified by Susan Jeffords as a defining feature of Hollywood masculinity ultimately eludes even the toughest woman.[20] Ultimately, Jordan overcomes the attempt to subordinate and exclude her through an appropriation of macho military culture.

Contemporary Hollywood action cinema embraces the implausible, deploying CGI, wirework and cosmetic surgery to stage fantasised and fetishistic figurations of gender. The military woman may be willing to fight but, within the cinema at least, her desire to do so is figured as immensely disruptive. Her presence is repeatedly seen to disrupt the very institution she aspires to join. Moreover, she is repeatedly cast as both source and subject of violence. The exuberance of the "postfeminist action heroine" is quite markedly at odds with Hollywood's visualisation of the military woman, a figure associated with real-world disputes and with media coverage of the ongoing wars in Iraq and Afghanistan. The military women seen here are very different to those located in Hollywood cinema, cast as heroic in some instances, perverse in others and occasionally simply as average soldiers. *G.I. Jane* is both fascinating and anomalous in its attempt to foreground the military woman as action protagonist. It is telling both that her willingness to fight becomes *the* narrative problem, and that the conflict is staged primarily over her body.

Notes

1. See my "Fantasizing Gender and Race: Women in Contemporary US Action Cinema," in *Contemporary Hollywood Cinema*, ed. Michael Hammond and Linda Ruth Williams (London: McGraw Hill, 2006), 410–28.

2. Another recent example, *Stealth* (2005) casts the white military woman (Jessica Biel), a naval pilot, alongside two male pilots, one white, the other African-American. The emphasis on Biel's sexualised female body is in line with Marc O'Day's characterisation of "action babe cinema." See Marc O'Day, "Beauty in Motion: Gender, Spectacle and Action Babe Cinema," in *Action and Adventure Cinema*, ed. Yvonne Tasker (London: Routledge, 2004), 201–18.

3. As Angela McRobbie has noted, popular media culture typically visualises feminism in terms of an aging parent generation whose concerns are no longer appropriate to the young women of today. See her "Post-feminism and Popular Culture," *Feminist Media Studies* 4, no. 3 (2004): 255–64.

4. Director Ridley Scott commented in one interview, "I really wanted to avoid making this a film about women's rights and all that nonsense. I've done one of them. It's really more about a woman trying to do a man's job." *Empire* (December 1997).

5. Amongst the mass of popular media coverage on this matter see, for instance, Nancy Mace with Mary Jane Ross, *In the Company of Men: A Woman at the Citadel* (New York: Simon & Schuster, 2001).

6. Jeanine Basinger, *The World War II Combat Film: Anatomy of a Genre* (New York: Columbia University Press, 1986).

7. The relatively few training camp films centred on women such as *Keep Your Powder Dry* (1945) or the much later *Private Benjamin* (1980) do not typically conclude with combat, a convention from which *G.I. Jane* departs in the Libyan scenes that serve to demonstrate the heroine's capabilities in active duty.

8. The hugely popular *Top Gun* (1986) involves Tom Cruise's character coming to terms with/living up to his dead father's legacy.

9. John Wayne's portrayal of Sgt John Stryker in *The Sands of Iwo Jima* (1949) is archetypal. The men he trains and toughens up detest him, but ultimately come to respect, understand and, following his death, mourn him.

10. For a succinct summary of some of the issues at stake in this much debated term see Sarah Gamble, "Postfeminism," in *The Icon Critical Dictionary of Feminism and Postfeminism*, ed. Sarah Gamble (Cambridge: Icon Books, 1999), 43–54. For other perspectives on postfeminism in popular media culture see *Interrogating Postfeminism: Gender and the Politics of Popular Culture*, ed. Yvonne Tasker and Diane Negra, (Durham: Duke University Press, forthcoming).

11. Cynthia Enloe, *Maneuvers: The International Politics of Militarizing Women's Lives* (Berkeley: California University Press, 2000), 238.

12. Yvonne Tasker, "Soldiers' Stories: Women and Military Masculinities in *Courage Under Fire*," *Quarterly Journal of Film and Video* 19, no. 3 (2002): 209–22.

13. Linda Ruth Williams, "Ready for Action: *G.I. Jane*, Demi Moore's body and the female combat movie," in *Action and Adventure Cinema*, ed. Yvonne Tasker (London: Routledge, 2004), 173.

14. As Cynthia Enloe and others suggest, the perceived need to maintain the femininity of military women has long been and indeed remains a preoccupation of the US military.

15. Barbara Creed has most famously explored these questions with respect to horror in *The Monstrous-Feminine: Film, Feminism, Psychoanalysis* (London: Routledge, 1993). Also relevant here is Creed's essay "Lesbian Bodies: Tribades, Tomboys and Tarts", in *Sexy Bodies: the strange carnalities of feminism*, ed. Elizabeth Grosz and Elspeth Probyn (London: Routledge, 1995), 86–103.

16. For an insightful discussion of some of these questions see Carol Burke, *Camp All-American, Hanoi Jane, and the High-and-Tight: Gender, Folklore and Changing Military Culture* (Boston: Beacon Press, 2004).

17. US military hostility to lesbian and gay personnel was a high-profile context at the time, and indeed remains an area of some contention. This is in sharp contrast to policies in other western nations. As I write, British newspaper *The Sun* carries a celebratory feature and front page headline devoted to the first lesbian soldiers to marry under the recently changed UK law allowing civil partnerships for same-sex couples. "Army Lesbians Get Wed," *The Sun*, February 2, 2006.

18. Susan Jeffords, "Performative Maculinities, or, 'After a Few Times You Won't Be Afraid of Rape at All,'" *Discourse* 13, no. 2 (1991): 106. Though Jeffords' analysis was produced in the early 1990s, reports of rape and sexual abuse of US servicewomen by their fellow soldiers continue to appear.

19. Alternatively films may deploy comedy, a strategy I discuss at length in my *Soldiers Stories: Military Women in Cinema and Television Since WWII* (Durham: Duke University Press, forthcoming).

20. Susan Jeffords, *Hard Bodies: Hollywood Masculinity in the Reagan Era* (New Brunswick: Rutgers University Press, 1994).

CHAPTER SIX

MILLION DOLLAR BABY:
THE MAKING AND UNMAKING OF THE FEMALE BOXER'S BODY

SILKE ANDRIS

Figure Seven: Hilary Swank in *Million Dollar Baby* (2004)

From the beginnings of cinema, the physical combat of two professional boxers in a ring, with its promise of spectacular and violent action, drama and a guaranteed resolution in the final fight, has become an elemental story line for documentaries and fiction films. The combat sport provides all of the spectacle, drama and punches that Hollywood attempts to capture and sell in motion pictures. More films have been made about boxing than any other sport.[1] Boxing is a favourite with moviemakers, but also with the public and critics. Portraits of boxers have regularly been nominated or awarded of film prizes such as the Academy Award. Boxing movies have been represented in many categories of achievement including Best Actor, Best Supporting Actor, Best Editing, Best Writing, Best Cinematography, Best Music and Best Motion Picture. Wallace Beery (*The Champ* [1931]), Marlon Brando (*On The Waterfront* [1954]) and Robert DeNiro (*Raging Bull* [1980]) all won an Academy Award for Best Actor. The movies *From Here to Eternity* (1953) and *Rocky* (1976) won Best Motion Picture. Prizes for editing went to *Body and Soul* (1947), *The Rocky* (1976) and *Raging Bull* (1980). *The Champ* (1931) and *From Here to Eternity* (1953) also won awards for Best Writing. The prize for best cinematography went to *The Champ* (1931) and *Somebody Up There Likes Me* (1956). The category of Best Actress has long been an obvious omission from the list. It was only in 2004 that Hilary Swank climbed through the ropes and took home the trophy for her portrayal of the female boxer Maggie Fitzgerald in *Million Dollar Baby* (2004). Additional awards for Best Director, Best Motion Picture and Best Supporting Actor went to Clint Eastwood and Morgan Freeman.

Million Dollar Baby is in many ways a straightforward reworking of the generic boxer-in-training story; where the rise and fall of the boxer's body is both the main spectacle and narrative of the film. Spectacular imagery of the "evolution", transgression and deformation of the fighter's body is a central and repetitive feature of the boxing movie. Action cinema often seems to reduce the protagonist to his/her body and this is nowhere more telling than in the boxing feature, where the body is the main instrument, weapon and target. In such movies, Roland Bergan explains "man is seen at his most elemental, stripped bare, literally and figuratively, with only his fists to defend himself against an equally unarmed opponent".[2] Once in the ring, the boxer's body itself seems to naturally narrate a story about the power of the creative and disruptive human body.

The boxing film uses training, sparring and fight sequences as important spectacles of physical action, punctuating the trial of the male hero at key intervals. The Hollywood boxing movie commonly moves steadily towards the extended bout that brings the film to its climax. As a result, the audience comes to anticipate the final fight, like the shoot-out in Westerns or the confrontation with the monster in horror films. The ring, elevated like a stage, illuminates the boxer's physical features, exposing them in detail. It brings the protagonist into sharp focus and ushers in the desire of scopophilia coupled with the anticipation and expectation of what might happen in the fight. With an appraising, anatomical gaze the camera lingers over the fighter's body, turning it into a proffered object.[3] The body becomes a coherent location and reference point for the audience, whose experience is not filtered through dialogue or verbal articulation but through corporeal experiences: and thus, the viewer is drawn into "complicity" with its point of view. This is supported further by a cinematography aimed at implicating the viewer deeply within the contender's pain. It shows us how it looks and feels to dispense and receive physical brutality.

The tale of personal transformation told in *Million Dollar Baby* closely follows these patterns. It is a familiar story. However, with a woman as its main contender it also differs from its cinematic predecessors. Boxing has long been portrayed as an exclusively male preserve—with no connections to women. It is essentially associated with male physique, psychology and aggression. As Frank Krutnik explains "the sport itself represents a primitive form of masculine testing, with the boxing scenes themselves often serving to present a stark spectacle of masculine triumph and defeat".[4] *Million Dollar Baby* transgresses the idea of masculine testing and heroism by putting a woman at the centre of the fight game. By doing so, it suggests that the boxer's body never just "naturally" narrates a story but rather narrates the story of a gendered body. Hence, the making and unmaking of the female contender's body in *Million Dollar Baby* is explored as the story of the rise and fall of a gendered body. My aim is to show how Maggie Fitzgerald's gender bears considerable influence on her development as a boxer, on the plot's direction and on its powerful ending.

Synopsis of *Million Dollar Baby*

Million Dollar Baby (hereafter *MDB*) is essentially a story about the personal transformation of Maggie Fitzgerald (Hilary Swank), a nobody who becomes a world contender through determination, discipline and physical ability and skill. Maggie's burning ambitions land her, literally, on the canvas of a boxing ring. Her flirtation with a physically demanding combat sport is dangerous and at the age of thirty-one she knows she is running out of time to realise her dream—yet she is ready to take her chances. She chooses Frankie (Clint Eastwood), the owner of The Hit Pit, a professional fighters' gym, as her coach. From Frankie's perspective, a fighter who is in her early thirties and without previous fighting experience is too old for a career in professional boxing.[5] Yet it is less Maggie's age than that she is a woman that is Frankie's main concern. For him, "girly tough ain't enough", and unlike many of his colleagues, Frankie refuses to train women. He regards women's boxing as a "freak show" which has nothing to do with the so-called "Manly Art".

However, Maggie perseveres and signs up at Frankie's gym, paying membership for six months in advance, suspecting that Frankie cannot afford to turn away a paying customer. With the help of the retired fighter and gym employee Scrap (Morgan Freeman), she eventually gets attention and training from Frankie, who is impressed by her willpower and skill. Maggie slowly turns her body into the muscular and fighting-fit frame of a boxer. Soon after, boxer and coach embark on a journey in which Maggie has to suffer some harsh rebuffs from Frankie, essentially a coach disillusioned with the fighting game and estranged from women. Yet their relationship gradually develops and their journey climaxes in Maggie having a shot at a title bout. She wins the title but pays a very high price for her ambitions. In her last bout she is illegally attacked by her opponent and is badly injured. She awakes in hospital to learn that she has become a quadriplegic. Showing no regret for her choice to take up boxing, Maggie explains that all she ever wanted was a chance to have a shot at a title bout. Yet with her dream of a career in boxing gone, she asks Frankie to help her commit suicide. Frankie's initial refusal allows the viewer to witness how Maggie's iron-will to build up her body turns into the will to destroy it and end her life. Seeing her determination, and knowing that nothing can stop her, Frankie gives in and fulfils her last wish. Maggie's sculpted fighter's body bears the mark of training and achievement. At first Maggie's body provides the key element of exceptional spectacle and success, and then an arresting and indelible defeat. *MDB* is, therefore, a transformation story that turns full circle: the making and unmaking of the boxer's body.

The Making of the Body

At the start of her career Maggie embarks on a battle with her body and trains excessively, but with little technical progress because Frankie refuses to have any part in her training. There is no supportive team of gym members or trainers and, as a result, Maggie is often isolated within both the film's frame and the narrative. The story strongly points to the stereotypes and prejudices female athletes face when they enter a so-called male sport. This is most prominent when Frankie refuses to train her, and later, when Maggie's mother describes her daughter as a freak because she participates in a male sport.[6] Despite the criticism of others, Maggie never stops training. Frankie comes to admire her dedication and endurance and eventually begins to coach her. He has a rigid set of conditions and Maggie must do exactly what he orders her to do. Like a drill sergeant, he does not tolerate questions or objections. As Frankie's student, Maggie fully "accepts his terms and devotes herself wholeheartedly to working up her craft. There is wisdom in the feminine: she knows what she needs".[7] According to Frankie, Maggie first of all needs to learn "to protect herself at all times"—the most important rule if she wants to succeed in the fighting game. Moreover, she has to "re-tool" her whole body and instincts. As Scrap's narration tells us, where instinct tells a boxer to go left, she/he must go right. Under Frankie's eyes she slowly masters the pugilist's skills. Thus, Maggie's first victory in the film is presented as personal—where a woman has successfully challenged her own body and has transformed herself into something new: a contender.

The main focus of boxing films is often on the overhaul of the body through rigorous physical preparation, and Maggie's story is no exception here. However, it differs from that of previous male contenders. Ideas about boxing and masculinity are closely entwined in society and in film, where the sport is represented as an essentially masculine, working-class activity, associated with male aggression, physique and psychology, and with no apparent connection to women.[8] As a result, the male boxer's physical ability is never questioned on the basis of his gender. Instead, the main test for him is to win the final fight. The challenge in the ring is to deprive another man of his masculinity in order to warrant one's own. Every win or loss in a boxing career thus becomes an indicator of masculine prowess, as a scene in *Rocky II* (1979) exemplifies: "I never asked you to stop being a woman", Rocky says to a pregnant Adrian who insists on his retirement, and he continues: "please don't ask me to stop being a man".

In comparison to male fighters, Maggie must not only defend her femininity but also prove her competence in doing a man's job. As a woman, she has to convince Frankie, the male gatekeeper of pugilist knowledge, of her abilities to be physically and mentally able to fight. Her gender becomes an issue where "the spectre of feminine physical unreliability [is] pitched against the certainty of muscular prowess".[9] Her first fight, therefore, takes place in the gym where she has to prove herself in training. *MDB* puts great emphasis on the rigours and indignities of physical and mental preparation. In this sense the film displays close affinities to the war film, and especially the subgenre of boot camp movies like *G.I. Jane* (1997), where the primary conflict is fought over the gendered body of a female soldier. In such training stories, as Williams shows, physical contest becomes emblematic of sexual struggle.[10] She explains further that the female soldier of the boot camp movie first has to wage and win a battle over her own body and, secondly, with fellow students of a different gender over the issue of her body.[11]

One particular poster tacked up in Frankie's office is emblazoned with the saying "Tough ain't tough enough". It functions as a constant reminder of

Frankie's doubts about women's participation in the sport, and his earlier comment to Maggie that "girly tough ain't enough". Amongst other posters and signs at the gym the sign "Winners are simply willing to do what losers won't" also gains a certain visual prominence. Maggie is shown training with this particular sign in the background so often that the sign acts as a caption for the image of the female body in training. It underlines that Maggie has a set goal and is willing to take a shot at a fight. Such posters, as Beltrán elsewhere shows, perform a similar function to the advertising slogans of major sports companies, which also reiterate "the sentiment that everyone, regardless of gender or ethnic background, can train to become powerful if they dare to struggle and persevere".[12] The voiceover narration further emphasises the idea that nobody is a "natural" but that everyone can learn to box—if (only) they want to. Maggie's body becomes the locus of transformation and self-production achieved through (the consumption of) workout. With its strong emphasis on self-creation, transformation and agency, *MDB* shows close affinities with liberal sports feminism as well as consumer culture's particular articulation of feminism as identity politics, and of consumption as self-production.[13]

The extended cinematography of training sessions and Maggie's successful transformation also clearly carry an air of idealisation. As Butler explains:

> The contour that marks the athletic body is a contour produced over time, established again and again, the spatialized result of a certain repetition. The contour we appreciate is one produced and established through a reflexive work, a working on oneself, but also a working on oneself in the service of an ideal, a belabored practice of the body in the service of an idealization of that body.[14]

The athletic body is therefore portrayed as attractive and desirable. It is the result of hard work, dedication and it becomes a symbol of Maggie's achievements and progress.

Maggie is constantly shown in training and the emphasis is on the everyday drudgery of such routine. To the extent that "the camera dwells on the wearing practice of these routines—whether they occupy the foreground or grind on in the background while the main protagonists are focusing on other matters".[15] As a workout practice, boxing "must continue, must reiterate itself in daily and regular ways, as a discipline and as a ritual ... [the athletic body] is always in the process of being made".[16] Maggie's time spent training implies her growing proficiency and mastery of pugilistic skill, and thus, results in her empowerment through increased movement or fighting potential. The film emphasises this potential to the extent that Maggie's relative empowerment seems to be discerned only through her movement and physical ability. Training and, later, fighting act as a sort of "movement-narrative"—which, as Anderson defines it, conveys its story through the protagonist's mastery and virtuosity of bodily movement.[17] In short, any pleasure and/or torment in training or fight scenes comes "simply" through watching Maggie's body in action.

Furthermore, the endless gym sequences imply a degree of readiness for physical confrontation with an opponent. Similar to a police officer, a soldier or a government agent, Maggie accepts and embraces aggression and competitiveness as part of her preparation and job. She rises quickly in the fight game as others fall to her devastating right. Physical aggression is a means to an end for her, a way to improve and advance in a sport. Hence, she embodies the idea that aggression and violence become integrated into the definition of the professional athlete. [18]

From the outset, Maggie is not only willing but also eager to enter a competitive combat sport and adopt its values of toughness and prowess. Heywood and Dworkin show in their discussion of *Girlfight* that such values are not only applicable to women but are associated with:

> human potential and development in a dog-eat-dog world where victimisation is
> the norm and everyone has to fight for a place. Access to the world of such
> values is necessary to even get in the game, to signify in the film's cultural
> context at all.[19]

In *MDB*, Maggie's eagerness to fight and to better her life through participation in an aggressive combat sport is also explained through her social context—a dysfunctional family and poverty. Participation in the "hurting game" is her ticket out of a desperate situation and the only way her life will become meaningful; otherwise, as Maggie herself explains "I might as well go back home and buy a used trailer and get a deep fryer and some Oreos". A life in which she would eat herself into a sedative state, exemplified by her greedy, over-weight and welfare-cheating mother.

As a working-class woman, Maggie's body and physical ability are her only "assets". Her bodily transformation is therefore represented as a way to realise her dream of a better life and climb up the class ladder.[20] Yet, in order to make some money, Maggie has to win and in the act risk her life in the ring. *MDB* leaves no doubt that professional boxing is a "hit pit", a brutal hurting game that is about a single sinister duality: winning or losing. The fate of a fighter is epitomised in the figure of Scrap, a half-blind former fighter who works at The Hit Pit and lives in a backroom of the gym. When Frankie warns Maggie to save her money otherwise "she might be left with nothing", he clearly refers to Scrap's fate as a prizefighter. The loss of the fighter's eye is told by Scrap as a lesson, threat, and prescient warning of Maggie's own fate. We learn that Frankie was with Scrap when he was seriously injured in his last fight. Frankie was Scrap's cut man and watched on in agony from the corner. The power to throw in the towel is exclusively reserved to managers, and Scrap's was off getting drunk, not interested in Scrap's fate. For every boxer who makes it to the top, there are thousands like Scrap who end up penniless, and often with a body and/or soul beyond repair. The fairy story promised by prizefighting is an "effective sop thrown to the have-nots to passify their discontent".[21] Many films, for example *The Set Up* (1949), *Fat City* (1972), and *Raging Bull* (1980), have described the illusions behind a contender's dream. The condemnation of the sport is put most blatantly in *The Harder They Fall* (1956), when Humphrey Bogart, playing a sports columnist, becomes so disgusted by the corruption and violence of the game that the opening words of his article, (which are also the closing disclaimer for the movie), tell the viewer that: "Professional boxing should be banned even if it takes an Act of Congress to do it". The boxing movie, as Bergan points out, is an exemplification of America as a land of opportunity, however:

> Hollywood has not always made the distinction between the American Dream and American reality. The idea that democracy in America provides equal opportunity for all and that sports are the best demonstration of this, is embedded in the American consciousness. From the earliest silent movies to *Rocky* (1976), screenplays have paid lip service to this ideal.[22]

Like many boxer-in-training-stories *MDB*, at first, closely follows this path. However, the film also goes beyond such lip service and explores in detail what happens to Maggie when her dream goes awry.

The Unmaking of the Body

MDB is exceptional in the sense that not only do we see Maggie's body in the making, being moulded to be fighting fit, but also being unmade, hurt and paralysed in the ring. First her body is represented as too old for a sporting career, then in the fights she bleeds, sweats, her nose is broken and her body becomes bruised. Extreme images of vulnerability and invincibility are often mobilised, to intersect, in the action genre. Yet *MDB* is especially exceptional in its gruesome and bloody portrayal of female aggression and violence. Female fighters in other films also risk their lives (for example *Charlie's Angels* [2000], *Lara Croft:Tomb Raider* [2001]), however, the audience can retain confidence that these heroines are rarely seriously injured. These fighters, especially those employing martial arts, represent a more stylised type of fighting. What *MDB* holds in common with many action heroines is an emphasis on training. The training and perfecting of the body into a fighting carapace, promises protection from harm and death and potently communicates human mortality and frailty (even when the viewer can rest assured that the heroine will not be seriously or fatally injured). Tasker argues that the manufacturing and later the endangerment of bodies, or, "the establishment and transgression of limits is the stuff of Hollywood rather than an occasional by-product".[23] She suggests that action films:

> operate in part to dramatise transgression—a transgression that may take the form of the breaking of official codes of the law as seen in *Thelma and Louise*. These codes can often be taken to stand in for symbolic codes of social behaviour. Transgression is a term resonant for feminism, implying the crossing of boundaries and the breaking of taboos.[24]

In the boxing movie, the power and dangers accredited to transgression are shown through the body. The main sites and functions of danger and weakness are located where transgression can be recognised by our senses: at its margins, such as the skin. The body is not invincible and it is this very corporeality that makes it a site of potential threat. Thus, Maggie tries in vain to overcome the vulnerability of the body by toughening and hardening her body through training. In one of her fights, Maggie breaks her nose, which starts bleeding heavily. The ring doctor takes the blood as a sign to warn Maggie that he might stop the bout. Back in her corner, Maggie begs Frankie to fix the nose so she can continue fighting. That Frankie and Maggie attempt to hide any sign of blood, in order to continue the fight, further points to the notion that borders, as the very edges of categories and classifications, are critical to the process of constructing symbolic meaning. As Mary Douglas formulates it:

> Any structure of ideas is vulnerable at its margins. We should expect the orifices of the body to symbolise its specially vulnerable points. Matter issuing from them is marginal stuff of the most obvious kind. Spittle, blood, milk, urine, faeces or tears by simply issuing forth have traversed the boundary of the body... The mistake is to treat bodily margins in isolation from all other margins. There is no reason to assume any primacy for the individual's attitude to his own bodily and emotional experience, any more than for his cultural and social experience.[25]

Ideas about preventing, regulating and even punishing transgression have as their main function the imposition of a system of symbolic order onto what is an inherently disorderly and "messy" experience. The act of symbolically (re)ordering this "matter out of place", as Douglas explains, is a means of ritually protecting the vulnerable margins and threatened borders of the broader body politic. Reflections on transgression, in other words, involve reflection on the relation of "order to disorder, being to non-being, form and formlessness, life to death".[26] The symbolic ordering of the (boxer's) body through training is double-edged, as Grosz describes it, depending for its very existence upon the darker, transgressive, side of human corporeality.[27] For Grosz, bodies are Janus-faced: purity and danger, order and chaos. Signs of bodily orifices, cuts, sweat and blood attest to the body's irreducible "horror" and "threat". They not only confuse cultural categories and transgress the symbolic boundaries of the broader body politic, but also highlight the impossibility of the "clean", the "pure" and the "proper".[28]

MDB relies extensively on these dualities for telling a captivating story. Through the depiction of extended training sessions, sparring and fight scenes, the so-called Janus-faced sides of the body are frequently displayed. The filmic representation of the boxer's story is striking in its sameness: in preparation for a fight the body is shaped, tuned, made into form—it is somehow waiting to go beyond its bounds. During the fight internal and taboo flows, such as sweat and blood, become visible. Looking closely at a boxer's body before, during and after a fight, one gets the impression that form has transformed back into matter. There is both an excess and lack of boundaries. The figures have become too active, too physical, they push their way forward and beyond containment. After the fight, the boxer returns to the gym, and prepares herself/himself for the next fight. Transgression is a repetitive pattern in a boxer's life and this is what makes it such an attractive story for the movies.

Female action stars are rarely seriously injured, and it is even more unusual for them to die, or that the viewer be allowed to witness their death in full detail.[29] Unsurprisingly then, for many viewers the ending of *MDB* comes as a shock. Two-thirds into *MDB* a horrific accident puts an end to Maggie's career. During the title bout and after hearing the bell, Maggie retracts her own punch. As she walks towards her corner, she is attacked with a blindside blow by her vicious opponent (played by professional boxing champion Lucia Ryker). Maggie falls against her stool, which has been carelessly put into the ring too early. Next, she wakes up in bed, paralysed. Her fighter's body, once the perfect athletic image of health and fitness, can only survive with the help of a machine. Eastwood's direction of the transition from the ring to the bed makes the outcome of the bout doubly shocking, as Chamberlain describes it:

> The first shot is banal, a visual cliché. It is the lights of the ring spinning in darkness. A voice tells her to breath. We are suspended in hope. And then he shows her on the bed, a slow push into her face as she realizes what happened. Horrified, she says, 'Oh God.' Eastwood cuts 30 degrees to the side, backs away, revealing the air tubes and the machine that is her new life. Fade to Black.[30]

Frankie tries to find ways to help Maggie adjust to life with a disability. Most of his attempts are closely connected to keeping Maggie "mobile", for example, getting a power wheelchair or thinking about a career in college. Yet Maggie does not want to adjust to her new life. After she has overcome her initial shock, she shows surprisingly little sadness and few signs of depression. Nor does she lose her fighting spirit and sense of justice. The latter is made particularly clear in a scene when her greedy family, months after the accident, pays her a visit to get their hands on Maggie's prize money. In one of the most appalling scenes of the whole film, Maggie's mother slots a pen between her daughter's teeth and asks her to sign over her money. Realising the family's intentions, Frankie's outrage is almost beyond containment. Yet Maggie, in a subtly authoritative way, tells him to leave the room so that she can deal with her family alone. The audience sees that Maggie has learnt to protect herself at all times, as she throws a blow that hits her family hard. At the early stages of her career Maggie had bought a house for her mother who thanked her by accusing her of jeopardising her illegal welfare claims with the gift. As a result the mother never signed the deeds for the house. In hospital, Maggie tells her family that she will sell that house if they ever pester her again. As witnessed in earlier fights, and as Scrap reminds us, Maggie always liked to knock her opponents out in the first round. Thus, even bound to her bed, Maggie remains a "knockout".

Clearly Maggie is still a fighter, yet one who has lost control over her physicality and with it her dream of a boxing career. Boxing captivated her whole life, a preoccupation that might be hard for some to understand, yet which each gym member of The Hit Pit seems to share. Again, Scrap's story enriches our understanding of a fighter's life and therefore Maggie's tragedy. Like many boxers, Scrap did not escape his impoverished life through a career in the ring. He lives in a room at The Hit Pit and is financially dependent on Frankie. Participation in boxing has cost him half his eyesight, his one luxury remains the pay TV broadcasts of professional boxing bouts. Thus, all he "can" see or wants to see is boxing—the sport that is responsible for his blindness. Moreover, in the vicious fight that lead to Scrap's loss, Frankie urged him to stop fighting, yet Scrap was unable to stop insisting that he could turn the fight around. Similarly to Scrap, Maggie's preoccupation with boxing has become so strong that it blinds her to other options in life. Far from being disillusioned or consumed by regrets, however, she is content with having been up there in the ring. She tasted success and experienced the loyalty and support of her fans. She tells Frankie: "I got it all—unless they keep taking it away from me". Yet the complications of bedsores, gangrene and leg amputation bind Maggie—a woman whose life and future dreams were defined by her physical activity—to her bed. Maggie tells Frankie she has had her moment of glory and asks him to assist her in euthanasia. At first, Frankie refuses. The same eagerness and élan that made Maggie train now turns into self-destruction. The viewer is shown in great detail how Maggie attempts suicide by biting off her tongue, trying to bleed to death. After her tongue is stitched back on she repeats the act. Frankie eventually steps in to help her die. Once again, Maggie has decided the outcome of her fight.

The hospital scenes are the climax of an interesting power reversal that takes place between coach and boxer. While Frankie takes the role of expert and gatekeeper at the beginning, it is Maggie who grows more and more powerful and independent over the course of the film. At the gym, she embraces the changes her training brings and steadily moves forward into a new life (and eventually her death). Frankie, however, is fully anchored in the past and cannot embrace the present or future. He has not found a way of coming to terms with the continuing risk, dangers and emotional cost inherent to boxing. Over the years he developed a false feeling of responsibility for his boxers' fate and destiny. This hinders him emotionally, in becoming a reliable trainer for Maggie, and then, once he is committed to training her, he is still driven by the "oppressive refusal to allow the people he cares for to take risks in the process of growing into full selfhood".[31] Frankie cannot bear the idea of letting his boxers face their own challenges. He is burdened by the idea of averting things that he has no means of preventing. The rule "to protect yourself at all times" has become his personal mantra.

What is eventually revealed as a pattern in Frankie's life is first seen when Frankie's most promising fighter, Big Willie (Mike Colter), leaves the gym because Frankie is tentative and over-cautious. Willie has recognised Frankie's inhibitions and under new management he succeeds in winning a title bout. Scrap, who narrates the film with great omnipresence, warns Maggie that if she really wants to make it to a title fight "Frankie won't take you there". He continues: "Sometimes the best way to deliver a punch is to step back, but step back too far and you ain't fighting at all". His words make the viewer realise that Frankie and Maggie are ill matched too. One has stepped back too far from the fight game, while the other is eager to step into the spotlight and risk everything. This is further emphasised through imagery which shows Frankie in the dark or lingering somewhere in the background of the frame, while Maggie never seems to rest and is always shown preparing and training for a fight. Maggie, unlike Frankie, is able to move on and grow into her full self. By the end of the film she has out-grown her mentor and now dictates the rules without objection. And, it is Frankie who fully accepts these conditions and helps Maggie to reach her new goal: to finish the unmaking of her body.

Conclusion

Building and re-building the body, using it in the ring and destroying it in the act makes *MBD* stand out with respect to issues of gender. First, with a female as protagonist the idea of boxing as a masculine preserve is lost forever and so is the confidence in a normative masculinity promoted in earlier boxing films. In the short story on which the movie is based, writer F.X. Toole directly quotes Joyce Carol Oates in order to emphasise the point of lost masculinity:

> Just as a boxer is his body, a man's masculinity is the use of his body...Boxing is for men, and is about men, and *is* man. A celebration of the lost religion all the more trenchant of being lost.[32]

The athletic performance of gender, has long been a battleground for ideas about gender norms and their transgression (see for example *Girlfight, Pumping Iron II: The Women* [1985]). Women's sports are a special case, as Butler explains, because they have shown just how radically gender norms can be altered through a spectacular restaging. Over the years, as Butler claims, bodies that have gone from being perceived as "outside" the norm are now perceived as some of the most progressive instances of the norm. Thus, Maggie's appearance and action in the gym and fight arena effectively unsettle "the rigidity of gendered expectations and broaden the scope of acceptable gender performances".[33]

Moreover, *MDB* also questions the idea that bravery or the "right" to die a heroic death are "reserved" to male contenders. As often seen in male boxing movies, for example *Raging Bull*, male contenders struggle to accept their loss in the final fight and move on. In fact, their loss seems to paralyse them. Given this cinematic history and its strong focus on winning, it is not surprising that the "movement-narrative" of *MDB* must somehow come to a halt when Maggie loses her ability to dance across the canvas. It is heartbreaking to watch her health collapse, because for the majority of the film Maggie's relative empowerment is represented through her athleticism and willpower. Thus, when Maggie loses her movement, we expect her to be powerless. Unlike most of her male predecessors, however, Maggie has neither lost her ability to fight nor her fighting spirit. Instead, her willpower never seems stronger than in the hospital scenes—she is unstoppable. This is further supported by a narrative emphasis that is not on the protagonist's suffering *per se* but on the ways Maggie decides, or rather dictates, her own death.

For Modeleski, Maggie's death is a mere "sacrifice to the gods of the lost religion of masculinity" and this sacrifice overrides any empowering meaning.[34] At the movies women who have traversed the boundaries of the body, and with it those of society, must die a symbolic or actual death (*Thelma and Louise* [1991], *Alien³* [1992]). Death becomes the punishment for their transgressive gender performances and actions. The woman who dares to do one's gender wrong, as Butler so famously pronounced, will be punished.[35] This might well be argued for Maggie, who is essentially an ageing woman whose flirtation with a high-risk sport, which is also regarded as a male preserve, becomes a question of life and death. Yet it is not Maggie's death itself but the exceptional way she actively endures the tragic outcome of the title bout and then dictates her own fate that sets her apart from previous male contenders. The way Maggie never looks back and always moves forward, especially when she loses her bodily ability to move, emphasises that Maggie's life is essentially about having a chance to choose; which includes deciding her whole life's trajectory, including its end. Maggie's dream of a boxing career has gone awry but rarely has a contender been so strong, determined and active in the act of being unmade as Maggie Fitzgerald in *MDB*. Never has heroism in a boxing movie been so utterly (self-)destructive than in its female form.

Notes

1. A good source on American sports movies, including boxing, is Roland Bergan, *Sports in the Movies* (London and New York: Proteus Books, 1982). The writings of historian Dan Streible give an invaluable insight into the history and development of a particularly strong kinship between boxing and the movies. See Dan Streible, "A History of the Boxing Film, 1894–1915: Social Control and Social Reform in the Progressive Era," *Film History* (3)3 (1989): 235–257.
2. Bergan, *Sports in the Movies*, 14.
3. Such tarry photography is a marker of the New Hollywood cinema action and adventure films. Yet it also has its predecessors, for example, Douglas Fairbank's performances in films like *Robin Hood* (1922) and *The Thief of Baghdad* (1924), the Errol Flynn and Tyrone Power films, as well as post war movies such as *Ben Hur* (1959), *Spartacus* (1961) and the numerous Tarzan serials and movies made from the 1930s to the 1960s. For a critical discussion of the objectification of the female and male action star—a discussion that aims to go beyond the claim that cinematic representations of gender are mainly organised around binary oppositions of active/male and passive/female encouraging the male gaze and thus eroticisation of the female star— see Yvonne Tasker, *Spectacular Bodies: Gender, Genre, and the Action Cinema* (London and New York: Routledge, 1993).
4. Frank Krutnik, *In a Lonely Street: Film Noir, Genre, Masculinity* (London: Routledge, 1991), 190.
5. Maggie's age is a deliberate choice. At thirty-one Maggie is too old for a career in amateur boxing, the only sport with an age limit reached at the end of thirty. Therefore her only chances lie in the more physically demanding and dangerous business of professional boxing/prizefighting.
6. There are many sport movies that show how the athletic body of a young woman becomes a contested site. See for example *Pumping Iron II: The Women* or *Girlfight*. *Girlfight*, the debut film of Karyn Kusama also tells the story of a female boxer, Diana Guzman, a working-class girl who is perceived as nothing but trouble succeeds in the sport through her unbreakable will and ambition. Several essays have been written on this particular film. Two especially interesting examples are by Mary Beltràn and Hilary Neroni. Beltràn writes on *Girlfight* with respect to the rise of the Latina action

protagonist in the Hollywood action genre. While the particular focus is on issues of race, gender and the evolution of Latina heroines in general, Beltràn shows how actress Michelle Rodriguez's role differs from the previous portrayals of Latinas as essentially tough and overtly sexual women. See Mary Beltrán, "Más Macha: The New Latina Action Hero," in *Action and Adventure Cinema*, ed. Yvonne Tasker (London and New York: Routledge, 2004), 186–201. For Neroni the movie *Girlfight* is the most intriguing depiction of a violent female fighter in American film. It stands out through its realistic depiction of female violence and the way it connects violent women and men in realistic (love) relationships. See Hilary Neroni, *The Violent Woman: Femininity, Narrative, and Violence in Contemporary American Cinema* (Albany: State University of New York Press, 2005). I discuss *Girlfight* with respect to the representation of gender in the history of sports and boxing movies in "On the Ropes: Gender Politics in the Boxing Movie," in *Visual Anthropology of Sport* (working title), ed. Peter Crawford (Denmark: Intervention Press, forthcoming).

7. John Izod and Joanna Dovalis, "*Million Dollar Baby*: Boxing Grief," *Kinema*, Fall 2005, (http://www.kinema.uwaterloo.ca/izod052.htm; accessed 16 May 2006).

8. Jennifer Hargreaves, "Bruising Peg to Boxerobics: Gendered Boxing – Images and Meaning," in *Boxer: An Anthology of Writings on Boxing and Visual Culture*, ed. David Chandler (London: Institute of International Visual Arts, 1996) 121-131.

9. Linda Ruth Williams, "Ready for Action: G.I. Jane, Demi Moore's body and the female combat movie," in *Action and Adventure Cinema*, ed. Yvonne Tasker, (London and New York: Routledge, 2004), 173.

10. Williams, "Ready for Action," 173.

11. Ibid.,173.

12. Beltrán, "Más Macha", 195.

13. For a discussion of the articulation of feminism at the movies see Jim Collins, Hilary Radner and Preacher Collins Ava, *Film Theory Goes to the Movies* (London: Routledge, 1993). For an extensive discussion of competing forms of liberal and radical feminism in women's sports see M. Ann Hall, *Feminism and Sporting Bodies: Essays on Theory and Practice* (Champaign, IL: Human Kinetics,1996). Leslie Heywood, and Shari L. Dworkin analyse the female athlete's impact on American popular culture in *Built To Win: The Female Athlete As Cultural Icon* (Minneapolis, MN: University of Minnesota Press, 2003).

14. Judith Butler, "Athletic Genders: Hyperbolic Instance and/or the Overcoming of sexual Binarism," *Stanford Electronic Humanities Review*, (6) 2, 1998, (http://www.stanford.edu./group/SHR/6-2/html/butler.html; accessed 5 May 2005).

15. Izod and Dovalis, "*Million Dollar Baby*: Boxing Grief".

16. Butler, "Athletic Genders".

17. Aaron Anderson, "Kinesthesia in Martial Arts Films: Action in Motion," *Jump Cut*, 42 (Dec.1998):1–11.

18. For an interesting discussion of aggression and violence enacted by women see Neroni, *The Violent Woman*. It is especially the discussion of the roles of police women, female soldiers and the female boxer in *Girlfight* that show how particular professions, seemingly by definition, encourage aggressive and violent behaviour.

19. Heywood and Dworkin, *Built To Win*, 118.

20. Most boxing films point to the body as the protagonist's main asset. For example, when Rocky (*Rocky*) is asked why he wants to be a fighter, he replies "Because I can't sing or dance." The suggestion being that for ambitious working-class people like him there is only the ring or the stage. In *Somebody Up There Likes Me*, Rocky Graziano is the exception to the rule that guys from the lower east side do not have a chance in life. Rocky becomes a star, his friend who can neither dance, sing nor fight becomes a criminal. The stage and the ring, both, put the body at the centre of display and make it the story's main spectacle, as Tasker argues, "if the performance of a show functioned to produce the showgirl as spectacle, then the equivalent sites of the action movie are the gym, a space for rehearsal, and the arena for a fight". See Yvonne Tasker, *Spectacular Bodies: Gender, Genre, and the Action Cinema*, (London and New York: Routledge, 1993), 79. The kinship of boxing and the stage, coupled with the dream of success, becomes most obvious in the movie *Kid Galahad* (1973), when Kid Galahad asks the question: "Everyone wants to be a champion, don't they?" Bette Midler answers him "Even I wanted to be one once. I was going to panic New York with dance and song." Her abandoned expectations clearly mirror his rising expectations.
21. Bergan, *Sports in the Movies*, 14.
22. Ibid., 9.
23. Tasker, *Spectacular Bodies*, 150.
24. Ibid., 150.
25. Mary Douglas, *Natural Symbols* (Middlesex: Penguin Books, 1970).
26. Ibid., 6.
27. Elizabeth Grosz, *Volatile Bodies: Toward a Corporeal Feminism* (St Leonards, NSW: Allen & Unwin, 1994), 194.
28. Grosz, *Volatile Bodies,*194f. Grosz, as Julia Kristeva's *Powers of Horror, New York* (New York: Columbia University Press, 1982), builds essentially on Mary Douglas' writings. In film studies, Barbara Creed uses Kristeva's idea of transgression and abjection as her hypothesis for an exploration of the cinematic representations of the monstrous woman in the horror genre. See Barbara Creed, *The Monstrous Feminine: Film, Feminism, Psychoanalysis* (London and New York: Routledge, 1993).
29. The movies *Alien*[3] (1992) and *Jean of Arc* (1999) are further exceptions here, as Barbara Creed explains in this volume.
30. James Chamberlin, "The Magic of Risking Everything for a Dream Nobody Sees: *Million Dollar Baby*: The Shadow Film," *Senses of Cinema* (2005), (www.sensesofcinema.com/contents/05/35/million_dollar_baby.html; accessed June 2006).
31. Izod and Dovalis, "*Million Dollar Baby*: Boxing Grief".
32. The story *Million Dollar Baby* is written by fight manager Jerry Boyd and published under his pseudonym F.X. Toole, *Rope Burns: Stories from the Corner* (New York: Ecco Press, 2000). See also Oates, Joyce Carol, *On Boxing* (London and New York: Routledge, 1987), 72.
33. Butler, "Athletic Genders".
34. Tania Modleski, "Million Dollar Baby: A Split Decision," *Cineast,* (30)3 (Summer 2005): 11.

35. Judith Butler, *Bodies that Matter: On the Discursive Limits of "Sex"* (New York and London: Routledge, 1993).

Chapter Seven

Fighting to be Seen: Looking for Women in the West, from *The Searchers* to *The Missing*

Martin Flanagan

Figure Eight: Cate Blanchett in *The Missing* (2003)

Why does the woman in the West fight? For many years in critical work on the Western, this sort of question was subordinate to an even more crucial one to do with whether filmic representations of the West actually allowed women *to exist* with any degree of complexity or agency. Where women do appear in classical Westerns, they tend to appear as "decent and long-suffering matron[s]"[1] or inexperienced young maidens who have few adventures, while the women defined as more aggressively sexual—say, Linda Darnell's devoted but tainted Chihuahua in *My Darling Clementine* (1946), or Jennifer Jones' self-confessed "trash" Pearl Chavez in *Duel in the Sun* (1946)—often prove their inner decency only in their death throes. Though there are honourable exceptions to characters of this nature (Joan Crawford as Vienna in *Johnny Guitar* [1954] is willing to fight and depends on no man), their presence in stylistically unusual Westerns places them outside the mainstream current of representation. Other Western women, including those defined as "tomboys", transform, reform or remake themselves, sometimes to win male approval (Doris Day in *Calamity Jane* [1953]), sometimes to secure a role outside the logic of sexual exchange and the need for male protection. Claudia Cardinale's Jill in *C'era una volta il West/Once Upon a Time in the West* (1968) exemplifies the latter trajectory, becoming matron of the railroad and thus a symbol associated with the civilising of the country through her own work rather than by simply representing a feminine ideal; yet the film does not discourage the reading that this is merely compensation for her romantic rejection by the hero (Charles Bronson's "Harmonica"). In some criticism, one wonders if it is enough that women appear on screen at all in the genre. Andrew Sarris, writing on the cinema of John Ford, notes the surprising "profusion of mothers, sisters, wives and sweethearts" in a genre that is usually taken to be concerned with rootlessness and adventure, and while it is true that some of Ford's women provoke interest and engagement beyond their function of aid or inspiration to the hero (Clare Trevor's Dallas in *Stagecoach* [1939], for instance), his frequent coding of gender within the conventional dichotomies that oppose domesticity with freedom, emotion with action, hardly puts Ford beyond reproach in terms of gender representation.[2] Indeed, perhaps Ford's most famous single image, from *The Searchers* (1956), is the sight of a returning male adventurer from the point of view of a waiting woman, and his films, according to Michael Dempsey, offer up such "waiting women" again and again.[3]

The Western itself, of course, regularly disappears from view in terms of mainstream regard and volume of production. Contemporary American cinema saw its last major Western cycle coalesce around the box-office successes *Dances With Wolves* (1990) and *Unforgiven* (1992) in the early 1990s. Out of this revival emerged *Bad Girls* (1994) and *The Quick and the Dead* (1995) as notable female-centred, studio-backed Westerns; the independent sector produced Maggie Greenwald's *The Ballad of Little Jo* (1993), a less conventional genre entry that explores issues of gender performance and impersonation (and the economic and class imperatives that drive them).[4] Although this phase of genre activity lost impetus after 1995, there have been scattered signs of a further revival in a series of popular fictions (sometimes Westerns in disguised form) since 2000. This series includes *Shanghai Noon* (2000), *All the Pretty Horses* (2000), *American Outlaws* (2001), *Texas Rangers*

(2001), *Open Range* (2003), *The Missing* (2003) and *Brokeback Mountain* (2005). We can arguably add Tarantino's *Kill Bill: Vol. 1* (2003) and *Kill Bill: Vol. 2* (2004), revenge narratives wherein "the elements of the classical Hollywood Western" are reshuffled.[5] During the same period, American television offered the critically acclaimed HBO serial *Deadwood* (2004-) and the sci-fi Western *Firefly* (2002-3). The latter show was later developed into a theatrical feature in the form of *Serenity* (2004).

Some of the texts in that group acknowledge the development of the post-feminist female warrior in popular culture (particularly in 1990s action-fantasy movies and television), and accordingly allot roles for female fighters and leaders. Others (generally those where the narratives mentioned unfold within the "proper" nineteenth century historical parameters of the Western), situate women in crucial but largely non-violent social functions where fearlessness, initiative and emotional strength can be proven; thus the more conventional genre designations of nurses, prostitutes and mothers find more complex, empowered manifestations in *Open Range* and *Deadwood* (the latter of which develops a key plotline around retelling the story of Calamity Jane, centring on her attempts to forge an identity after the death of her idol, "Wild Bill" Hickok). Freed by fantasy into an unspecified time-zone that nevertheless strongly indicates an allegorical relation to the Reconstruction era after the American Civil War,[6] *Firefly* and *Serenity* make the most capable member of their crew of mercenaries a black woman pilot (although Zoe, played by Gina Torres, is still second-in-command to Nathan Filion's errant officer Mal).

Maggie Gilkeson (Cate Blanchett) fights to restore her all-female family unit in a film, *The Missing*, that is perhaps the most significant recent attempt to reinvent the Western woman in a way that transcends simple gender inversion, as is arguably the case in the enjoyable but formulaic *The Quick and the Dead*. The primary intertext for Raimi's typically referential film is the quotably iconic work of Sergio Leone,[7] while *The Missing* stands as a reworking of Ford's *The Searchers* (which is also referenced visually in a key scene in *Kill Bill: Vol. 2*, as noted by McGee).[8] Commonly recognised as an "explicit retread"[9] of Ford's movie, *The Missing* can also be justifiably construed as a new reading of the sexual (and, to a milder extent, racial) dynamics of *The Searchers*, even a *corrective* to certain ideological oversights in the earlier film, principally the treatment of women as functional "abstractions", serving only to inspire and be rescued by the masculine protagonists.[10] Indeed, the very title cues us to the film's possible agenda, to rework Ford's monolithic canonical Western by shifting narrative emphasis and spectatorial contemplation from the heroic "manly" activity of searching, to a consideration of the feeling and consequences of *absence*, of "the missing" understood as a person (the women abducted by Indians) or sensation (their experience, virtually untold in the abduction scenario of Ford's film), or as something *lacking* (the absence of women in central roles in the genre as a whole).

The problematic, largely essentialist treatment of women in *The Searchers* has been the subject of much discussion;[11] female narrative marginalisation in the film is perhaps best encapsulated by Peter Lehman:

> Many viewers will respond to an analysis of the place of women in the film by saying, "But that's the way things were in the West and its wrong to judge them by contemporary standards". This response is naively inadequate...First of all, that is not the way things were in the West in 1868. Women and Indians, for example, all lived twenty-four hours each day then as now, and we can explain nothing about their place within the narrative structure of the film with reference to actual conditions. A story about Texas in 1868 could just as well centralise women and Indians and peripheralise white men as do the reverse.[12]

Lehman, echoing many others, suggests that what is really at stake in the Western is a self-justification of the national cultural centrality of white men. Robert Warshow's abiding expression of the same problem tells us that what the Western hero *really* defends is "the purity of his own image".[13] The status of the gender or racial other in the Western thus poses a particular epistemological problem for a genre mainly concerned with the "knowability" of types of men. If the history of the Western can be seen at least in part as a slow, incremental progression towards recognition of the agency of gendered and racial others— their right to live twenty-four hours each day (paraphrasing Lehman)—then we must ask if women are still a problem in the Western. In terms of representation, is the mission of *The Missing* to deliver some kind of updated gender-conscious rebuke to *The Searchers*? Looking at notable equivalences and divergences between the two texts will aid our understanding of the encounter between the two films. The question is whether *The Missing*—compromised and uneven as it is in places, and perhaps too much in thrall to its model *The Searchers*—can nevertheless claim to renew the Western by adding strong representations to its limited repertoire of formidable females.

Looking for Women, Looking at Women

Whether the phallic male identity of the Western hero is taken to be unproblematically affirmed and celebrated by the genre, or is seen as fragile, fragmentary, and contingent, there can be no doubt that to be a Western male is to *look* like one. Critics agree that "the Western hero's phallic identity utterly depends on his being the proper object of vision",[14] with the violence that seems essential to the genre being deployed towards the ultimate end of "constituting one's physical self as a male. The purpose is less defeat, or destruction, than display";[15] or put another way, "a hero is one who looks like a hero".[16] Studies of the centrality of performance and spectacle in the Western abound, and have also been extended to the female presence in a genre where the "eroticised display of masculinities as spectacle" often translates into activities of "dressing up and putting on a show".[17] The "show" may involve more than one gender, just as easily accommodating the showgirl, cowgirl or female gunfighter (whose frequent lesbian connotations are noted by Tasker) as the stoic male. Less numerous are Westerns that are driven by powerful and active maternal figures; *The Missing* certainly qualifies as one.[18]

In such an epistemologically unstable textual environment, first looks take on extra symbolic weight, for one must of course be *seen* to be recognised. The catalogue of iconic first glimpses of protagonists in the genre is appropriately long and memorable.[19] Rather like George Stevens' *Shane* (1953), the opening of *The Searchers* definitively associates the male Western adventurer with a desiring female vision as Martha Edwards (Dorothy Jordan) opens her front door to see Ethan Edwards (John Wayne) materialise from the landscape. Studlar notes that this manner of entrance underscores the general coding of the (feminine) domestic realm as that which is known with Ethan/the wilderness representing the unknown, "the question mark, an uncertainty".[20] This romantic intrusion of mystery and unfettered masculinity into the home inhabited by Martha, Ethan's brother Aaron (Walter Coy) and their children anticipates the forthcoming shattering of their fragile façade of civilisation. The children, including Debbie (played as a child in this scene by Lana Wood) gather around Ethan and show their fascination with the tokens of violence—his sabre and war medals—that mark all the ways in which he is different from their peaceable farmer father. The film thus opens with a somewhat disruptive arrival and Ethan's (temporary) re-integration into the family. Yet some things remain confusingly obscure; Ethan mistakes Debbie for her older sister Lucy (Debbie's age and size when he last saw the family), and Ethan's undocumented history since the end of the Civil War is brought up by his brother. Ethan does not qualify as completely familiar; he is still, to some extent, "unknowable", resembling a mirage or ghost when he appears out of the landscape. Peter Lehman notes that in *The Searchers*, issues of naming and identification around both men and women, American and Indian, reach the level of a "contagion".[21] Little wonder that Ethan—in biographical and moral terms—is such a mystery, his enigmatic introduction setting up the film's essential hermeneutic.[22] Although *The Missing* is also greatly concerned with problems and barriers to identification, and the slippage between reputation and core personality, its introduction of Maggie Gilkeson could not be more different to that of Ethan. Our first sight of Maggie is prosaically intimate, her reverie in the privy disturbed when a door once again swings open—to reveal daughter Dot (Jenna Boyd), telling Maggie that her first client has arrived for the day's healing tasks. We next see Maggie as a figure in the landscape, an extreme wide shot placing her modest ranch in a mountainous terrain and allowing us to just make out her trudging body behind the graphic legend "New Mexico, 1885". Despite the pictorial drama of this shot, its position in the narrative appears to be intended to underline the hardness and repetition of Maggie's routine and to situate her in the material history of the time rather than place her in a mythical register (as in Ethan's epic, mysterious entrance). Her first act in the film is to rouse herself from a rare moment of rest and privacy to get up and *work*, and as a worker she is not out of place in the West, proving her centrality and belonging in the harsh landscape; this is vital to the modern Western which must not treat the female presence as incongruous, and therefore a subject for comedy.[23] Having said this, the next scene qualifies this incipient gender discourse around Maggie's independence by signalling the inappropriateness of traditional female vanity, in such a time and place, as very much a comic matter. The aged Mexican woman who has come to Maggie for help with a lone painful tooth asserts her right to value her own appearance (her granddaughter explaining, "she don't worry about pain...it is her only tooth. She worry how she *look*"). Compounding this ambiguity is the fact that we will soon see this indictment of vanity transferred to a more serious register as Maggie's teen-aged daughter Lilly (Evan Rachel Wood)—marked in early scenes as fatally open to the temptations of civilised modernity (she is depicted, for instance, sullenly skinning a deer while dressed in her Sunday finery)—is abducted, and finds herself having to tap into a self-reliant strength that we suspect her mother never credited her with. Before this, Maggie treats Lilly's modern urban aspirations with bemusement if not contempt. She perceives Lilly's playing up of her menstrual cramps (an excuse to avoid working with the cattle, aimed at farmhand Brake Baldwin [Aaron Eckhart]) as an affront to her own sense that one should not make oneself look pitiable to gain favour with a man. Lilly— drily asserting her education as one of the ways she is different from her mother—corrects Maggie and suggests the word is "pitiful".

Despite these moments of friction, which hint at the family's vulnerability, the early scenes of the film code Maggie as a working mother and healer, productive and valued within the locality. Her main priority is to keep her family together and develop the ranch; she is undoubtedly domesticated but she owns and controls her own property and employs two men, Brake and Emiliano (Sergio Calderon), to tend the ranch. Brake is also her lover (problems of privacy arise around this arrangement as well), and although we are not told why Maggie has refused the repeated offers of marriage referred to by Brake, this does not seem connected to any pining for escape. Maggie is not tempted by

the marvels of the nearby town, or far-off Cleveland, which so absorb Lilly—
nor any other form of adventure. This explains her disturbed feeling when her
estranged father, Samuel Jones (Tommy Lee Jones), arrives at the farmstead.[24]
The "contagion" of (mis)recognition and being judged by how one looks is
developed with Jones, whose otherness as marked against the white male norm
is even more pronounced because of his adoption—some time ago, we
assume—of the apparel, hairstyle and customs of the Chiricahua nation. Jones is
forced to justify his arrival to the suspicious Brake and Emiliano in terms of
asserting his humanity: "I'm not a coyote", he tells Brake as Emiliano shadows
his approach, rifle drawn. Unlike Ethan, no-one has been waiting for Samuel
(least of all Maggie), and the door is not flung open to him—he is invited to
sleep in the barn by Brake, who, isolated from so much of Maggie's emotional
life, does not know Jones' identity as Maggie's father. Yet youngest daughter
Dot *does* regard Jones as a figure of spectacle and fascination, with the camera
in these establishing scenes repeatedly rendering Dot's point of view as she
steals glances at the enigmatic sight.[25] To her, Jones' difference is as thrilling
and unlikely in these familiar domestic surroundings as the promise of the fair
and its "expositions of the future" (such as recorded sound) are to her sister.
Thus, the film's two younger women are established as looking in two very
different directions—one to modernity, urbanisation and the East, one to
atavistic founding myths, masculine-coded adventure and the West.

In an indication of the film's wish to compensate for the Western's
problematic tradition of racial representation, Dot expresses her delight at the
thought that she and Lilly might have Indian blood in them (that Dot is
associated with hybridity is also expressed in her tomboy-ish clothing, as
compared with Lilly's traditionally feminine apparel and tendency to "dress up"
in fancy duds).[26] The film self-consciously asks the spectator to note a contrast
with *The Searchers* in regard to race; Dot, although young, is presented as
entertaining a positive relation to the racial other, and sees her personal borders
in different terms to her mother and sister. Attracted to the exoticism of Indians,
she welcomes the connection represented by the protective charm and
moccasins offered to her by Jones, over Maggie's objections. In terms of the
film's attempt to construct an acceptable racial dynamic, Dot, resembling
Martin Pawley (Jeffrey Hunter) in *The Searchers* as described by Brian
Henderson, becomes "the national subject that can integrate the other into its
own myth".[27] If we can agree that Howard's film seeks to re-examine the
problematic racial values often attached to interpretations of *The Searchers,* it is
clearly important that Dot—the symbolic "hybrid" character who mirrors her
grandfather but does not show signs of wanting to abandon her family—is not of
a sexually mature age (unlike the abducted Lilly, who shows no such desire to
assimilate and indeed is characterised by Maggie as unlikely to trust an Indian).

As many commentators have pointed out, in 1956 *The Searchers* was unable or unwilling (or both) to embrace even the "idea of a conversation"[28] between white woman and Indian male, even as its narrative posits that the older Debbie (Natalie Wood) has spent five years with the Comanche, presumably some of those years as a wife to Chief Scar. Of course, the two films do not match up exactly in any area. In transposing *The Searchers* onto *The Missing*, those familiar with the earlier film are less likely to correspond Maggie to Ethan than to the younger, more compassionate "searcher", Martin Pawley; instead identifying Jones as a version of Ethan (thus recognising the reconfigured but still present Oedipal dynamic in the later film). Yet Maggie, identified by Brake as "a good Christian", has a problem with Indians in a way that Dot does not. Ethan's racism is explicit and made an obvious issue by *The Searchers*, although this is not the same as saying that the text's feelings on race issues, so vivid in America in 1956, can always be clearly separated from its protagonist simply because he is not always shown in a good light. After all, Ford reserves his most disturbing and haunting imagery—and Ethan/Wayne's most disgusted expression in grim close-up—for the depiction of a group of white women gone crazy from the effects of living with Indians (in the scene where Ethan checks for Debbie at the fort). *The Missing* strives for balance in issues of race, binding up Maggie's attitude to Indians with her emotional rejection of the culture that took her father away. Her desire to build a permanent home, signified by the frequent scenes depicting her at work, adumbrate her need to live as different a life as possible from that of her rootless drifter father. Her objection to Indians (she admits that she does not normally practice her healing on them) could be read as a racist fear of the other, but rather seems to express a concern that the same kind of spell that made Jones abandon his family could emerge from the charm he proffers Dot. If Jones is allowed back in, Maggie can see her own family—vulnerable even before the restless Lilly is taken—breaking up.

The Missing frequently comes across as confused or hesitant when it comes to strongly critiquing or revising the Western's dubious gender/race assumptions. Although an ostensible aim of the overall text appears to be to assert Maggie's strong maternal character, the narrative nevertheless punishes Maggie by causally linking Lilly's abduction to her maternal fears. Fundamentally distrusting the maturity both of Lilly and of the nascent civilisation in the territory, Maggie insists that Lilly accompany Dot, Brake and Emiliano in taking the cattle for branding, dashing Lilly's hopes of heading to the town fair.[29] It is the wrong advice; en route, their party is attacked and Lilly is captured by Chidin (Eric Schewig), an Apache "witch" or "brujo", recently escaped off the reservation with a band of former scouts. In the attack, Brake and Emiliano are murdered but Dot manages to escape to be reunited with her mother; consequently, they take up the search for Lilly, accompanied by Jones.

If the culturally hybridised Jones, the returning "bad father", is initially represented as a source of threatening difference to Maggie's life and home only to be recuperated by his actions, the main antagonist Chidin is the genre's traditional inscrutable Indian whose difference is inscribed here, literally, as supernatural. The film's construction of a discourse on female representation is crystallised in the strand of the narrative dealing with Lilly and Chidin; reminding us of the centrality of epistemological doubts around vision and knowing to the genre as a whole, an elaborate photographic metaphor is built around the enslaved women, with their value as images repeatedly emphasised. Chidin literally wears the haunted visages of his previous victims on his person, and captures Wittick (Ray McKinnon), a white male photographer, forcing him into his retinue as he gathers a sufficient number of women to make a prosperous trade trip across the Mexican border. Yet women can also manipulate this value as a mode of self-preservation; after a failed escape, Lilly makes the furious Chidin back off by taunting him: "Go on, hit me. You won't fetch as many pesos with my face all swollen and you know it". Lilly—the farm girl who yearns for modernity—buys time by asserting the value of her difference, emphasising that one of the features of that coming modernity will be an ambiguous status for women when it comes to technological reproduction (almost as if Lilly is predicting something about how gender will inform the popular culture versions of the West that will come along in the next century). The only way Lilly can effectively protect herself at this juncture is to confirm the inscription of women in the West as property, but by buying this time, she makes possible the ultimate rescue by her mother.

Absences and Compromises

Despite its many ideological and narrative ambiguities and gaps,[30] *The Searchers* is classically structured around a clear goal that is commensurate with a staunchly patriarchal notion of where white women "belong". This is the goal of recovering Debbie and restoring her to white civilisation where she will take up a place within a new family headed by Martin Pawley and his sweetheart Laurie Jorgensen (Vera Miles), and presumably repress her Comanche experiences. This putative new family will famously lack Ethan's presence, as the final shot informs us that he will remain outside of society, making the restoration of patriarchy through Ethan's actions slightly more ambivalent. Still, the film makes it clear that for men, to embrace the domestic and take a nurturing role within civilisation is to be trapped. This is made clear in the fact that the farmers Aaron Edwards and Lars Jorgenson (John Qualen) are never visually represented with the stature of Ethan/Wayne, and reinforced in Laurie's dialogue as Martin departs for the second phase of his and Ethan's search: "I was hoping I might be able to hold you here but I guess I knew better". Better to be out there searching than "held" at home on the ranch, pacified, castrated, "missing" something. There is no disputing that the film demonstrates that this wanderlust and drive for vengeance exacts a high emotional cost on Ethan (including, the text allows us to infer, the loss of a possible romantic life with Martha, who chose his more reliable brother Aaron instead). It also has to be said that the film's address frequently allows the spectator to bypass Ethan's worldview; in gender and race attitudes, the text often draws us to the part-Cherokee Marty's more tolerant, less rigid perspective, particularly around whether Debbie is *worth* saving or not.[31] Yet Ford's "arbitrary"[32] narrative dependence on the rescue of a helpless woman—moreover, a woman whose sexual taint from her time in the hands of "others" can apparently only be removed by the purity of the rescuer's motivation—is insistent enough that it found itself being reproduced in a number of New Hollywood films two decades later.[33]

We might have expected *The Missing* to make better progress than those movies of the 1970s, and surely the premise of reworking *The Searchers* for new audiences was a promising one. However, many critical views found the film's ideological manoeuvrings insipid, misjudged or worse. Charles Taylor articulated the film's fatal compromise and hesitancy in establishing a credible ideological worldview: *"The Missing* is...entertainment for anyone who likes either a dollop of feminist uplift or family values (or both!) with their bloodletting". The byline for Taylor's review evaluates the film as "a gruesome and thoroughly unpleasant Western that can't decide whether it's racist or overly P.C. Guess what? It's both".[34]

Certainly, *The Missing* sacrifices dramatic edge and conflict in a bid to avoid being accused of misrepresentation. On the subject of race it works hard to apportion blame for the harshness of 1885 society "across [the] ethnic divide",[35] with white men supporting Chidin's abhorrent activities and Chiricahuan braves aiding Maggie and Jones. The film acts cautiously in constructing Apaches as the source of evil, taking care to compensate by identifying normative white male authority (the ineffectual cavalry and local sheriff) as responsible for creating the moral vacuum within which such activities can prosper. The Apache "witch", Chidin, is separated from the "mainstream" of Indian life in the film in more than one way. His savagery matches the most brutal Native American characters of post Production Code-era Westerns such as the titular character of Robert Aldrich's *Ulzana's Raid* (1972). Yet, though made thirty years earlier, Aldrich's film establishes Ulzana's motivation and feeling of responsibility for his Apache nation in social terms, unlike *The Missing*, which almost without exception displaces Chidin's negative actions onto his supernatural qualities (thus, if anything, reinforcing his otherness). Only once are Chidin's actions placed in anything like social terms, when he confronts Jones (whom Chidin will not recognise as Indian), and rejects the money Jones offers to free Lilly as insufficient compensation for the "evil done to [his] people" by the white man. Chidin and his group of rebellious former scouts prey on white (female) society but they also appear to have opted out of Native American society (they abduct Indian women too). Reconsidering the captivity narrative of *The Searchers*, Patrick McGee cites recent historical work that suggests that communal aspects of Native American social structures declined as a result of colonial displacement, with unequal wealth distribution beginning to influence social mores.[36] *The Missing* can thus acceptably blame Chidin's perversion of capitalist enterprise (his slaving business) on the Euro-American worldview and exonerate the Indian. Yet, simultaneously, Euro-American capitalist expansion and modernity (as represented by the town fair) is posited as an alternative to Lilly's abduction (if Maggie had allowed her to go to town, she would have remained safe). Compared to John Ford's rigidly atavistic view of the relationship between wilderness and civilisation, *The Missing* communicates a deep ambivalence about the American future.

Striving to avoid offence, Howard's film does appear to self-censor beyond the point of coherence on several complex issues. Sex, for instance, is one of the most obvious "missing" things in the film. The racist fear of sexual miscegenation that runs through *The Searchers* is rightly avoided in *The Missing* (the women's fates once they are sold in Mexico is held in abeyance by the narrative's race-against-time structure); for instance, Jones' romantic and sexual history while living with the Chiricahua is discussed seriously more than once (unlike Ford's film, which treats the notion of a white man/Indian woman marital relationship in broad comic terms). Laudable though the removal of the stigma of miscegenation is, *The Missing* has a bigger problem in reconciling sex with positive and honest depictions of gender. If, as David Thomson asserts, Ford's film could not bear to represent the "idea of a conversation" between Indian man and white woman in 1956, resorting therefore to implanting the idea as fantasy in the spectatorial imagination, *The Missing* seems to remove sex from the frontier completely in its bid to modernise or recuperate the Western's gender perspective.[37] There are understandable and largely positive narrative outcomes to this in that, for instance, Brake's death galvanises Maggie's singular identity as a mother who, as she says, does not "know how to leave" her children behind (unlike her own father, who she at first cannot forgive or empathise with). Yet Maggie must suffer terribly when Brake is brutally killed, while another prospective heterosexual union—that between Chiricahua brave Honesco (Simon Baker) and his young bride, another abductee—is tested by Honesco's injuries and the death of his father, Jones' friend Kayitah (Jay Tavare).[38] Perhaps most implausibly, Chidin's band of Apaches, although in the business of trading slave women, do not appear interested in sex and, as already discussed, appear outside of any family structures.

Chidin himself is represented as disfigured, "gross, unkempt, unwashed, dentally disadvantaged with blackened fingernails".[39] He seems to be voyeuristically obsessed with the images of his captive women, which he wears as trophies, but shows no sign of wishing to possess them sexually. This marks a significant difference with Chief Scar, the Comanche antagonist of *The Searchers*, whose clearly signalled sexual threat is the source of that film's racial dread (expressed through Ethan's values). At one point Lilly is almost raped by a white member of Chidin's retinue; this is prevented by Chidin's Apache second-in-command, who makes clear to her that he considers himself "better" than her, implying that his intervention is as much about proving his self-control as measured against the base desires of the white American as it is about ensuring her right to live free from such abuses. Lilly returns to her family, of course, and is much safer there, but what are audiences to make of the apparent message that, for her, a destiny outside of that life experienced by her mother is too dangerous? Will Lilly ever exercise her yearning for modernity again? Ultimately, it seems as if every avenue that might lead to sexual or romantic congress in *The Missing* is truncated and ultimately displaced onto the familial; reinforcing an impression of chaste conservatism in the film and a curious lack of courage in exploring gender progress as linked to sexual relations.

Conclusion

Prior to the abduction and its ensuing events, Maggie's ambition has been to maintain a farm and raise her daughters; her dilemma has been to romantically accept Brake and, in so doing, battle her own instincts about the reliability of men. Neither is easy for her. The film begins with a depiction of a far more fraught family than that of *The Searchers*, and Maggie's fighting with Lilly at the beginning of the film resembles a contemporary mother–adolescent daughter relationship as much as anything from New Mexico in 1885 (this reading is enhanced by the casting of Evan Rachel Wood as Lilly, whose breakout role was in the "problem teen" film *Thirteen* [2003]). Discourses of family as understood in the 1950s and early 2000s no doubt apply here (a major American film of the mid-1950s was more likely to examine the Oedipal confusion of the post-war male in an age of consumerism than the resistance of the young female). The visitation on Maggie's modestly cultivated life of the "natural" threat of the Apache forces her into a new conflict, even as she relives the hardest emotional trial of her life (abandonment by her father). We learn from dialogue that Jones' departure was the catalyst that powered Maggie's uncompromising attainment of her independent life; now all those resources must be used again in a new battle that tests her implacability as a mother. Unusually for a Western woman, Maggie is in the position not simply of aiding or inspiring a rescue but of defending the part of this hard world which she has carved out for herself and her daughters with little help from men. The text makes clear that physical survival and aggression is not Maggie's only test; still mourning Brake's horrific death, she has to conquer her own instinct to refuse Jones' offer of help in tracking Lilly. Yet if Maggie's life was built on a premise of independence from men like her father, it is difficult to resist reading Jones' intervention as a textual reassertion of gender traditionalism (it is his final act of self-sacrifice that defeats Chidin and effectively saves Maggie's life). Confused in how to justify a female fighter without alienating itself from the genre's history, the film dismantles the patriarchal family structure with Brake's death, only to resurrect it with Jones' return, qualifying Maggie's independence.

The Missing strives to make many parts of Maggie's identity—emotional, physical, intellectual, spiritual, maternal—resonate in her journey. Yet the film seems finally unable to reconcile the barbarous and violent world of the West with a version of femininity that incorporates all parts of a woman's life, leaving Maggie bereft of sexual identity at the end of the film. Although it does spell out certain things left unsaid by the various lacunae of *The Searchers* (for instance, Dot's desire to "be" Indian, which reconnects the two forms of otherness previously used to structure the Western's ideology of white male centrality), *The Missing* disappoints in its presentation of an only marginally less conservative sexual world than Ford's film. In terms of textual importance, the familial displaces the sexual; though Maggie's history of romantic suffering is repeatedly stressed, evoking the thematic territory of melodrama, the film arguably bypasses the "subversive" angle on feminine desire explored by the likes of *Johnny Guitar*.[40] Unlike the "notorious ladies" discussed by Patrick McGee—sexually assertive Western characters like "the Lady" (Sharon Stone) in the "feminocentric"[41] *The Quick and the Dead*—Maggie seems almost a victim of sex.[42] What powers her willingness to fight is depth of maternal feeling, which the film strives to associate with Maggie Gilkeson as vividly as vengeance is redolent of Ethan Edwards. The narrative concludes, of course, with Maggie's identity as a mother affirmed, her children safe, and her property intact; the family is secured, but romantically Maggie will have to start again. In terms of gender representation, it is thus chiefly around Maggie's strength as a mother, and the serious treatment of her as in control of her property (a status which is not denoted as special or incongruous), that the film can claim to have expanded the representation of the Western woman.

Notes

1. Peter William Evans, "Westward the Women: Feminising the Wilderness," in *The Movie Book of the Western,* ed. Ian Cameron and Douglas Pye, (London: Studio Vista, 1996), 211.

2. Andrew Sarris cited in Gaylyn Studlar, "What Would Martha Want? Captivity, Purity and Feminine Values in *The Searchers,*" in *The Searchers: Essays and Reflections on John Ford's Classic Western,* ed. Arthur M. Eckstein and Peter Lehman (Detroit: Wayne State University Press, 2004), 172.

3. Michael Dempsey cited in Studlar, "What Would Martha Want?", 174.

4. Interestingly, these are similar issues to those invoked in a more popular register—and at a time when the Western was enjoying its peak years—by *Calamity Jane* (David Butler, 1953).

5. Patrick McGee, *From Shane to Kill Bill: Rethinking the Western* (Oxford: Blackwell, 2006), 236.

6. The aftermath of the Civil War is also represented in two other recent fictions that owe much to the Western—Ang Lee's *Ride With the Devil* (1999) and Anthony Minghella's *Cold Mountain* (2003).

7. Although Raimi's narrative—through the conceit of the Oedipal-themed flashback hinting at formative childhood trauma—does establish a relationship with a more eccentric Western, Raoul Walsh's *Pursued* (1947), wherein Robert Mitchum plays the tormented and notably "feminised" hero.

8. McGee, *From Shane to Kill Bill,* 237.

9. Ben Walters, "*The Missing* (review)." *Sight and Sound* 14, no.3, n.s., (2004): 50.

10. Dempsey, cited in Studlar, "What Would Martha Want?, 172.

11. See for example Susan Courtney, "Looking for (Race and Gender) Trouble in Monument Valley," *Qui Parle* 6, no. 2 (1993): 97–130.

12. Peter Lehman, "Texas, 1868/America, 1956: *The Searchers,*" in *Close Viewings: An Anthology of New Film Criticism,* ed. Peter Lehman (Tallahassee: University of Florida Press, 1990), 401.

13. Robert Warshow, "Movie Chronicle: The Westerner," in *Film Theory and Criticism: Fifth Edition,* ed. Leo Braudy and Marshall Cohen (Oxford: Oxford University Press,1999), 658.

14. Courtney, "Looking for (Race and Gender)", 99.

15. Lee Clark Mitchell, "Violence in the American Western," in *Violence and American Cinema,* ed. David Slocum (London: Routledge, 2001), 181.

16. Warshow, "Movie Chronicle: The Westerner," 667.

17. Yvonne Tasker, "Cowgirl Tales," in *Genre, Gender, Race and World Cinema: An Anthology,* ed. Julie F. Codell (Oxford: Blackwell, 2006), 197. Some classic accounts of how performativity, sexuality and spectacle function in the Western are Warshow (1999); Steve Neale, "Masculinity as Spectacle," in *Screening the Male,* ed. Steven Cohen and Ina Rae Hark (London: Routledge,1993), 9–20; Martin Pumphrey, "Why Do Cowboys Wear Hats in the Bath?: Style Politics for the Older Man," in *The Movie Book of the Western,* ed. Ian Cameron and Douglas Pye, (London: Studio Vista, 1996), 50–62; and Corey Creekmur, "Acting Like a Man: Masculine Performance in *My Darling*

Clementine," in *Out in Culture,* ed. Corey K. Creekmur and Alexander Doty (London: Duke University Press, 1995), 167–82.

18. It should be noted that two recent televisual incarnations of the Calamity Jane legend deal with the character as a mother—a biological one in miniseries *Buffalo Girls* (1995) and as carer for the child of another in *Deadwood.* The *Kill Bill* films recount the revenge of "the Bride" (Uma Thurman) as she attempts to regain her child from its "bad father", figured as a journey towards her "final identity" as "Mommy." *From Shane to Kill Bill,* 243.

19. Dramatic entrances abound in Westerns. Some of the most well-known concern the first glimpses of John Wayne/Ringo Kid in *Stagecoach* (John Ford, 1939) and Alan Ladd as the eponymous *Shane* (George Stevens, 1953). As for female entrances, it is notable that the titular character of *Johnny Guitar,* played by Sterling Hayden, is given a less visually imposing entrance than Joan Crawford as Vienna, revealing to the audience that Vienna is the film's true protagonist.

20. Studlar, "What Would Martha Want?", 180.

21. Lehman, "Texas, 1868/America", 388.

22. Ibid., 394.

23. Tasker, "Cowgirl Tales", 199.

24. This character is also referred to by the Chiricahuan name of "Chaa-duu-ba-its-iidan" in the text.

25. The depictions of Dot's fascinated looks at Jones strongly recall the opening of *Shane,* where the cowboy's arrival is related through the gaze of Joey Starrett (Brandon De Wilde).

26. Tasker notes the importance of tomboy characters—archetypically in the figure of Calamity Jane—in constructing the "'masculine' Western heroine". "Cowgirl Tales", 203.

27. Brian Henderson cited in McGee, *From Shane to Kill Bill,* 108.

28. David Thomson, "The Last Frontier," *Sight and Sound* 14, no.2, n.s., (2004):14.

29. Lilly expresses her wish to hear her own voice played back to her on a recording apparatus scheduled to appear at the fair; later, this technology is ruefully witnessed by Maggie as she pleads with the disobliging local sheriff to call out a search.

30. Lehman, "Texas, 1868/America", 396.

31. Ethan's original intention is to track Debbie down simply to kill her rather than let her live tainted by her sexual involvement with the Comanche; strangely acting as "the voice of patriarchal sexual norms" (Studlar 2004, 186), Laurie Jorgensen argues that this is what her mother would have wanted. If that were true, a point of real difference with *The Missing* would be the treatment of how the maternal responds to the sexualised captivity scenario. However the text is inconclusive about whether Martha would in fact feel far more compassionately for Debbie than Laurie and Ethan suggest.

32. Studlar, "What Would Martha Want?", 191.

33. In "After the Rescue: *The Searchers*, the Audience and *Prime Cut* (1972)," *Journal of Popular Culture* 28, no. 3 (1994): 33–53, Arthur M. Eckstein identifies *Prime Cut* (Michael Ritchie, 1972) and *Hardcore* (Paul Schrader, 1979) as examples, while the Schrader-scripted *Taxi Driver* (Martin Scorsese, 1976) has long been recognised as an

intextual companion to *The Searchers*. See David Weaver, "The Narrative of Alienation: Martin Scorsese's *Taxi Driver*," *Cine-Action*, (Summer/Fall 1986): 13–14.

34. Charles Taylor, "*The Missing* (review)," 2003, http://dir.salon.com/story/ent/movies/review/2003/11/26/missing/index.html (accessed October 13th, 2006); See Walters, "*The Missing* (review)," 50; and Thomson (2004) for further examples.

35. Walters, "*The Missing* (review)," 50.

36. McGee, *From Shane to Kill Bill,* 97.

37. McGee points out that most Comanche raids on white women (as depicted in *The Searchers*) were not sexually motivated but intended to furnish slave labour for the horse and cattle businesses, thus underlining the film's feverish horror of miscegenation as rather ahistorical. *From Shane to Kill Bill,* 98.

38. Indeed, it is not completely clear in the film's concluding shots whether Honesco has actually survived the preceding battle, leaving the possibility that the group we see heading for home in the penultimate shot is all female.

39. Thomson, "The Last Frontier," 14.

40. McGee, *From Shane to Kill Bill,* 76.

41. Ibid., 75–6.

42. The message about women's freedom is mixed throughout the film. A further unrepresented sexual act that can be inferred by the spectator is that Maggie's conception of Lilly may have occurred through an act of rape; among other suggestive lines of dialogue, Dot tells Jones that her mother talks and cries in her sleep and gives Lilly strange looks the next morning. Of course, the film concentrates on Maggie's maternal attempt to recover Lilly rather than to avenge her (or Brake's death), and does not explicitly deal with the repercussions of any appetite for vengeance arising from that possible rape. Generally, the motivation of revenge is far less strong in *The Missing* when compared with *The Searchers*.

CHAPTER EIGHT

BELLES WITH ATTITUDE:
GENEALOGIES OF THE NEW HOLLYWOOD
WISECRACKING ACTION HEROINE

POLONA PETEK

handwritten annotations:
difference between identity;
the woman and the → because of different
superheroine - different expectations
personalities

Natasha Romanoff
'Whip It'
Carol Danvers

Figure Nine: Sandra Bullock in *Miss Congeniality 2: Armed and Fabulous*
(2005)

After a great deal of anxiety, anticipation, prediction and speculation, the new millennium arrived with fireworks, yet without any cataclysmic events. Or did it? According to the most enthusiastic reviewers, the release of *Miss Congeniality* (2000) was precisely such an event. The film, produced by its star, Sandra Bullock, has been described as heralding the birth of an utterly new, empowered and triumphant female protagonist in mainstream cinema. Of course, *Miss Congeniality* was marketed and greeted with the familiar taglines highlighting the film's mixed generic heritage and the largely intertextual dimensions of its conception and reception—"Dirty Harriet goes to the prom", "She's got a killer to catch…right after the swimsuit competition", "She's about to give crime fighting a makeover".[1] Yet the reviewers and, even more emphatically, the scholars seem to agree that the resultant wisecracking girl-next-door turned action heroine is without precedent in the century-old history of cinema. In this essay, I seek to disprove this contention. *Miss Congeniality* might seem like a refreshingly novel, that is, light-hearted and entertaining take on the female detective character, previously confined to the more sombre scenarios of *The Silence of the Lambs* (1991), *Copycat* (1995) and a plethora of their televisual cousins.[2] Yet an "archaeological" trip to the archives of early cinema and even a quick glance beyond the walls of Hollywood studios reveal that *Miss Congeniality*'s Gracie Hart (Sandra Bullock) is a rather pale incarnation of "belles with attitude", who have graced the cinema's screen ever since the inception of the medium.

In this essay, then, I will map out the generically, culturally and historically diverse genealogies of the wisecracking protagonist of *Miss Congeniality*. I will begin by locating Gracie Hart in the growing body of films featuring female characters in professional investigative roles, ranging from feminist classics such as *Blue Steel* (1990) to the more problematic blaxploitation films of the 1970s. Next, I will compare *Miss Congeniality*'s feminist agenda with that of another group of its predecessors—the films featuring women as assassins, vigilantes and other outlaws, immortalised in films such as Ridley Scott's *Thelma and Louise* (1991) and Luc Besson's *La femme Nikita/ Nikita* (1990). I will also argue that a more comprehensive map of Gracie's genealogical tree must run through Asia, whose cinematic female action heroes not only predate their Hollywood counterparts but have in fact, unlike the latter, garnered a very popular genre in its own right. Another branch of Gracie's family tree I identify are the superheroines, whose roots lie in media other than cinema and who share with Gracie not only the tendency to fight their battles single-handedly but also a desire to resist the patriarchal expectation that women be beautiful rather than witty or funny. In conclusion, I will draw attention to Gracie's oldest cousins, the feisty heroines of the early cinema's serial-queen melodramas.

Gracie Hart is a young female federal agent negotiating her place in a male-dominated environment with plenty of wit and spirit, yet with little grace and, as it happens, not much success either. The first time we see her in her capacity as an undercover agent, she is impersonating a nerdy student sitting in a restaurant and spying on a group of Russian gangsters. Everything seems to be going well until one of the mobsters chokes on a peanut; Gracie helps him and, as a result of this display of (maternal?) life-preservation instinct and (feminine?) compassion, she is taken hostage. The situation is eventually resolved and the thugs are captured, but all the credit goes to agent Matthews (Benjamin Bratt), who has caught one of the runaways. Gracie is reprimanded for putting the lives of her colleagues at risk and assigned to desk; however, the squad's next case requires Gracie's "natural assets". A terrorist, who calls himself the Citizen, is threatening to blow up the Miss America beauty pageant, and the best plan the FBI can muster is to send in an undercover agent posing as a beauty queen. Since all other female agents under the age of 35—a bewildering threshold, given the criteria applied in the majority of beauty contests[3]—are unavailable (due to maternity leave or similarly "becoming" reasons), the unkempt, unpolished and, in the eyes of her colleagues, rather unfeminine Gracie is assigned the task of infiltrating the competition as Miss New Jersey. After a tremendous amount of effort by a team of FBI grooming experts, assisted by Victor Melling (Michael Caine), a veteran beauty pageant consultant who of course also happens to be gay, Gracie metamorphoses into a ravishing beauty, who blends perfectly with the other contestants and has no trouble persuading everyone (including, hopefully, the viewers of the film) that her ascent to the final is perfectly legitimate. While parading in swimsuits, evening gowns and, what else, a Bavarian garb, Gracie also manages to figure out the identity of the Citizen and, albeit not before stumbling into a couple of embarrassing situations, she eventually single-handedly saves the day. She might have missed the title of the new Miss America, but Gracie wins three other trophies: her suspension is called off; her fellow beauty contestants award her the title of Miss Congeniality; and—at least until the sequel, *Miss Congeniality 2: Armed and Fabulous* (2005)—she has won and tamed the heart of her womanising colleague, agent Eric Matthews.

Hardboiled, High Heeled and Educated

How could this happy-go-lucky *mélange* of the Cinderella story and the Pygmalion myth make a powerful enough impression to be hailed as "funny, irreverent, feminist"?[4] To begin answering this question, Linda Mizejewski, in her recent book on the figure of the female detective in cinema, draws attention to Gracie's professional status.[5] The fact that Gracie is a federal agent is important for it allows Mizejewski to situate *Miss Congeniality* within a relatively new category of Hollywood films. As she observes, the amateur female sleuth might have been a staple of crime and mystery fiction since the middle of the nineteenth century,[6] but "the *professional* female character is an exhilarating newcomer to a market long dominated by men".[7] Mizejewski thus identifies the first branch of Gracie's genealogical tree: *Miss Congeniality* belongs to a recent but steadily growing group of films featuring female characters in professional investigative roles. From a feminist point of view, this body of work is extremely diverse and not without problems. On the one hand, it includes groundbreaking features such as *Blue Steel* and *The Silence of the Lambs*. These films critique and rework the codes and conventions of the genre (the cop film and thriller respectively) to accommodate their most radical intervention—the introduction of the professional female protagonist into a previously "testosterone-heavy" mainstream genre.[8] On the other hand, the earliest examples of such a character belong to the group of films whose role in women's emancipation feminists cannot but view with suspicion. The first federal agents, cops and private detectives on the big screen were the characters Cleopatra Jones[9] and Sheba Shayne, played by Tamara Dobson and Pam Grier in blaxploitation films of the 1970s.[10] As Mizejewski notes, the spirited African-American heroines were well ahead of their time, particularly since "Hollywood's nonvillainous white women with guns at this time were mostly James Bond's girlfriends"; yet these powerful, stunning women were also a peculiar blend of "sexist cartoons and Amazon avengers".[11] Moreover, they had no mainstream Hollywood counterparts; in "the era of *Dirty Harry* (1971) and *Magnum Force* (1973)...the action-style woman investigator or cop would be a novelty item at best, and certainly a box-office risk".[12]

Such a mapping of the emergence of a female protagonist in the role of a professional investigator of course invites the conclusion that *Miss Congeniality* is quite a progressive text. In contrast to her blaxploitation forerunners, whose professional status remains vague (for instance, we never find out whether Cleopatra Jones is an agent of the FBI or the CIA) and is thus ultimately reduced to little more than just another fashion accessory, we know exactly what Gracie's job is and we are offered some insight into the bearing of her gender on the way she is treated by her peers and superiors. She is introduced to us through a narrative of her difficulties at work, which are explicitly related to the fact that she is a woman, rather than through exploitative shots such as those that fetishised Grier's and Dobson's bodies in the seventies. (When such shots do appear, as for example in the scene where we first see the "new" Gracie, they are executed with a heightened sense of self-consciousness and irony.) In this sense then, Gracie is closer to Clarice Starling (Jodie Foster) of *The Silence of the Lambs* or *Blue Steel*'s Megan Turner (Jamie Lee Curtis), whose stories are articulated emphatically as the stories of women struggling to make it in a man's world. Yet Gracie fares better than Clarice or Megan, for she can have it both ways, so to speak. In the vocabulary of Mulvey-style feminist film theory, she is the subject and the object of the gaze, and she is ultimately not punished but rather rewarded for assuming the role of the agent of the narrative:

> A generation ago, that movie would have ended with Gracie giving up life in the Bureau for life with a beau. In turn-of-the-twenty-first century Hollywood, with a full decade of woman investigators elbowing their way onto the screen, Gracie is allowed both.[13]

Such an interpretation of *Miss Congeniality* could be disputed on several counts. It preserves the traditional framework of binary oppositions; it reveals teleological tendencies; it has a limited understanding of the pleasures afforded by exploitative cinematography; and so on. What interests me more in the context of this essay, however, is Mizejewski's privileging of mainstream appeal, sizeable budget and box-office success as well as her evaluation of the importance of representing women as competent members of the law enforcement. In other words, commercial success and the ability to fit into the (patriarchal) system are key to Mizejewski's appraisal of *Miss Congeniality*'s significance and feminist achievements. This is a problematic choice of criteria, to say the least, and not only because it signals a certain degree of complicity in the power structures and tastes of patriarchy. What is more problematic is the fact that it obscures *Miss Congeniality*'s affinities with, and differences from, another cluster of powerful female characters, the one comprised of action heroines as assassins, vigilantes and other outlaws. What creeps into Mizejewski's reading of *Miss Congeniality* then is her allegiance to a liberal rather than radical feminist agenda, which eclipses Gracie's kinship with, and departure from, the more radical versions of women fighters, such as the eponymous protagonists of Ridley Scott's *Thelma and Louise*, Sigourney Weaver's Ripley in the *Alien* films,[14] Linda Hamilton's Sarah Connor in *Terminator 2: Judgement Day* (1991), or Anne Parillaud's Nikita in Luc Besson's *La femme Nikita*.[15]

(S)elective Affinities

Nikita is an interesting character to compare to *Miss Congeniality*'s Gracie, particularly within the parameters of Mizejewski's discussion. Both women are undercover agents; however Besson's film refuses to gloss over this institutionalisation of women fighters. In contrast to *Miss Congeniality*, which takes for granted Gracie's desire to be "one of the boys", Besson's film focuses precisely on Nikita's recruitment and stages it as a matter of life and death for the female protagonist, whose decision to join the French secret service is a result of ruthless and sanctioned extortion. What is more, despite its anarchist edge, Besson's feature meets Mizejewski's other criterion; the independently produced film proved such a hit with audiences that it yielded not only a slick Hollywood remake, *Point of No Return* (1993), but also a long-running Canadian television series, *Nikita* (1997–2001), as well as a Hong Kong filmic reworking, *Black Cat* (1991). As such, *La femme Nikita* is extremely valuable; it points to the necessity of tracing Gracie's precursors and contemporaries in cinemas outside Hollywood.

Black Cat is particularly interesting here, for while this film is an instance of Hong Kong action cinema incorporating Western influences, the situation is usually reversed. Discussing the development of the American action movie in the eighties and nineties, Yvonne Tasker notes a "clear debt to Hong Kong action films",[16] and even Mizejewski,whose exploration of the "hardboiled and high heeled" in Asian cinemas is limited to a single statement, observes that the development of the female action hero in Hong Kong martial arts movies predates her New Hollywood examples.[17] However, regardless of how one maps the flow of influences between culturally diverse incarnations of the fighting woman, that is, regardless of whether one sees the late twentieth century action heroine as born in America, Europe or Asia, it is important to acknowledge that Asian cinemas do have a more developed cinematic tradition of representing such characters. While American and European "action films in which women *have* taken central roles were not developed in a *separate* generic space",[18] this is precisely what happened with the deadly females in Japanese and Hong Kong cinemas. It might have taken *Zero Woman: Red Handcuffs* (1974) two decades to spawn sequels, but when it did, they emerged in masses.[19] At about the same time, the Hong Kong film industry produced a number of films featuring gun-toting, fist-fighting or sword-wielding heroines such as the glamourous assassins of *The Naked Killer* (1992), *The Heroic Trio* (1993) and *The Heroic Trio II: Executioners* (1993). The significance of these texts for contemporary Western filmmakers cannot be overestimated. They are perhaps most readily acknowledged in Quentin Tarantino's *Kill Bill* films,[20] which pay tribute to this subgenre of Asian martial arts movies not only through an appropriation of their aesthetics, special effects and action-scene choreography but also, more importantly, through an unrestrained glorification of the deadly female protagonist.

Both Besson's Nikita and Tarantino's "The Bride" (Uma Thurman), as well as *Miss Congeniality*'s Gracie, are interesting from yet another perspective. Unlike their Asian counterparts, who forge strategic (and often emotional and/or sexual) allegiances with other women to better their chances in combat, the Western female fighter is more likely to fly solo. Whether because of her outlaw status, the failure of her (male) colleagues to come to her aid, or as a more pervasive symptom of Western individualism, the Western action heroine does not make friends easily.[21] This could be seen as the ultimate statement on woman's power: the Western action heroine needs no one to save her; she is invincible even, or especially, when she is completely alone. However this is not necessarily a sign of empowerment. Drawing on Barbara Creed's work, Tasker suggests that female buddy movies might be more threatening to patriarchal audiences than films featuring single action heroines. Noting that the eighties and the nineties produced virtually "no examples of an action movie with female pairing", she opines that the "reluctance to put money into such vehicles is telling on a number of counts: perhaps it is the lesbian potentialities of the active body identified by Creed that so often preclude narratives involving two women together".[22] Tasker does, however, also insist that an "*equivocal* play with gay and lesbian desire and identity has become a defining feature of the [action] genre".[23]

The two *Miss Congeniality* films confirm Tasker's assessment. They attempt, and fail, to acknowledge lesbian desire, just as they fall short of developing a full-blooded friendship between Gracie and another woman. In the first film, there is a "small but priceless moment", as Mizejewski calls it, when Miss New York comes out on stage.[24] Never off-guard, Gracie is the first to applaud her, yet one cannot get rid of the feeling this is because the agent in her estimates that this is the safest and least disruptive way to go. Moreover, the way Gracie herself forms romantic attachments locates her within an exclusively heterosexual realm. The film's anxiety as regards its protagonist's sexuality is all the more obvious if one considers how peripheral the romantic story-line is to the crime plot of the movie. The sequel approaches lesbian desire and friendship between women in an even more traditional manner. Eric has just dumped her and, on her new assignment, the now utterly feminine Gracie must join forces with an excessively butch (but never openly gay) African-American woman, Sam Fuller (Regina King). Yet *Miss Congeniality 2* does little in terms of an exploration of the dynamic between the two women; instead, it merely exploits the slapstick potential of such a coupling.

The decision to make Gracie's sidekick a woman of colour is equally tokenistic. Drawing on Judith Mayne's work, Tasker observes that "genre mixing may serve a particular function in movies that centrally involve fantasies about 'race' and difference"; it conveys a "muted articulation of an interracial relationship".[25] Indeed, *Miss Congeniality 2* consistently ignores Sam Fuller's racial identity, except in a brief moment when the two women go undercover as performers in drag and Gracie cannot understand why it is Sam who gets to impersonate Tina Turner. This moment is also priceless, for it encapsulates, and for a split second exonerates, the film's overall indifference to racial difference;

and as Tasker predicts, it does so through a blending of action, crime and comedy.[26]

A consideration of the female action hero as a solo warrior brings into focus another branch of Gracie's family tree. Such a character displays a strong affinity with a relatively large group of female protagonists who, like the female sleuths with their literary roots, migrated to the silver screen after establishing themselves in other media—comic books, graphic novels and, more recently, video games. While some of them might have a *doppelgänger*-like sidekick, Wonder Woman, Catwoman, Lara Croft and other superheroines are ultimately very much like Gracie—women left to their own devices.[27] Some critics see Gracie, Clarice Starling or Cleopatra Jones as a progressive development of these characters. Mizejewski, for instance, sees superheroines as a transitional phenomenon, occurring "in the interim", before the development of female action heroes proper, and offering "more thrill than threat".[28] The perceived advance embodied in Miss Congeniality and her fellow agents in other movies is the fact that these women manage to kick-ass without possessing any superpowers. Gracie's physical prowess is perfectly realistic and, as we are shown, maintained through rigorous training. Even more, her power stems equally from her physical strength as it does from her gender or, more accurately—at least in the first film—from her ability to *perform* gender. This indeed seems to be a move towards more realistic representations of women, which could serve as feasible role models rather than impossible blends of computer-enhanced glamour and power. Yet it is important to keep in mind, as Mizejewski does, that even Gracie and her likes "aren't useful measures of social change, but they're good measures of social fantasy—in this case, fantasy about the place of women in high-level law enforcement, at the forensic autopsy or with a giant flashlight in the labyrinth".[29]

The trouble with the fantasy of *Miss Congeniality*, however, is the fact that both movies try too hard to "create a strong female character without offending anyone".[30] All Gracie's traits that could be seen as genuine and nonconformist (her healthy appetite, her imperfections, competitiveness, her disregard for the latest fashion) are eventually channelled into a "more acceptable" version of liberated femininity through the popular scenario of the late twentieth and early twenty-first centuries—the makeover.[31] More importantly, before and during her metamorphosis into beauty-pageant material, Gracie's less feminine characteristics are toned down through comedy.

Girls Just Wanna Have Fun

The function of comedy—as a genre in its own right or as an inflection of an otherwise less cheerful genre—is a complex issue. Writing about British screen culture and drawing on George Orwell, Jerry Palmer asserts, "[w]hatever is funny is subversive".[32] Similarly, Kathleen Rowe compares comedy and humour to carnival:

> Almost all comedic forms—from jokes to gags to slapstick routines to the most complex narrative structures—attempt a liberation from authority. Like carnival, comedy levels the lofty and erases distinctions, replacing the exalted hero of tragedy with one reduced to the level of Everyman, or lower.[33]

According to such accounts, the function of comedy, like that of carnival, is to provide an outlet for acting out various fantasies of social upheaval and subversion and a general loosening of cultural norms, such as those pertaining to gender. Comedy mocks authority and facilitates a transgression of social conventions. Yet the transgressiveness of carnival, and that of comedy as its modern-day legatee, is limited. During the officially sanctioned carnival, anyone could be "a king for a day"—as long as everyone knew that the day after meant a return to "normality". Contemporary comedy, in turn, "provides a space in which taboos can be addressed, made visible and…negotiated"; however, precisely because this transgression occurs at a designated time and place (such as Hollywood comedy), the breaking of taboos is "contained" and kept in check.[34]

This is a fairly accurate description of the comic relief afforded by Gracie's antics. Her clumsiness, wisecracks, lack of grooming, snorting and so forth may be portrayed as funny and endearing rather than repulsive or abject; yet the frequency of these comic moments steadily recedes as we are witnessing Gracie's transformation. The film's stance towards its protagonist is disturbingly patronising; we are invited to laugh *at* Gracie rather than *with* her and, as the film's sentimental resolution reminds us, our laughter has an imminent expiry date. It would seem then that Mizejewski's assessment, that the comic veneer of *Miss Congeniality*'s crime plot constitutes a radical novelty in the body of films featuring female action heroes, requires a careful reconsideration. For Mizejewski, the "comedy of *Miss Congeniality* stems from turning Gracie from 'one of the boys' into a girl".[35] Such an interpretation seduces Mizejewski into seeing Petrie's film as a much more insightful and subversive text than it actually is:

> the entire premise of *Miss Congeniality*—the makeover of a tomboy FBI agent into a swimsuit contestant—poses anatomy and fashion as combined problems for this relatively new Hollywood character…the female FBI agent made over into Miss Congeniality suggests a lingering anxiety about how to picture this character—hardboiled but high heeled.[36]

My reading of *Miss Congeniality*'s comic effect is significantly different. In my view, the characterisation of Gracie is most forcefully geared towards entertaining the viewers during her initial "tomboy phase", whereas her transformation anticipates a more serious response from the audience, their approval and, possibly, relief.[37] *Miss Congeniality* thus dramatises, yet not quite parodies, Tasker's observation: "women are not expected to be funny, in conventional terms, they are expected to be beautiful".[38] Indeed, Gracie the tomboy may not have been expected to be beautiful, but she wasn't exactly perceived as funny either; rather, she was the Bureau's (and, possibly, the audience's) laughing stock—a humiliating position with little pleasure for Gracie. However, as soon as Gracie has mastered the girlie behaviour and grooming she used to mock, having fun—at her expense or, even more disturbingly, with her—becomes redundant. Gracie the beauty queen embodies, yet hardly critiques, the traditional patriarchal expectations regarding women and humour; as Siân Mile writes, women "are not expected to attempt humour, nor are they expected to succeed at it".[39]

It would seem then that being tough, funny *and* a woman in a male-dominated *milieu* is no laughing matter, if not a downright impossibility. Yet there are films that suggest this need not be the case—although, unsurprisingly, they are much more likely to be found outside Hollywood's mainstream production. *Tank Girl* (1995) is a particularly illuminating case in point. The low-budget feature, starring Lori Petty in the title role, became an instant cult favourite upon its release.[40] The film's protagonist is a girl with eyes bluer than the sky and a smile worthy of a toothpaste ad. However, Tank Girl is anything but your typical blond cheerleader kind of gal. Not unlike Gracie, she is a fiercely independent young woman with a foul mouth which, more often than not, gets her into trouble. To save her skin and the lives of her few remaining friends, the sassy vigilante must fight the corrupt ruler of the drought-stricken world, Kesslee (Malcolm McDowell), who controls all the water supplies. In a Nikita-like scenario, Tank Girl is "invited" to join Kesslee's troops—an offer she almost cannot refuse for the only alternative seems to be death. Tank Girl rejects the proposition, hooks up with another girl (Naomi Watts), and wipes the floor with the all-male apparatus of global control. Clearly, the film's feminist politics are partisan, and rather crude at that: all Tank Girl's male allies are half-human, half-kangaroo mutants and their intellectual capacities are, to put it mildly, dubious; all surviving human males are crooked and greedy to the point of becoming equally dim-witted. Yet the intrepid heroine of *Tank Girl* need not undergo a makeover, not even as an undercover ruse, to do away with her adversaries. Cracking jokes and having a ball all along, she remains as girlie as she likes, as maternal as she feels, and as scruffy as she pleases.

It is significant, however, that the Tank Girl's unconventional, combative and witty femininity thrives in a science-fiction scenario (the story is taking place in 2033). The natural habitat of such a character, even in a non-mainstream text, is more readily imagined in a not-too-remote future than as a viable possibility for the present. It would be premature to argue that cinema, and our society at large, have yet to invent a representation of woman defined by a quality of "musculinity",[41] capable of taking care of herself and others, *and* having fun doing it. In fact, it was precisely characters like this that inaugurated the action movie genre, when feisty heroines, played by reportedly equally headstrong and fearless actresses such as Pearl White, Ruth Roland and Helen Holmes, took over the silent screen in the so-called serial-queen melodramas nearly a century ago.

Between 1912 and 1920, American filmmakers produced more than sixty serials, comprising about 800 episodes, featuring female stars in roles that saw them embarking upon amazing "exotic" adventures and performing—often without doubles—breathtaking stunts.[42] While stylistically and thematically decidedly heterogeneous,[43] the genre of the serial-queen melodrama was nevertheless extremely consistent in its pronounced interest in "violent, intense action—abductions, entrapments, brawls, hazardous chase sequences, and last-minute rescues" and, even more so, in its remarkable emphasis on female heroism.[44] The serials were tremendously successful, which makes it all the more perplexing that they have been so "thoroughly forgotten…only *The Perils of Pauline* seems to have lingered in the recesses of popular or scholarly memory".[45] Ben Singer identifies an aetiological link between the serial-queen melodrama and the emergent women's liberation movement. Yet the genre was not a straightforward and unproblematic celebration of womanhood. While it clearly drew on the mythology and iconography of the New Woman, it habitually interspersed these empowering images of women with a "sadistic spectacle of the woman's victimisation"[46] and with commercial ploys designed to lure female viewers.[47] The serial-queen melodrama was thus "paradoxical", for it was "animated by an oscillation between contradictory extremes of female prowess and distress, empowerment and imperilment", emancipation and consumerist entrapment.[48]

I would argue, however, that the serial-queen melodrama was far less paradoxical than *Miss Congeniality* and the rest of its contemporary mainstream ilk. The Paulines, Helens and Ruths of the silent screen might have been routinely abused during their unconventional, "unfeminine" exploits; yet these women's predicaments served as nothing but the springboards for the display of female power, from which the early cinema's action heroines emerged triumphant, draped in high *couture*, and not in the least less emancipated. The serials offered their female audiences:

the best of both worlds: a representational structure that indulged conventionally 'feminine' forms of vanity and exhibitionism while it refused the constraints of decorative femininity through an action-packed depiction of female prowess.[49]

Moreover, as Lewis Jacobs contends, the adventures of the serials' protagonists were neither produced nor received as entirely impossible, fantastic and technologically manipulated wish fulfilments; rather, they "paralleled, in a sense, the real rise of women to a new status in society".[50] A hundred years or so later, in a presumably much more enlightened society, *Miss Congeniality* attempts a similar task: it deploys twenty-first century marketing strategies (the makeover as the modern-day counterpart of the tie-in); its spectatorial address, to a large extent, relies on the economy of female narcissism; and the film purportedly sets out to challenge the remaining "constraints of decorative femininity". This is precisely where Miss Congeniality pales in comparison with her early-twentieth century siblings. Gracie's "final package" is not, as Mizejewski believes, "femininity, boyfriend, good looks, plus powerful kick-ass competence",[51] but rather an unreliable boyfriend, conventionally feminine good looks, a diminished (and, by *Miss Congeniality 2*, utterly abandoned) kick-ass competence, and a pronounced inability to articulate anything but a weak echo of the most pathetic beauty-pageant-queen statements. A scary development, given that Gracie's early-twentieth century forerunners managed to convey poise, intelligence and wit effortlessly, even without colour or sound.

And yet *Miss Congeniality* is not necessarily a mindless instance of feminist defeat. Just as the "serial-queen melodrama's investment in images of female power implies women's disenchantment and frustration with conventional definitions of gender, while at the same time it celebrates tangible transformations in women's status after the turn of the [nineteenth] century",[52] *Miss Congeniality*'s paradoxical blend of antifeminist backlash and (post)feminist spunk is symptomatic of the cultural experience of womanhood at the turn of the twentieth century. Gracie Hart may not be the role model for girls at the dawn of the twenty-first century that their second-wave feminist mothers would have hoped for; she is, however, a valuable barometer of the ambivalence that marks the construction and circulation of femininity in the current cultural climate. Gracie is a composite character welding together a range of historical and contemporary cinematic visions of empowered femininity; she may not be raising the stakes of the still unfinished feminist project to unprecedented heights, yet her family tree is inspiring enough to provide a strong antidote against complacency.

Notes

1. http://miss-congeniality.warnerbros.co.uk (accessed 17 Dec 2005).

2. Other frequently discussed films featuring female federal agents or cops include *Black Widow* (1987), *Fatal Beauty* (1987), *Betrayed* (1988), *Blue Steel* (1990), *Impulse* (1990), *Bodily Harm* (1995), *Serial Killer* (1995), *Fargo* (1996), *Out of Sight* (1998) and *The Bone Collector* (1999). Television series featuring similar protagonists include *The X-Files* (1993–2002), *Profiler* (1996–2000), *Alias* (2001–), *Crossing Jordan* (2001–) and *Cold Case* (2003–). The trend, which arguably started with *Cagney and Lacey* (1982–1988), continues with *The Closer* (2005–) as the latest addition. Linda Mizejewski goes as far as to argue that, "[i]n the long run, Clarice Starling's legacy would develop not in cinema but on television, through complicated characters such as *The X-Files*' Dana Scully, *Profiler*'s Sam Waters, *Crossing Jordan*'s Jordan Cavanaugh, and *Alias*' Sydney Bristow". Linda Mizejewski, *Hardboiled & High Heeled: The Woman Detective in Popular Culture* (New York: Routledge, 2004), 142.

3. The *Miss America* website states that eligible candidates for this beauty pageant must be between 17 and 24 years of age (http://www.missamerica.org/competition-info/become-a-contestant.asp; accessed 16 Dec 2005). Similar age limitations apply in the world's top female beauty contests *Miss Universe* (http://www.missuniverse.com/index2.html), *Miss World* (http://www.missworld.tv/), *Miss Earth* (http://www.missearth.tv/), and *Miss International* (http://www.miss-international.org/).

4. Laura Weinstock, "*Miss Congeniality* directed by Donald Petrie. Starring and Produced by Sandra Bullock. A Must-See. Funny, irreverent, feminist," *Feminist Filmtakes* (Winter 2001) http://www.awakenedwoman.com/filmtakes7.htm. (accessed 7 Dec 2005).

5. Mizejewski, *Hardboiled & High Heeled*.

6. Famous examples, quoted by Mizejewski, include Nancy Drew and Miss Marple. Nancy Drew, the amateur girl sleuth from a series of stories written by various authors under the pen-name Carolyn Keene, first appeared in literature in 1929. By the end of the 1930s, she had been the star of four films—*Nancy Drew – Detective* (1938), *Nancy Drew, Reporter* (1939), *Nancy Drew, Trouble Shooter* (1939), and *Nancy Drew and the Hidden Staircase* (1939)—and in the seventies she just as smoothly moved onto the small screen in the popular TV series *The Hardy Boys/Nancy Drew Mysteries* (1977–1979). Nancy's youngest cousin is Veronica Mars, the protagonist of the new American television series, *Veronica Mars* (2004–), which yokes together the elements of the early-twentieth century adolescent detective fiction with the aesthetics of classic *film noir*. Screen adaptations of Agatha Christie's Miss Marple, whose first adventure appeared in print in 1930 (*The Murder at the Vicarage*), are virtually endless. Interestingly, the latest additions, the British Independent Television's four made-for-TV features—*Marple: The Body in the Library* (2004), *Marple: 4.50 from Paddington* (2004), *Marple: The Murder in the Vicarage* (2004), and *Marple: A Murder is Announced* (2005)—were met with disapproval for their fairly successful attempt to make Christie's protagonist less spinsterish, more world-savvy, and decidedly wittier.

7. Mizejewski, *Hardboiled & High Heeled*, 2. As Mizejewski points out, there is a socio-historical reason for this late emergence of the professional female detective: "if the female sleuth was most typically the curious old lady, the spunky spinster, or someone's girlfriend, this was mostly due to real-world constraints. The professional woman investigator was a historical rarity until the 1970s." Ibid., 17.

8. Ibid., 118.

9. Cleopatra Jones, played by Tamara Dobson, is the protagonist of two features, *Cleopatra Jones* (1973) and *Cleopatra Jones and the Casino of Gold* (1975). Jennifer DeVere Brody discusses how the two films differ as regards the representation of Cleopatra's sexuality. Jennifer DeVere Brody, "The Returns of *Cleopatra Jones*". *Signs: Journal of Women in Culture and Society* Vol. 25, no. 1 (Autumn 1999), 91–121.

10. Sheba Shayne (Pam Grier) is the protagonist of William Girdler's *Sheba, Baby* (1975).

11. Mizejewski, *Hardboiled & High Heeled*, 115.

12. Ibid., 118.

13. Ibid., 13.

14. *Alien* (1979), *Aliens* (1986), *Alien3* (1992), *Alien Resurrection* (1997). Yvonne Tasker considers Ripley a "reference point for the contemporary female action hero". Yvonne Tasker, *Working Girls: Gender and Sexuality in Popular Cinema*. (London and New York: Routledge, 1996), 71.

15. Mizejewski's box-office-privileging criteria force her to posit the genealogical rapport between the female detective and the female action hero differently; she sees the woman detective as paving the way for the female action figure: "*The Silence of the Lambs* was a turning point because it made the female investigator respectable and visible…More to the point, the day had come when it was possible to imagine a woman's body as an *action body*." Mizejewski, *Hardboiled & High Heeled*, 142. According to Mizejewski, it was only in the late nineties that "a new kind of character was emerging in Hollywood, the action heroine, first cousin of the woman detective and popular enough to draw a market and an audience". Ibid., 141.

16. Ibid., 73.

17. Ibid., 143.

18. Tasker, *Working Girls*, 68.

19. *Zero Woman: Red Handcuffs* was followed by *Zero Woman 2* (1995), *Zero Woman: Final Mission* (1995), *Zero Woman: Assassin Lovers* (1996), *Zero Woman: The Hunted* (1997), *Zero Woman: The Accused* (1997), *Zero Woman: Dangerous Game* (1998), and *Zero Woman Returns* (1999).

20. *Kill Bill: Vol. 1* (2003) and *Kill Bill: Vol. 2* (2004).

21. The television series *Charlie's Angels* (1976–1981) and its big screen adaptations, *Charlie's Angels* (2000) and *Charlie's Angels: Full Throttle* (2003) are of course glaring exceptions to this rule. Yet, the kickboxing triplets of these texts are less a trio of women bonding together to boost their power than an all-female team working for a man.

22. Tasker, *Working Girls*, 84.

23. Ibid., 72. Emphasis added.

24. Mizejewski, *Hardboiled & High Heeled*, 168.

25. Tasker, *Working Girls*, 11.

26. The racial blindness of the recent Hollywood "female dick" output is perplexing, particularly in view of the aforementioned debt of this group of films to the seventies blaxploitation movies. In the last two decades of the twentieth century, only two women of colour investigated crime in a professional capacity in Hollywood cinema—Whoopi Goldberg in *Fatal Beauty* (1987) and Jennifer Lopez in *Out of Sight* (1998).

27. Wonder Woman is a *DC Comics* superheroine, who first appeared in 1941. Her first screen adaptation was a made-for-TV feature *Wonder Woman* (1974), followed by a television series of the same title (1975–1979). The release of her first big-budget cinematic incarnation, directed by Joss Whedon, is announced for 2007. Catwoman is another *DC Comics* character. After making numerous appearances in *Batman* texts, she finally got her own screen adaptation with Pitof's *Catwoman* (2004). Lara Croft, originally the heroine of the *Tomb Raider* series of video games, appeared on the big screen in *Lara Croft: Tomb Raider* (2001) and *Lara Croft Tomb Raider: The Cradle of Life* (2003).

28. Mizejewski, *Hardboiled & High Heeled*, 115, 144.

29. Ibid., 16.

30. The quote, cited by Mizejewski, appeared in the *New York Times* in reference to *V.I. Warshawski* (1991). Mizejewski, *Hardboiled & High Heeled*, 140.

31. Mizejewski finds *Miss Congeniality*'s synthesis of the beauty pageant and the makeover fascinating. In her view, the makeover is "a potent cocktail of mixed messages, ranging from Cinderella magic to cynical consumerism"; however, grafted onto the Miss America beauty pageant, the makeover creates ironic distance from the gender myths underpinning beauty contests: "In *Miss Congeniality*, the awkward FBI agent Gracie Hart needs a makeover to 'pass' as a girlie girl for the pageant…Gracie needs not just a physical makeover, but a gender makeover as well." Ibid., 169.

32. Jerry Palmer, *The Logic of the Absurd: On film and television comedy* (London: BFI, 1987), 11.

33. Quoted in Tasker, *Working Girls,* 163.

34. Tasker, *Working Girls,* 163.

35. Mizejewski, *Hardboiled & High Heeled,* 13.

36. Ibid., 13, 20.

37. It is, however, interesting to note that this makeover—during which Gracie is stripped of the majority of her "unfeminine" qualities, including her comic potential—does not diminish the physicality of this character's fighting abilities. Gracie continues to fight with her fists rather than with her brains. As such, Gracie's transformation suggests that a physically strong woman is nevertheless less threatening and therefore more palatable than an intellectually empowered and witty one.

38. Tasker, *Working Girls*, 165.

39. Siân Mile, "Roseanne Barr: Canned Laughter—Containing the Subject," in *New Perspectives on Women and Comedy*, ed. Regina Barecca (Amsterdam: OPA, 1992), 43.

40. Like the aforementioned Wonder Woman, Catwoman and Lara Croft, Tank Girl, too, is a comic book based character, first drawn by Jamie Hewlett and written by Alan Martin in the late eighties in the UK. Her last adventure, written by Peter Milligan, was published in 1995, the year Talalay's film was released.

41. The term, coined by Tasker, denotes "an enactment of a muscular masculinity involving a display of power and strength over the body of the female performer". Tasker, *Working Girls*, 70.

42. Famous serial-queen melodramas include *The Perils of Pauline* (1914), *The Hazards of Helen* (1914–1915), *The Exploits of Elaine* (1914), *The New Exploits of Elaine* (1915), *Ruth of the Rockies* (1920), and *A Woman in Grey* (1920).

43. As Ben Singer reports, the serial-queen melodramas covered "a range of sensational-melodramatic subgenres (e.g., Western, Gothic, Patriotic, and Working-girl melodramas)". Ben Singer, "Female Power in the Serial-Queen Melodrama: The Etiology of an Anomaly," [1990] in *Silent Film*, ed. Richard Abel (New Brunswick & New Jersey: Rutgers University Press, 1996), 167.

44. Ibid., 167.

45. Ibid., 163.

46. Ibid., 164.

47. The serial-queen melodramas promoted "'fashion interest', apparent both in the *mise en scène* of the serials and in extratextual merchandising tie-ins with fashion houses". Ibid., 172.

48. Ibid., 164.

49. Ibid., 172.

50. Lewis Jacobs, *The Rise of the American Film: A Critical History* (New York: Teachers' College Press, 1969), 270.

51. Mizejewski, *Hardboiled & High Heeled*, 171.

52. Singer, "Female Power", 176.

CHAPTER NINE

ZHANG ZIYI, "MARTIAL ARTHOUSE" AND THE TRANSNATIONAL *NUXIA*

LEON HUNT

Figure Ten: Zhang Ziyi in *House of Flying Daggers* (2004)

Zhang Ziyi is arguably China's biggest contemporary star. In 2002, *Teen People* magazine included her as one of their "25 Hottest Stars Under 25" while she made *Time* magazine's "100 Most Influential People" list in 2005. She has already enjoyed a strong inter-Asian career, with films in Japan, Korea and Hong Kong, as well as her native China, working with a number of key Asian auteurs—Ang Lee, Suzuki Seijun, Wong Kar-wai, and most notably Zhang Yimou. *Crouching Tiger, Hidden Dragon/Wo Hu Zang Long* (2000) quickly attracted Hollywood's attention, leading to a supporting role as the fighting villainess of *Rush Hour 2* (2001). More recently, she made her English-speaking debut in *Memoirs of a Geisha* (2005). If speaking English with a Japanese accent in the latter did not already tell the tale of transnational mutability, the change in her billing does—from *House of Flying Daggers/Shi Mian Mai Fu* (2004) onwards, Western press and publicity have billed her as "Ziyi Zhang", following the Western convention of given name first. Zhang has been described as "the new Gong Li" or "Little Gong Li", primarily through her association with director Zhang Yimou, but also perhaps because Gong Li is often associated with roles which place female desire in conflict with a restrictive social system, such as *Ju Dou* (1989) and *Raise the Red Lantern/Da Hong Denglong Gaogao Gua* (1991). Berenice Reynaud suggests that Gong's star persona is predicated on an "exquisite mixture of pain and sensuality", while her popularity with Western "arthouse" audiences might rest on "her ability to signify Chineseness, femininity and mystery outside her own culture".[1] Zhang Ziyi's debut, *The Road Home/Wo De Fu Qin Mu Qin* (1999), a love story set partly during the Cultural Revolution, suggests a degree of continuity between the two stars, but from *Crouching Tiger* onwards, Zhang would be distinguished from her predecessor by her physicality. A graduate of Beijing Dance Academy, she adapted to the rigours of martial arts choreography so impressively that one might feel cheated when *The Legend of Zu/Shu Shan Zhen Zhuan* (2001) visibly doubles her for most of her one fight scene.[2] In *Hero/Ying Xiong* (2002), one might be forgiven for thinking that she is as extensively trained in Chinese martial arts as co-stars Jet Li and Donnie Yen.

Given the change of direction—geographic as well as generic—that *Memoirs of a Geisha* seems to represent, one might hesitate to describe Zhang Ziyi as a martial arts star. However, while her film roles have always been varied, her international success rests on three pan-Chinese *wuxia pian* (martial chivalry films)—*Crouching Tiger, Hero, House of Flying Daggers*—which provided many Western viewers with their first exposure to the figure of the *nuxia* (chivalrous or martial arts heroine).[3] I have adopted the term "Martial Arthouse", first coined by *Sight and Sound*'s cover copy (December 2000), to distinguish these films from earlier *wuxia pian*.[4] Director Zhang Yimou describes *Flying Daggers* on its DVD commentary as an "arthouse film with action elements". These films are further distinguished by their transnational funding, arthouse auteurs and, to borrow a term from Charles and Mirella Jona Affron, "design intensity", a luxurious spectacle that is *spatial* as well as *kinetic.*[5] In the Peony Pavilion sequence in *House of Flying Daggers*, Zhang Ziyi's heroine Mei is part of the design, with its *Dunhuang* colours,[6] silks, beaded curtains that surround sunken baths, painted paper screens that reflect the movement of water in a semi-darkened room, a floor patterned with butterflies and a floral design at the centre.[7] In contrast to the stoicism and Confucian duty of the traditional *nuxia*, Zhang's "Martial Arthouse" heroines are wilful, romantic, capricious and fully sexualised. In *Crouching Tiger,* her rebellious anti-heroine Jen threatens to disrupt the patrilineal structures of martial learning, while Mei in *House of Flying Daggers* fights (and sacrifices herself) for desire rather than loyalty to the *jianghu* underworld. *Jianghu*— literally "rivers and lakes", but sometimes translated as the "World of Vagrants" or "the Martial World"—refers to the subcultural world inhabited by martial arts heroes and heroines in the *wuxia pian.* Its inhabitants include wandering *xia* (chivalrous knights), security guards (like *Crouching Tiger*'s Yu Shu-lien), bandits, and street performers, amongst other itinerants and outsiders. While it overlaps with the everyday, more respectable world, it also has its own codes, values and hierarchies. For the purposes of this paper, one of *jianghu*'s distinctive features is its comparative gender egalitarianism, which is partly a legacy of Daoism. According to Zhang Yimou, *House of Flying Daggers* is:

> not your typical Martial arts film, where the rules and morality of *jianghu* are placed on a pedestal. Everyone usually follows all the rules, maintains the interests of the organisation…Very rarely do you see people do things for love where they don't care about anything else (DVD commentary).

The "Martial Arthouse" heroine's fight is explicitly linked to desire—both sexual desire and a longing for "freedom" that goes beyond even the idealised mobility of the *jianghu* underworld. In this respect, her fight is also connected to modernity, destabilising traditions, rules and authority. Kwai-cheung Lo sees Jen in *Crouching Tiger* as embodying "a new trans-Chinese form of modernity represented by woman" that is in conflict with "the old conservative paternal power of China".[8] However, it is harder to see Mei's fight in *House of Flying Daggers* as being against "paternal" authority when she transgresses the rules of a predominantly female team of fighters. Moreover, Zhang's heroines have coincided fortuitously with Western populist discourses about "kick-ass" heroines, leading to some interesting cross-cultural debates about the films' perceived "feminist" credentials. Zhang Ziyi's *nuxia* heroines can be seen as either "inauthentic" or revisionist, orientalist or signalling a new kind of transnational action heroine.

'Who are you really?' The Power(s) of the *Nuxia*

Some comment is necessary on the nature of the *nuxia*'s fighting abilities, given the parameters of the present volume and its focus on "mortal women". While the *wuxia pian*'s subgenre, the kung fu film (*gongfu pian*),[9] hinges on comparatively plausible physical capabilities (and the "authentic" abilities of its performers), swordplay-based *wuxia* frequently blur the line between the extraordinary and the preternatural. While Western audiences have probably grown accustomed to the "flying" effects in "Martial Arthouse" films, they may still wonder where the line is drawn between *wushu* masters and Western "Superheroes" or whether the Green Destiny Sword's empowerment of Jen rests on magical qualities rather than her own proficiency. To complicate matters, there is a subcategory of martial arts film that comprises a kind of Daoist *fantastique*, or what Sam Ho terms the *shenguai* (Gods and Demons) *wuxia*.[10] The heroine of the Shanghai serial *Red Heroine/Hong Xia* (1929) simply flies— the intertitles refer to her as a "Maiden of the Clouds" to underline her uncanny powers. The "New Style" *wuxia* of the 1960s—most notably the output of Shaw Brothers studios and directors like King Hu and Zhang Che—are generally seen as more "grounded" in mortal corporeality. However, "magical" elements did not disappear entirely—Shaw Brothers' *Dragon Swamp/Du Long Tan* (1969), a vehicle for the actress Zheng Pei-pei, features dragons, Daoist "Palm Power" (allowing fighters to fire lightning bolts from their hands), pills and potions that allow voices to switch gender or age in a storyline that otherwise features many of the tropes reworked by *Crouching Tiger* (stolen swords and elite martial sects).

In Wang Dulu's "Crane-Iron Pentalogy" (1938–42), of which *Crouching Tiger, Hidden Dragon* is the fourth volume, the characters' abilities are rooted in a heightened version of "hard" Shaolin and "soft" Wudang martial arts, with Daoist *xia* Li Mu-bai (Chow Yun-fat) and Jen practitioners of the latter. The characters acquire their abilities through training and their knowledge is gained from a master (*shifu*) or book, or both. Jen's story in the film hinges on her "illegitimate" acquisition of knowledge from a partially understood Wudang manual and the outlaw Jade Fox (Zheng Pei-pei). What appears to be preternatural "flight" is an exaggerated version of "light foot" *gongfu*, achieved through the control of *qi* (internal energy). The characters do not possess "Palm Power" (unlike the more powerful characters in the otherwise "grounded" *Come Drink with Me/Dai Zui Xia* [1966]) or use sacred scrolls to change gender, as Invincible Asia (Brigitte Lin) does in *Swordsman II/Xiao'ao Jianghu II Dongfai Bubai* (1991).

The reference to actual styles of fighting is one way of "grounding" the *nuxia*, but two moments in *Crouching Tiger* also seem designed to remind us that these powers are embodied in corporeal mortality. In the first instance, Jen pauses to register the pain in her wrist after an exchange of blows with the burly fighter, Iron Arm Mi, while seated at an inn. Even though she subsequently defeats him (and virtually everybody else in the vicinity), this brief moment registers the difference in their bodies, significantly during an episode when she adopts a male guise. The second example happens during Jen's second duel with Yu Shu-lien (Michelle Yeoh), the security guard who shares an unspoken love with Li Mu-bai. As Shu-lien switches weapons during the duel, she is literally stopped in her tracks by a huge crescent spade, its weight preventing her from wielding it effectively and prompting a smirk from Jen. Taken in itself, the second scene might be seen to illustrate the difference between Yu Shu-lien's "hard" *gongfu*, which is ultimately limited by the practitioner's physical strength, and the "soft", yielding power of Jen and the Green Destiny sword. But taken together, these scenes explicitly gender corporeal frailty. The Western female fighter may achieve a degree of "muscularity", but the *nuxia* never does—she is frequently delicate in appearance, a mixture of "soft" and "hard".

Crouching Tiger's narrative is preoccupied with the question of Jen's training—when Li Mu-bai asks her who her master is, he is asking her where she acquired such tremendous ability. Jen has easily transcended her illiterate master Jade Fox, in spite of partly misinterpreting the Wudang manual herself; consequently, one of the film's central enigmas is how she came to be such a prodigy. But it isn't just the film's arthouse credentials that allow this kind of open-endedness. Even when the *wuxia pian* alludes to the *nuxia*'s training, it is reluctant to show it. As Berenice Reynaud puts it:

> while the acquisition of fighting skills is the result of a *process* for a man, no such narrative development seems to exist for a woman. Like Athens, she comes out in the world dressed in full warrior regalia.[11]

The most blatant example of this can be found in *wuxia* literature; the Maiden of Yueh trained herself while growing up in a forest. Where did she gain knowledge of martial arts? "I just got it", she proclaims enigmatically.[12] Reynaud argues that this is a source of anxiety in the genre—the apparently inexplicable source of her ability is part of the *nuxia*'s duplicitous appearance, a figure who "looks like one thing and right in front of your eyes…becomes another thing".[13] In *House of Flying Daggers,* Mei is in a constant process of "becoming another thing"—when it transpires that she isn't blind, as we have been led to believe, the duped and increasingly love-struck deputy Jin (Kaneshiro Takeshi) asks what seems to be the film's key question, "Who are you really?"

To qualify Reynaud's proposition slightly, the genre's reticence about the *nuxia*'s training is less a matter of narrative development than a spectacle being withheld from the viewer. Films may allude to her training, they may name a master figure, but they always seem reluctant to show the pedagogic process. In *Red Heroine*, we know that titular *nuxia* Yun Mei is trained by a Daoist hermit, White Monkey, who rescues her from a rapacious general. But the film elides the three years in which this tutelage takes place, and the "Maiden of the Clouds" does, indeed, emerge fully formed. Jen's training clearly is central to *Crouching Tiger*'s narrative development, and we see Li Mu-bai attempt to teach her in two fight sequences, including the celebrated bamboo forest sequence. But she resists his teaching, and we never see her put any of his ideas into practice. Jen is *between* teachers for the duration of the film—she has outgrown Jade Fox and reached an impasse in interpreting the Wudang manual, but she rejects Li Mu-bai and Wudang at the cost of her further development. What we see of Jen the fighter is largely a result of a process that took place outside the film, enhanced by her acquisition of the Green Destiny. Thus the question remains: how did she get to be so good?

Figure Eleven: Uma Thurman and Gordon Liu Jiahui in *Kill Bill: Vol. 2* (2004)

There is no female equivalent in Chinese cinema of the spectacle of the male body transfigured by discipline and pain in films like *The 36ᵗʰ Chamber of Shaolin/Shaolin Sanshiliu Fang* (1978). Interestingly, it took Quentin Tarantino to map this sado-masochistic scenario onto a (white, blonde) female body in *Kill Bill: Volume 2* (2004). The Bride/Beatrix (Uma Thurman) endures the "cruel tutelage" of Pai Mei/Bai Mei (Gordon Liu Jiahui), a villainous mainstay of numerous Hong Kong films about the Shaolin Temple here doubling up as the traditional patriarch of the pedagogic *gongfu* narrative. If this process is traditionally patrilineal, Pai Mei's most powerful students seem to be women. He teaches the Five-point Exploding Heart Technique—a flamboyant variation on Wudang "internal" techniques—to The Bride, presumably in recognition of her martial excellence. Bill (David Carradine) recognises the technique the hard way, by being the recipient of it. Interestingly, he does not seem to have been taught it himself. On the other hand, Pai Mei unwisely underestimates Ellie Driver (Daryl Hannah), who avenges the loss of her eye by poisoning him. However, even *Kill Bill*'s training sequence, staged as a crash-zoom tribute to Hong Kong movies that focus in great detail on the acquisition of specific fighting styles, conceals as much as it reveals. We see The Bride learning Shaolin-based Tiger and Crane techniques, and the Wing Chun one-inch punch that will save her from a (literal) early grave, but her possession of "internal" power is withheld from both Bill and the audience until the revelatory climax. *Kill Bill* sticks with the male *shifu*, however, whereas Jen and Mei's skills are linked, at least in part, to female mentors—Jade Fox is explicitly identified as counter-*shifu* (who, like Ellie Driver, kills male *shifu*s through stealth and deceit), while the Flying Daggers group seems to derive its power from its enigmatic matriarch, Nia.[14] Pai Mei and Jade Fox may, in different ways, constitute bad *shifu* figures—one is xenophobic, misogynist, sadistic and (even in *Kill Bill*'s alternative mythology) destroyer of the Shaolin Temple,[15] the other consumed by bitterness and hatred. But even though Jade Fox is the more sympathetic character—one might even reclaim her as a tragic figure—she is an incomplete (and failed) *shifu*, overtaken by her student. Pai Mei, on the other hand, embodies transcendent knowledge, the source of ultimate mastery. As he is worthy of being avenged, The Bride plucks out Ellie's other eye. In both *Kill Bill* and *Crouching Tiger,* women can only acquire the most advanced martial mastery from men, even though only The Bride takes up the offer. Only Nia, in *House of Flying Daggers*, embodies a power to rival this in recent martial arts films, but there is a sense that she cannot be represented, that she is as much primal mother as martial arts master.[16]

In *Crouching Tiger*, Jen's drama as a fighter is the acquisition of power without sacrificing her autonomy. When she defeats all-comers in the inn fight, she does indeed seem to be the "invincible sword goddess" that she declares herself to be. However, Yu Shu-lien and, particularly, Li Mu-bai put her abilities in context. Yu Shu-lien accuses her of being over-dependent on the Green Destiny, a weapon that is both hysterically phallic ("Don't touch it", she yells at Jen, "That's Li Mu-bai's sword!") and the epitome of *yin* power.[17] But as the sword passes between Jen and Li, it also seems to epitomise the young "Hidden Dragon", "beautiful and yet dangerous" as one character describes it. Li disarms Jen as one might a child, and identifies a lack in her nevertheless extraordinary martial prowess. One might infer that she has mastered the moves, but not grasped the essence—the softness, the effortlessness or stillness that underpins Wudang styles like Tai Chi.[18] Some of this "essence" is distilled into the language adopted by Li Mu-bai—"True strength is light as a feather", "Learn to defeat movement with stillness". Sometimes, the male *wuxia* hero falls between the cracks of the learning process, lacking a living master or left with a damaged, incomplete book. But he is less likely to find himself in a pedagogic void than a space of innovation in which he may create a new style of fighting. The hero of *Executioners from Shaolin/Hong Xiguan* (1976) struggles with his father's damaged *gongfu* book and a bronze dummy that uses ball bearings to simulate the flow of *qi*, but progresses by combining aspects of his father's Tiger fist with his mother's Crane style. Jen, on the other hand, does not get to be her own master. She might reject Li Mu-bai as a mentor, but she is equally terrified of her untutored development, particularly when she realises her superiority to Jade Fox—"I had no one to guide me, no one to follow, no one to learn from".

In some respects, Jade Fox offers Jen more freedom than Li ever can—she has "enchanted" her "with a dream of the *jianghu* underworld"—but is circumscribed by her limited comprehension of Wudang techniques. Two masters fight over an exceptional student, both framed as a seduction or courtship. What the film leaves open-ended is whether Li's interest in her is sexual, as she believes ("Is it me or the sword you want?"), or whether Jade Fox's sexual exploitation by Wudang has soured her towards the title of master that she declares "meaningless".

If the *nuxia* undergoes an (off-screen) process of training, what motivates her to acquire these abilities and to use them? She may be an anti-heroine, like *The Deaf and Mute Heroine/Longya Jian* (1971) or the demonic avengers played by Brigitte Lin in the early 1990s. She may be a security guard, like Yu Shu-lien. But most frequently, she is dutiful, which might take the form of filial piety or patriotism—the fighting women in the films directed by King Hu are mostly underground rebels taking on corrupt governments and officials.

If Gong Li is one of the referents for Zhang Ziyi's *wuxia* persona, then the other one is arguably Zheng Pei-pei, the 1960s "Queen of the Swordswomen".[19] Also a trained dancer, Zheng made her *wuxia* debut with *Come Drink with Me*, her most iconic role and the film that *Crouching Tiger* seems to reference more than any other. She plays a governor's daughter (like Jen in *Crouching Tiger*), who enters the world of *jianghu* in the guise of Golden Swallow, a male *xia* (chivalrous knight). We first meet her in drag, routing the bandits who are holding her brother hostage. Like Jen, she is an incongruous presence at the inn, betraying her privileged background by ordering something that isn't on the menu, but is able to easily defeat her opponents with her twin daggers. When Jen fights at the inn in *Crouching Tiger*, it is largely because she flouts the rules of *jianghu*, showing blatant disrespect for the local martial artists. Golden Swallow, on the other hand, has an established underworld reputation and acts out of political and familial duty. However, *Come Drink with Me* works to reposition her as the narrative shifts towards the drunken hero, Fan Da-pei (Yueh Hua), who even becomes a master figure to her—"I told you to observe more and fight less", he chides her at one point. Kwai-cheung Lo describes Jen as a "trans-subject", characterised by "mobility, to the point of transgression".[20] Golden Swallow, too, is a mobile, if not necessarily transgressive figure—she does not disrupt the boundaries she crosses. However, while the "Martial Arthouse" films adhere to the conventions of crossing gender boundaries—both Jen and Mei adopt male clothes, with Jen passing for Master Long (Dragon)— they make less of the *nuxia*'s cross-gender mobility than the traditional *wuxia pian* sometimes does. *House of Flying Daggers,* in particular, seems to me to in some ways reinvest in gender essences—its concern with shedding duplicitous surfaces can be seen as a desire to see its characters' authentic selves. When all guises are dropped, its central love triangle comprises two violent male rivals (but former friends) and a self-sacrificing girl who dies for a fantasy of romantic love.

The *wuxia pian's* drag act is undoubtedly rooted in the "transvestite theatre"[21] of Beijing Opera, but there are historical precedents too, such as the late Qing era revolutionary Qiu Jin who unbound her feet, wore men's clothing, carried a sword and aspired to possessing "the mind of a man".[22] The cross-dressing of the *wuxia pian* poses a conundrum—how "subversive" can such representations be when they are so rooted in convention? For Western audiences more accustomed to the machismo of the *gongfu pian*, this gender play can be dizzying. Almost thirty years before Brigitte Lin's gender-bending roles, 1960s *wuxia* star Connie Chan specialised in male roles. In *Six-Fingered Lord of the Lute/Liu Zhi Qin Mo* (1965), her (biologically) male character interacts with female characters who adopt male guises in the course of the narrative. Reynaud suggests that the *wuxia pian* betrays a real anxiety about "femininity as *essence*".[23] Certainly, one promotional item in Shaw Brothers' fan magazine *Southern Screen* appears to have lost track of Golden Swallow's gender identity. In a pictorial feature, "Golden Swallow" is initially referred to as a male guise adopted by the governor's daughter, Hsi-yen, to negotiate the release of her brother. Subsequently, she is "advised to revert to her real identity" when tracing the villains to a Buddhist temple. However, visiting as "a dainty, innocent girl Golden Swallow reveals herself when a bandit tries to molest her".[24] So where does Hsi-yen end and Golden Swallow begin? What is his/her "real identity", "dainty innocent girl" or "male, expert swordsman"?

Golden Swallow is a resolutely chaste heroine, her only sexual contact subtextual as Fan Da-pei sucks poison from her shoulder. When Yang Hui-ching (Xu Feng) seduces a largely ineffectual scholar in *A Touch of Zen/Xia Nu* (1971), it transpires that her real motive is the perpetuation of the family line, a motive that unites familial and patriotic duty. Zhang Ziyi, on the other hand, plays conspicuously sexualised heroines. In *Hero*, which only seems to recognise men as being nobly heroic, Snow (Zhang) is motivated solely by her libidinous devotion to the swordsman and calligrapher Broken Sword (Tony Leung), attempting in vain to avenge his death at the hands of her rival in one of the film's competing narratives, defending him in another. In both *Crouching Tiger* and *House of Flying Daggers*, she appears to choose love objects who represent mobility and freedom rather than romantic commitment as an end in itself—the desert bandit Luo (Chang Chen) in the former, Captain Jin's alter-ego Wind, "a free spirit" who is "always moving", in the latter.

"Kicking-Ass" with Unbound Feet: The *Nuxia's* Transnationality

When the narrator of Maxine Hong Kingston's *The Woman Warrior* wonders whether "women were once so powerful that they had to have their feet bound", the prelapsarian fantasy of the *nuxia* is simultaneously aligned with an image of modernity.[25] The brutal image of the mutilated female foot—a foot that the *nuxia* uses for kicking and defying gravity—condenses the social constraints of Confucian patriarchy onto a circumscribed female body. The "Golden Lily" might promise social mobility, in the form of an advantageous marriage, but was designed to curtail any other kind of mobility. As a Manchurian, Jen would be less likely to be subjected to this kind of disfigurement than a Han like Yu Shu-lien,[26] for whom *jianghu* offers freedom of at least a physical kind. In her book on Chinese female athletes, Fan Hong argues that the athletic female body is "an icon of modernity, reconstruction and rehabilitation" in China.[27] In the trajectory "from cripples to champions", "unbinding the feet" represented a discourse that wedded modernity to the liberated female body. The emergence of the literary *nuxia* has been connected to the anti-Confucian May 4th Movement of 1919 and the emergence of a notional "new woman".[28] The athletic Chinese woman could be conscripted into larger agendas, including discourses of national strength or political revolution. Sometimes, she had to negotiate Neo-Confucian revivals, such as Chiang Kai-shek's "New Life Movement", which revived the four virtues of *li* (propriety), *yi* (righteousness), *lian* (integrity) and *chi* (sense of shame), while the obsession with "hygiene" (moral and physical) had the unexpected benefit of physical activity programmes that extended to women.[29] The emerging dichotomy—"a modern body and an ancient morality"—can be seen to inform the mixture of mobility and constraint experienced by the *nuxia*.[30] The *jianghu* of popular culture is, in many ways, a meeting point of the Confucian and the modern.

The cinematic *nuxia* can be linked to three further Chinese encounters with modernity—the economic boom of 1960s Hong Kong as more women entered the workforce,[31] Hong Kong's impending postcoloniality in the 1990s, and the growing transnationality of "Greater China". It is the latter that provides the context for "Martial Arthouse" and Zhang Ziyi. Zhang Zhen finds the most recent conscription of Chinese women into a discourse of modernity in the "rice bowl of youth", a new sexual politics in which "feminine youth…is simultaneously the trope and implement of modernisation and globalisation with Chinese characteristics".[32] The desire to "catch the last train of global modernity" is condensed into an idealised image of youth, beauty and consumption.[33] The emergence of a "pink collar class" in China may have been driven by economic imperatives and ambitions, but can be seen to offer a degree of empowerment, with the domestic priorities of marriage and childbirth deferred in favour of an extended "youth" partly defined by gratification. This new subjectivity is defined by "learning to want, to gratify desire rather than to sacrifice".[34] In *Crouching Tiger*, Jen's initial relationship to *jianghu* is as a consumer—she is a reader of *wuxia* fiction, seduced by the romance of the martial arts world.[35] In *House of Flying Daggers*, Mei seemingly abandons her long-term relationship with Leo (Andy Lau), the underground rebel posing as a local deputy, for the more mercurial Jin. But in fact it isn't Jin who captures her heart, but his phantasmatic alter-ego, "Wind", the representation of a knight-errant that doesn't otherwise exist in the film. In her analysis of *Crouching Tiger,* Catherine Gomes suggests that, in fleeing her arranged marriage to the unprepossessing Gou, Jen remains within the patriarchal order by sleeping with the bandit Luo and thus becoming his "de facto" wife, but there is no evidence that she maintains her "loyalty and obedience" to Luo; it is he who disrupts her marriage, and she abandons him on Wudang Mountain at the end of the film.[36] In *House of Flying Daggers,* on the other hand, Mei's antipathy towards commitment and devotion to gratification leads her to walk away from not only the *jianghu* world, but the political struggle that the film has lead us to believe is noble and just.

This is one way of contextualising Zhang, but global circulation exposed her to other readings. The comparative invisibility of the *nuxia* in the West lead some critics to see female-centred narratives as a new development in Chinese martial arts cinema or to see the films in the context of Western "kick-ass" heroines (particularly as many of those heroines used Asian martial arts in order to "kick-ass"). At the same time, others saw "Martial Arthouse" as rendered generically "inauthentic" by its concessions to a Western audience.[37] There have been some interesting debates about the cross-cultural reception of *Crouching Tiger*'s gender politics. Felicia Chan is sceptical of Western feminist readings of the film—given that *jianghu* is a hierarchical framework, she suggests that the male characters struggle with its restrictive social rules as much as the female ones do.[38] Catherine Gomes is insistent on the need to place the film within a Confucian framework, but seems slightly undecided about whether it is a critique of Confucian repression or an embodiment of it.[39] On the other hand,

Marc O'Day, while by no means insensitive to cultural difference, discusses *Crouching Tiger* as an example of "action babe cinema", which is characterised by:

> beautiful, sexy and tough heroines who command their narratives, invariably driving vehicles, shooting guns, wielding weapons or fighting in hand-to-hand combat better than their (frequently male) adversaries.[40]

Some eyebrows might ascend over O'Day placing the film alongside *Lara Croft: Tomb Raider, Charlie's Angels* and *The X-Men*, and yet this is arguably one of the interpretive contexts in which "Martial Arthouse" films are consumed. It is well-known that *Crouching Tiger*'s script grew out of a cross-cultural dialogue between James Schamus and his Chinese co-writers Wang Hui-ling and Tsai Kuo-jung, while Ang Lee claimed that "Western" techniques such as psychoanalysis were necessary to penetrate the depths of Chinese culture—"to be more Chinese you have to be westernised".[41] According to Kwai-cheung Lo, "youthful and energetic go-getter Jen...acts far more like a contemporary American teenage girl than a Chinese woman in the martial arts genre" [42]—the subtitles' (otherwise inexplicable) transformation of "Yu Jiaolong" into "Jen" seemingly supports this Americanisation and sets her apart from the other characters in the film.[43] On the other hand, O'Day observes that what sets Jen apart from Lara Croft or the Angels is that her "personal motivation" is the desire to "escape patriarchal oppression and find freedom".[44] With her delayed global crossover and cross-cultural dialogue over her "feminist" credentials, the *nuxia* has enjoyed an unprecedented (some might say, disproportionate) visibility as an icon of Chinese cinema's modernity.

Destroying Cities with a Glance: *House of Flying Daggers*

At the Peony Pavilion Pleasure Palace, a beautiful blind girl performs a slow dance—the movements of her waste and hips accord with the conventions of traditional Chinese dance, yet, simultaneously, seem strangely modern. She sings a song, *Jia Ren Qu*, the words based on a famous Han Dynasty poem:

A rare beauty from the North
She's the finest lady on earth
A glance from her, the whole city goes down
A second glance leaves the nation in ruins
There has been no city or nation
That has been more cherished than a beauty like this.

The film quickly progresses to another, more elaborate, performance, the "Echo Game", where graceful dance combines with athleticism and a potentially deadly precision—her leaps and mid-air turns suggest the balleticism of martial arts more than the seductive poise of her slow dance. She strikes a circle of drums with the long sleeves of her dress, her targets determined by Captain Leo propelling nuts at the drums. Without warning, one of her sleeves snakes towards the Captain's sword, removes it from its sheath and performs a slashing sweep that nearly takes his head off. From exoticised object of the gaze to deadly fighter, femme fatale and warrior (with an Amazonian rebel clan behind her), *qingcheng qingguo* (beautiful girl) and authority-defying rebel, Mei inhabits a series of roles in the film—showgirl, helpless captive, wild flower, androgynous boy. She is as dangerous in male garb—fighting in a field of flowers or a bamboo forest—as the hyper-feminine guise she adopts at the Peony Pavilion, objectified and (given the film's global reach) orientalised. In some ways, she reverses the gender expectations of some of her generic predecessors, who, like Golden Swallow, appear in "masculine" form and soften into a "girl" as the film goes on.

If the Peony Pavilion constitutes *House of Flying Daggers'* most spectacular sequence, its nearest rival is a sequence in a bamboo forest as airborne soldiers pursue Mei and then engage her in intense combat. This is undoubtedly the sequence the film's Chinese title "Ambushed on Ten Sides" has in mind, but it also finally brings the eponymous "Flying Daggers", an underground rebel group, into the action as an onscreen presence. The Flying Daggers' recently assassinated leader is male, and in one of a rapid sequence of plot twists, Leo turns out to be a member (as well as being Mei's lover). But the film largely presents *female* rebels in opposition to a corrupt male order. Leo may not be the silky sadist he poses as earlier in the film, but he is murderously jealous, attempting to rape and later kill Mei when he learns that she has fallen for Jin. The forest-dwelling Flying Daggers are suggestive of Amazons, but also Buffy-style slayers (one of their attacks substitutes stakes for blades), while the green hues of their costumes and environment suggest *The Matrix* as much as the bamboo forests of King Hu. Their current leader, Nia, is a more mysterious and powerful figure—it is hard to imagine that she will be as easy a target as her predecessor. Augusta Lee Palmer and Jenny Kwok Wah Lau argue that the *nuxia* is always presented as an exception in an otherwise male-dominated world.[45] King Hu's films sometimes feature teams of female fighters, such as the soldiers who appear alongside Golden Swallow towards the end of *Come Drink with Me* or the fighting waitresses in *The Fate of Lee Khan/Yingchun Ge zhi Fengbo* (1974). These tend to be fairly unindividuated characters, but they also suggest that the heroine isn't so unique. When Mei drops at least some of her guises, it is revealed that she is neither blind nor (as Jin was told by Leo) the daughter of the assassinated leader, but "just one of many girls" in the organisation. On the surface, this is not the patriarchal *jianghu* of *Crouching Tiger*, but one that is unambiguously female, even matriarchal.

By investing so much design (as well as kinetic) intensity into two of the film's (implicitly feminine) spaces, the film invites some analogies between the brothel and the forest lair. Yee (Song Dandan), Nia's second-in-command, initially appears as the madam of the Peony Pavilion. Are we then to infer that all of the girls at the brothel are also skilled freedom fighters? According to Zhang Zhen, the "rice bowl of youth" has attracted criticism for its sexualisation of Chinese female youth, seen as "akin to prostitution", but also arousing an "anxiety of impotence" at this new economic power enjoyed by young women.[46] Mei's skills clearly go beyond martial arts—we are told that she has used her seductive powers in the revolutionary struggle before.[47]

If *jianghu* is feminised in *House of Flying Daggers*, the film does not equate this with the empowerment of its heroine. The World of Vagrants is ultimately still identified with restrictions, rules, prohibitions and limitations—"this is not the time for love", judges Nia before ordering Mei to kill Jin. Just as Jen fights with Yu Shu-lien and abandons Jade Fox in *Crouching Tiger*, Mei walks away from any intimations of martial sisterhood that Western critics might want to read into this scenario. She abandons her comrades to an unknown fate—an inconclusive shot shows the General's troops closing in. As she dies in Jin's arms, surrounded poetically by snow, the film both romanticises and punishes Mei's selfishness—one can read Jen's climactic leap from Wudang Mountain in a number of ways, but Mei's fate is all too conclusive.

In their essay on women in contemporary Hong Kong cinema, Augusta Lee Palmer and Jenny Kwok Wah Lau contrast what they see as the "regressive" portrayals found in art cinema with the "playfulness" of certain female-centred action movies. Art cinema burdens its female characters with "the allegorical weight of nation, the people, or cultural identity" often through tropes of suffering and suicide, while *wuxia*-derived action movies featuring warrior women are "progressively inflected".[48] As the heroine of "Martial Arthouse", Zhang Ziyi combines these two personas, usually within the same films. Is *Crouching Tiger*, for example, an allegory of the conflict between tradition and modernity or a high-flying adventure with a very cool (anti)heroine (or both)? In *House of Flying Daggers*, Mei embodies the two archetypes of female resistance identified by Lee Palmer and Lau, the courtesan and the warrior. Does her melodramatic snowbound death conform to orientalist images of "Chineseness, femininity and mystery"? And yet, while the "Martial Arthouse" *nuxia* is in some ways a more essentialist figure than her predecessors, she remains a revisionist—perhaps even transgressive—heroine, too. The genre's name refers to both martial arts (*wu*) and chivalry *(xia)*, but while both Jen and Mei are consummate martial artists, they are not in any way chivalrous, their ambiguous climactic self-sacrifices notwithstanding. While *Crouching Tiger* still embodies chivalry in the noble Li Mu-bai, in *House of Flying Daggers* one glance from this "rare beauty from the north" does indeed seem to bring everything tumbling down. Zhang Ziyi's heroines threaten to topple not only the restrictions of the *jianghu* world, but the very heroism that underpins the *wuxia* genre.

Notes

1. Berenice Reynaud, "Gong Li and the Glamour of the Chinese Star," *Sight and Sound* 3, no. 8 (1993): 12,15.
2. To add insult to injury, she appears to have been doubled by a stunt*man*.
3. While *Musa* (2001) is not a *wuxia pian* and casts Zhang in a non-fighting part, her billing in the film helped sell the DVD to Western action fans.
4. More "Martial Arthouse" films have appeared more recently, such as Chen Kaige's *The Promise/Wu Ji* (2005). Tsui Hark's *Seven Swords/Qi Jian* (2005) and Ronny Yu's *Fearless/Huo Yuanjia* (2005) have some of the same qualities—epic scale, high production values—but have a less character-driven, flavour that is more typical of Hong Kong crowd-pleasers.
5. Charles Affron and Mirella Jona, *Sets in Motion: Art Direction and Film Narrative* (New Brunswick, New Jersey: Rutger University Press, 1995).
6. On the DVD commentary for the film, Zhang Yimou explains that the colours used in the Pavilion were based on the paintings in the Dunhuang Grottoes in Gansu Province, where monks carved the caves into the cliffs as a site for Buddhist art over a six hundred year period.
7. One reviewer was so enraptured by the Peony Pavilion that he wanted to "step through the screen and wander around this incredible, dream-like place". Peter Bradshaw "*House of Flying Daggers*," *The Guardian*, December 24th, http://www.film.guardian.co.uk/News_Story/Critic_Reviews/Guardian_review/0,4267,13 79290,00.html, 2004 (accessed April 7, 2005).
8. Kwai-cheung Lo, *Chinese Face-Off: The Transnational Popular Culture of Hong Kong*, (Urbana and Chicago: University of Illinois Press, 2005), 191.
9. The *gongfu pian* shares many of the themes of the *wuxia pian*, but the films of Bruce Lee, with their emphasis on physical authenticity and real fighting techniques, made empty-handed fighting films look more like a distinct subgenre.
10. Sam Ho, "From Page to Screen: A Brief History of *Wuxia* Fiction," in *Heroic Grace: The Chinese Martial Arts Film,* ed. David Chute and Cheng-sim Lim (Los Angeles: UCLA, 2003), 14.
11. Berenice Reynaud, "The Book, the Goddess and the Hero: Sexual Politics in the Chinese Martial Arts Film," *Senses of Cinema* 26, 2003, 6. http://www.sensesofcinema.com/contents/03/26/sexual_politics_chinese_martial_arts.ht ml (accessed February 16, 2006).
12. James J. Y. Liu, *The Chinese Knight-errant* (London: Routledge and Kegan Paul, 1967), 85.

13. Reynaud, "The Book, the Goddess", 4.

14. One can only infer that a woman—Nia or someone else—trained Mei because there is no reference to how she learned to fight.

15. In Tarantino's version, Pai Mei destroys the Shaolin Temple over an imagined slight when a young monk fails to acknowledge his nod. The Pai Mei/Bai Mei of *wuxia* literature and popular cinema was one of the Shaolin elders, but defected to the rival Wudang school and collaborated with the Manchu government in the burning of Shaolin. *Kill Bill* briefly alludes to the gender ambiguity of Bai Mei's popular representation when The Bride ineffectually attacks his genitals and finds nothing there—in some films he is able to retract his testicles at will and use his groin to trap his opponents.

16. One probably cannot separate this entirely from the death of Hong Kong actress Anita Mui, who was originally intended to play Nia. When Mui passed away, Zhang Yimou reduced the character to the shadowy presence of the final film and built up her second-in-command, Yee. Nia is consequently both an absence and a mobile signifier, one that can be inhabited by different characters, such as Yee, who briefly poses as her. Compounding this impression, Zhang Yimou sometimes conflates Nia and Yee in his DVD commentary.

17. In Daoist cosmology, the "feminine", passive *yin* complements the "masculine", dominating *yang*.

18. What my Tai Chi teacher calls "not making a move".

19. Zheng won this accolade in a 1969 poll in *Sing Tao Evening News and Express*, Frank Bren, "Fighting Women: Cheng Pei-pei (and King Hu Legacy)." *Metro* 113/114 (1998): 81.

20. Lo, *Chinese Face-Off,* 190.

21. Marjorie Garber, *Vested Interests: Cross-Dressing and Cultural Anxiety* (London: Penguin, 1992), 244.

22. Hong, *Footbinding, Feminism and Freedom*, 91.

23. Reynaud,"The Book, the Goddess", 6.

24. Unknown Author, *"Come Drink with Me"*, *Southern Screen* 96 (1966): 79–80.

25. Maxine Hong Kingston, *The Woman Warrior: Memoirs of a Girlhood Among Ghosts* (London: Picador, 1977), 25.

26. At the start of the Qing Dynasty (1644–1911), the Manchurian invaders attempted to abolish footbinding amongst the Han Chinese. Not only were they unsuccessful, but some Manchus adopted a practice ostensibly forbidden to them. See Hong, *Footbinding, Feminism and Freedom*, 50.

27. Ibid., 36.

28. Reynaud,"The Book, the Goddess," 2.

29. Hong, *Footbinding, Feminism and Freedom*, 235.

30. Ibid., 235.

31. Law Kar and Frank Bren, *Hong Kong Cinema: A Cross-Cultural View* (Lanham, Maryland: Scarecrow Press, 2004), 258.

32. Zhang Zhen, "The 'Rice Bowl of Youth' in Fin de Siècle Urban China," in *Globalization*, ed. Arjun Appadurai (Durham and London: Duke University Press, 2003), 133.

33. Ibid., 131.

34. Ibid., 150.

35. Moreover, Zhang Ziyi may be the face of the contemporary *wuxia pian*, but she has also been the face of Maybelline, Pantene, Visa and Dior, and first worked with Zhang Yimou on a shampoo commercial.

36. Catherine Gomes, "Crouching Tiger, Hidden Genre: An Investigation into Western Film Criticism's Reading of Feminism in Ang Lee's *Crouching Tiger, Hidden Dragon*", *Limina* 11, 2005, http://www.limina.arts.uwa.edu.au/current_volume?f=79246. (accessed February 8, 2006), 53.

37. Stephen Teo, "*Crouching Tiger, Hidden Dragon*—Passing Fad or Global Phenomenon?" in *Heroic Grace,* ed. Chute and Lim, 23–26.

38. This may be true of the central characters, but risks overlooking the larger patrilineal structures and the power wielded by dead men (Li Mu-bai's slain master, Yu Shu-lien's dead fiancé who prevents her relationship with Li). Felicia Chan, "*Crouching Tiger, Hidden Dragon*: Cultural Migrancy and Translatability," in *Chinese Films in Focus: 25 New Takes*, ed. Chris Berry (London: British Film Institute, 2003), 60.

39. Gomes, "Crouching Tiger, Hidden Genre".

40. Marc O'Day, "Beauty in Motion: Gender, Spectacle and Action Babe Cinema," in *Action and Adventure Cinema,* ed.Yvonne Tasker (London and New York: Routledge, 2004), 201.

41. Quoted in Lo, *Chinese Face-Off,* 183.

42. Lo, *Chinese Face-Off,* 187.

43. And "Jen" she has remained in virtually every English-language critique of the film, this one included.

44. Then again, that sets her apart from most Chinese action heroines, too, who no more fight "male oppression" than Lara Croft does. See O'Day, "Beauty in Motion", 211.

45. Augusta Lee Palmer and Jenny Kwok Wah Lau, "Of Executioners and Courtesans: The Performance of Gender in Hong Kong Cinema of the 1990s," in *Multiple Modernities: Cinemas and Popular Media in Transcultural East Asia,* ed. Jenny Kwok Wah Lau (Philadelphia: Temple University Press, 2003), 217.

46. Zhang Zhen, "The 'Rice Bowl'", 141.

47. *The Intimate Confessions of a Chinese Courtesan/Ai Nu* (1972) offers the most sustained analogy between martial and sexual training—both will be crucial to its heroine's revenge.

48. Palmer and Kwok Wah Lau, "Of Executioners and Courtesans", 207, 216.

CHAPTER TEN

SUPERHEROINE:
WOMEN AS MARTIAL ARTISTS IN EARLY
TWENTY-FIRST CENTURY CINEMA

CATHERINE DRISCOLL

Figure Twelve: Maggie Cheung in *Hero* (2002)

This essay assembles a history of the woman martial artist, focusing on how Hollywood film distributes, deploys and intervenes in images of fighting women from Chinese-language martial arts films. It begins by considering the possible conjunctions between two films released at the beginning of this century in terms of the way they articulate the history of women and fighting on screen that unfolded in the previous century. Using these films I want to point to some changes in representations of how fighting and the fighter are gendered on screen. There certainly has been a proliferation of screen images of women who are fighters in the 1990s and 2000s, but these women are often clearly coded as unrealistic—whether in science-fiction, fantasy or the more general action hero genres there is usually something very remarkable about the woman who fights. This essay will focus on the way in which the martial arts film genre has participated in this shift, tracing the ways in which the superhero and the martial artist interacted to produce two distinct new figures—the superheroine and the woman warrior.

The two films I will use to anchor this discussion are Zhang Yimou's *Hero* (2002), successfully disseminated on an international scale with an acclaimed cast of Hong Kong film stars, several of whom specialise in martial arts films, and the Pitof film *Catwoman* (2004), a vehicle for the supermodel presence of Halle Berry. These are radically different examples of the woman as martial artist in contemporary film. Their aims and audiences are too different to be easily compared, but the juxtaposition of *Hero* and *Catwoman* maps a field of exchanges between different film cultures around the image of the woman who fights. Both films foreground the influence of Chinese-language martial arts films on the fighting skills and attitudes of women in US film and television. And both also foreground the contemporaneous but not necessarily reciprocal influence of the genres and styles that have defined women for Hollywood film, particularly film and television melodrama, on Chinese-language martial arts film.[1] I want to begin this essay, then, by considering the key historical influences on each of these films' central fighting women.

Hero

Hero is set in feudal China, telling a story about power on an immense scale—the power of love, home, death and nation. A nameless civil servant is summoned to tell his King how he defeated three powerful assassins, and the frame narrative of this interview encompasses five interlocking but incompatible stories about the warriors Sky, Broken Sword and Flying Snow, each of which is told in a separate colour-infused sequence: grey, red, blue, green and gold/white. While this use of colour and the epic scale of the cinematography help to translate the Chinese narrative for a range of audiences, the success of *Hero* with English-language audiences cannot be credited to any single cause. Among reasons for its success I want to focus on its renovations of the traditional Chinese-language *wuxia pian* genre which change, first and most dramatically, the gender of the martial arts film for English-language audiences. *Hero*, as framed by the dominant conventions of Hollywood film, is more artistic or beautiful, more emotional or sensitive, more focused on melodramatic narrative and character and less focused on physical torment, than martial arts films are generally presumed to be. It was also given new life in English-language markets by the box office success of the female-centred *Crouching Tiger, Hidden Dragon* (2000), a film to which I will return later, a fact which highlights the importance of female martial artists in *Hero*. But understanding this reception of *Hero* as regendering the martial arts film requires more attention to the history of *wuxia pian* behind it.

Based on a traditional Chinese story—one that has been told before, including in Chen Kaige's acclaimed *The Emperor and the Assassin* (1999)— *Hero* premiered in the Great Hall of the People. Alongside its nationalist narrative about Chineseness, this film is also shaped by the success of the martial actress in contemporary Chinese-language cinema. In *Hero*, even the scenes which do not include the lead female character, Flying Snow, incorporate her as a central narrative force. Before cutting to the grey sequence in which he fights Long Sky, the Hero explains that he needed to prove Flying Snow's infidelity, and this is the narrative context encompassing the grey-themed fight scene, like the falling rain and the *qin* music. When Flying Snow herself appears in the red sequence, this idea of her treachery is immediately reinforced by framing and *mise-en-scene*. Everything about her impassive face, off-centre and looking off-screen, tells us that she is in pain, but not exactly why. While the inferences we are invited to draw from this scene turn out to be wrong, the red ink symbolising the tension between husband and wife here becomes the central motif of the rebel's plan. Snow, and the slowly revealed story of her vengeful determination to kill the King, hang suspended on a scroll above him as the diegetic story unfolds, and they hover in red plumes over the Hero's funeral at the end.

Even in the sequence where Sword is tortured by betrayal and jealousy, it is Snow's pain we watch and her red that drowns out the screen with each tragic death, and thus her wound and her mode of fighting are always especially significant. In the scene where she and the Hero fight alongside one another, her clothes are the weapon aligned with his swords, crafting a concretely feminised form of martial skill. We subsequently see her use more traditional fighting styles, but her principle weapon remains both her femininity and her emotion, sometimes indecipherable amidst a frenzy of leaves and dresses and swords and sometimes as nakedly apparent as her suicide. While the character and motives of the other characters seem clear and consistent, who Snow is and what she wants changes in each narrative sequence within the overall frame of her need to kill the king. Although its precise inflection changes with each colour, Snow is always seeking personal vengeance of some kind, rejecting the interdiction that "one person's pain is nothing" that the men all endorse.

If *Hero* exemplifies a regendering of the Chinese-language swordplay drama it is not because women fight in it. *Wuxia pian* always left a place in which women were able to fight while remaining within dominant gender paradigms.

Wuxia stories proper began as nineteenth-century interpretations of Chinese mythology. They generally involve battles for the good of the family, state or world, telling a story about the community or way of life the hero stands for in which personal struggles symbolise social struggles. But *wuxia* also commonly revolves around a martial spirituality, meeting magical obstacles with magical fighting skills.

Film was particularly successful at interpreting the *wuxia* genre, because of its mechanisms for spectacle and fantasy, and many of the characteristic techniques of Hong Kong martial arts cinema, such as wirework, were developed in order to tell these stories. *Wuxia* on film was never a static genre, left behind by new tastes in and conventions for film. Hong Kong filmmakers in particular, more directly and successfully interacting with Hollywood film, both adopted new conventions for realist action to *wuxia* and blended *wuxia* motifs and plots with new urban contemporary drama. Even in the high fantasy mode of *wuxia*, fighters began to tire, were depicted as more dependent on training, and employed fewer surreal fighting moves. In more recent examples, such as *Hero,* a new dependence on characters with complex private emotional narratives has also been emphasised. Emotion increasingly takes over as combatants tire, and private dramas are just as central as social ones. The display of emotion has come to signal failure for the *wuxia* hero, as the failure of emotional control represents failure of fighting skills as well, but this increasingly important narrative convention means something more ambivalent for the increasingly significant female martial hero. Failure, or at least the impossibility of success, may in fact be the centrepoint of her story, just as emotional displays are central to her story. I want to call this the melodrama of the martial actress, and it is at full force in *Hero* despite its key narrative of male heroes battling for control of themselves and the state.

The meaning of "melodrama" has changed since it was a term used to describe simplistic dramatic narratives in which good triumphed over evil. Refracted through its revision by classic Hollywood film and the serial narrative forms of popular melodrama on radio and television, melodrama consistently refers to suspenseful drama with stark characterisation and soaring emotional excess matched by soaringly excessive performance. Martial arts films have frequently used a similar kind of excess to give texture to their schematic plot and heighten the dramatic effect of their martial spectacle. This also opens a place in which traditional femininity is an asset rather than an obstacle to the martial arts film. It does not necessarily relegate them to being the victim, the bereaved or the chorus for the martial drama. Because martial skills in *wuxia* are often metaphysical, women were never as restricted by narratives about sexed physical capacity in this genre as they were in many others. Women warriors were popular even in early *wuxia* in comparison to the "kung fu" films that were *wuxia*'s main competition in the Chinese-language film market, and also in comparison to Hollywood action films of the same period. This is partly because *wuxia pian* are period films where spectacular violence in a woman character is not as confronting as it might be in a film with a contemporary setting. There were nevertheless other filmic influences on the changing roles of women martial artists in those Chinese-language film that reached Anglophone cinemas; influences which exoticised the violence of the woman martial artist in quite different ways, indicating that it is not only period setting that made the woman martial artist in earlier *wuxia* accessible to a mainstream audience.

In Hong Kong film's watershed year, the landmark film was *Enter the Dragon* (1973), the last film completed by martial arts legend Bruce Lee. This is an American production in cooperation with Hong Kong's Golden Harvest, and, while clearly a kung fu film designed to break kung fu and Lee in America, it did so using the success of the James Bond films as a template.[2] *Enter the Dragon* not only takes up the cackling Asian villain from *Dr. No* (1962), down to his fluffy white cat, but also a score that sounds like the Bond theme remixed as muzak, and the Bond girls. Han's "daughters" fight very little, just like the Bond girls of this period, but they are introduced as sexy martial artists demonstrating extraordinary skills with darts and daggers. This film is clearly addressed to an audience who understand martial arts prowess as the province of a male audience and revolving around men, with one notable exception. Another female martial artist provides the key motivation of the plot. Li (Bruce Lee) refuses the quest he is offered by the British government until he hears the story of his sister's death and realises the quest will allow him personal revenge. The legendary Angela Mao plays this sister in a brief flashback cameo. Cornered by a gang of thieves under obvious but undeclared threat of rape she fights back desperately and, when she has obviously lost, kills herself with a large shard of glass rather than submit. While the suicide was unusual for an artist of Mao's standing, the wounded girl and the rape victim are common tropes in kung fu films that provide another lens for considering the success of women martial artists in *wuxia*.

This melodramatic role for women in Chinese-language action films was often taken up by women who themselves did not fight. In John Woo's *The Killer* (1989), the protagonists are motivated by their encounter with a wounded girl, the emotive singer Jennie, who is blinded in the film. As in Zhang's most recent *wuxia* film, *House of Flying Daggers* (2004), the blind girl here heightens both the melodramatic tensions of the plot between the two principle men and provides a different identificatory point for the audience. Jin in *Flying Daggers*, whether carried through beautiful fields or dressed in a staggering robe, is a melodramatic figure requiring an affective identification that both suspends disbelief and disavows literality for a symbolic or, as Ien Ang would have it when talking about soap-opera, an emotional realism.[3] The difference between Jin in *Flying Daggers* and Jennie in *The Killer* is, of course, that Jin is revealed as a fighter. In fact, despite the star quality and martial prowess of the two male leads, the central martial artist of *Flying Daggers* is undoubtedly Jin herself.

However, the new *wuxia* films like *Hero* and *Flying Daggers* should be seen as an entirely different trajectory for Chinese-language film than the "bullet ballets" of Woo's *oeuvre*.[4] Woo also draws on *wuxia* films in emphasising both aesthetic and affective style in his representation of violence. His film style asks you to look at violence as art, strategically focusing the audience on specific moments, slowing them or dwelling on them, stressing their real effects somewhat less than their symbolic standing and visual form. This strategy of delay, of suspension, is used in different ways to heighten the affective impact of the *wuxia* battle, emphasising that it is a spiritual as well as physical contest. Such tactics ask the viewer to linger over the aesthetics of movement, form and affect. They ask the audience to respond to violence not in terms of its effects but in terms of impact on characters and the audience—how it feels and how it looks. These strategies are the stylistic centre of *Hero*, which consists of one after another fight scene as artistic tableau, played out in beautiful detail along the chain of interlocking possible storylines within the diegetic frame of the film. It would be a terrible generalisation to claim that this *wuxia* style of representing fight scenes is itself feminine, but when such films are consumed by Western audiences they fit into the gendered schema of cinema as things to-be-looked-at, and thus fit neatly with the ways in which Hollywood film treats the aesthetic appeal of the feminine.

Catwoman

My second starting point is a superhero film, one of many following the success of Sam Raimi's *Spider-Man* films in 2002 and 2004 and billed, moreover, as a spinoff from the successful Batman film series. *Catwoman* was never so commercially successful, but it is interesting for its attempt to reshape the successful superhero film genre into a story centred on a woman. In considering the history of *Catwoman* I want to also flesh out its interaction with Chinese-language martial arts films.

Catwoman was never designed to be a superhero, but neither was she originally a villain. Appearing in the comic *Batman* #1, in 1940, creator Bob Kane described her as Batman's love interest, adversary and alter-ego.[5] The first story of Catwoman's origin appears in *The Secret Life of Catwoman* of 1951. While Batman belongs to the new popular gothic heroes like hard-boiled detectives, with a double-life marked out by the secret underground of his mysterious mansion and a traumatic past that drives his crime-fighting vocation,

Catwoman combines the femme fatale role of film noir with some of its hero's violent struggles. However, Catwoman manipulates and incites violence rather than fighting Batman claw to glove. She was initially a criminal but not a fighter, and her revealing costume enabled her spectacular crimes and escapes rather than any martial style.[6]

Figure Thirteen: Halle Berry in *Catwoman* (2004)

The martial arts style that comic book Catwoman eventually develops is a product of the TV renovations of Catwoman that transformed her from femme fatale to superheroine. In the 1960s TV spoof, *Batman*, even though Catwoman could never be hit by gentlemen like Batman and Robin, her occasional kicks in high-heeled boots are significant. They not only show her physically fighting her nemesis but make it clear that she is fighting as a woman. In this series, Batgirl's fighting style is similarly confined to balletic kicking with high heels or hitting people with handy objects. Yvonne Craig, who played Batgirl, has reflected on this: "I admired Diana Rigg, who was in *The Avengers* then with all that karate, but my producer didn't want Batgirl doing any martial arts at all. He didn't think it was feminine to karate-chop people".[7]

When Batgirl was added to the comics after the TV series, she was a karate expert, but on television the transformation from Barbara Gordon to Batgirl was a process of dressing up rather than training. Almost every episode shows her secret wardrobe, wigs and makeup stand. This daring single girl's life in fact aligned her with Catwoman's sexual ambivalence, and Batgirl's wigs and Catwoman's whip represent their fight as a game with femininity. However, their dance moves in place of combat do have a martial context provided by the visibility of "karate" at the time. Bruce Lee was on the talk show circuit, cop shows featured karate-kicking villains, and James Bond and other spy-heroes used a combination of boxing and kung fu moves. Also under planned production was *Charlie's Angels* (1976–81), where girls did get to karate-chop, and the *Kung Fu* series (1972–5) starring David Carradine, a role originally suggested for Lee. Lee also appeared in *Batman* as Kato, sidekick to The Green Hornet. Kato was the orientalised houseboy, marked by both deference and secret knowledge, but also bringing to the series a new way of fighting that resembled that of Catwoman and Batgirl rather than Batman and Robin. After Kato's appearance, women also seem to fight more physically on *Batman*, paving the way for Batgirl's arrival.

Although Catwoman in the TV series is only superficially characterised (and Batgirl's motivations were even more scantly treated), in the comics Catwoman eventually became a superhero—a child from the streets who aims to fight for good. In both feature films that give her a starring role she has a more ambivalent part to play, not a fighter for justice itself so much as a wounded girl seeking revenge that also happens to address a social ill, after the mode of many *wuxia* fighters. Catwoman becomes not quite a superhero but what we might call a "superheroine", as distinct from the superhero, as two different elements are foregrounded: first, as she develops a personal revenge narrative justifying her violence, and second, as her body becomes a weapon. This is made explicit in the 1992 Tim Burton film, *Batman Returns*, starring Michelle Pfeiffer as Catwoman.

The motivation for Catwoman's vengeance in *Batman Returns* is both different and similar to that in Pitofs *Catwoman*. Selina (Michelle Pfeiffer) in the earlier film and Patience (Halle Berry) in the later one are humiliated at work and at home and constantly derided as inadequate, but the scene in which Selina becomes Catwoman after having been thrown through a window by her boss takes up the feminine masquerade of the TV series in a more explicit (and yet more camp) manner. While Patience in *Catwoman* also falls to her death, she then finds herself possessed by an alien cat-goddess persona. Selina, on the other hand, is personally transformed. Having been bitten back to consciousness by stray cats, Selina goes through the routine of her single girl's life out of synch—pouring milk on the floor and smashing the answering machine on which her mother leaves belittling messages. Finally, she drags out a vinyl coat and a sewing machine and makes her sexy catsuit. This costume reflects both the streamlining of her body into a weapon, incorporating metal claws and pointed boots, and the fashioning of herself as a wounded body, marked out in the stitches criss-crossing the taut shiny vinyl.[8]

All film versions of Batman, and his associated villains, reference the trauma that transforms them into superhuman figures, but there is a gendered dimension to this gothic double-life of the superhero. In *Batman Returns*, despite Batman's insistence that he and Catwoman are the same, Catwoman does not pursue social evils but exacts personal revenge. She is humiliated and dismissed as a woman and because she is a woman, and that underpins how she fights. About to attack her first victim, a man harassing a woman in an alley, 1989 Catwoman says, "Be gentle; it's my first time". In case we miss the point she stops mid-fight to quip, "I am Catwoman, hear me roar". Her fighting style here is still more acrobatic than martial and indeed Catwoman never kills anyone except the real villain, her old boss, whom she kills with an electrically charged kiss in a melodramatic self-sacrifice. Catwoman returns to life, of course, but continues to define herself as a victim remaining alone on the city skyline.

Catwoman intends to be more subtle with its "girl power" than *Batman Returns*, casting Sharon Stone as Laurel Hedare, the evil force of industrialised femininity against which Catwoman must fight. It is Laurel, rather than Catwoman, who attempts the feminist quips in this film. When the hero suggests to Laurel that she doesn't really want to kill him, Laurel spits back, "I'm a woman. I'm used to doing all sorts of things I don't want to do". We also cannot take an anti-beauty culture narrative from the evil supermodel turned murderer with skin like living marble. Patience can move on her life as a beautiful girl undisturbed by any social critique, and her friend, addicted to the dangerous cosmetic, can not only move on to another product but wins her handsome doctor through the effects of the dangerous one. Nevertheless, it is in this reflection on a conflicted femininity that *Catwoman* takes up a place amongst popular heroines which foreground the impact of feminism on US popular culture and where she appears in a context where fighting girl heroines are mainstream prime-time fare.[9]

The traditional superhero, developed in comic books and in episodic television, is a hyper-masculine man in most if not all elements. His body is usually his weapon too, although some superheroes have bodies transformed by the use of weapons. Batman, for example, is a normal man in the physical sense, but attached so closely to so many weapons and other tools that his body becomes one with the Bat-weapons. The female superhero, however, is more often the user of magical weapons that impart some of their magic to her, like Wonder Woman or She-ra, her superpowers are not explicitly weapons at all (like Mystique and Rogue in the *The X-Men* [2000]). She rarely uses her body as a supernatural weapon per se, but usually insofar as she has superhumanly enhanced strength as a martial artist. There is no question about Catwoman's status as a superheroine in *Catwoman*, but there is also no question that she articulates this role through her martial arts skills. Halle Berry's Catwoman knows how to flip, kick and punch and has the usual martial arts film crew of choreographers and stunt doubles to help her do so.[10] The history of Catwoman's coming to fight is produced in relation to Chinese-language martial arts genres emerging in US film culture and emphasising the two types of girl who fight in *Enter the Dragon*: the highly trained sexual object come fighting machine, and the hyper-victim with her dramatic gestures.

The high emotional drama of the female martial artist resembles the ambivalence of the female comic book superhero in ways that superheroine films like *Catwoman* or Rob Bowman's *Elektra* (2005) do not. Like Catwoman, Elektra is the love-hate counterpart of a superhero, Daredevil, and appears in his first volume. Most spectacularly, however, from 1983–92 Elektra appeared in volumes of her own devised and drawn by comic great Frank Miller and focusing on her violent tragic backstory, every bit as indebted to violent Asian cinema as is *Kill Bill: Vol. 1 & Vol.2* (2003, 2004). Like many martial artists before her, after Elektra Natchios' father is murdered she becomes a ninja assassin and she seeks rather indiscriminate revenge for her suffering. In film form, however, little is made of Elektra's traumatic experiences, and without her melodrama Elektra is a supermodel with knives. *Elektra*'s tagline is "If looks could kill", stressing the degree to which the cinematic objectification of the superheroine dominates this film, as it did *Catwoman*.

If the superheroine's fight is not necessarily for good and her quest more self-centred and self-referential, it is perhaps easy to see this as a weak version of heroism however able the martial performance. Their emotional quests or, in its weaker form, their spectacular displays of emotional strength, have as much in common with soap-opera as with action heroes. But what continues to link the somewhat abortive narratives of Laurel's ageing and Patience's struggle to recognise herself in *Catwoman*, connecting them to other privately wounded superheroines, is a rhetoric of self-care. This foregrounds an element of the woman as martial artist which is not present in *wuxia* film but is central to the superheroine narrative. The superheroine is not just a female superhero who now uses martial arts but a quite differently gendered version of the action hero. Drawing on the comparative weakness but exotic spectacle of female superheroes, the superheroine is also filtered through the power of film to both summon identification with and representatively challenge gender roles shaped by the social context of her emergence.

The superheroine, and the subcategories of supervillainess and supernormal girl, produce themselves out of available modes of self-criticism. Whether as excessive self-defense or to vengefully exact reparation for what has been done to them, and usually both, these characters employ what Michel Foucault would call "technologies of the self" to produce themselves as someone who can make a difference.[11] By "technologies of the self" Foucault refers to the way discourses on the self produce versions of the self by taking the self as an object. Foucault's examples include confession and sexuality, both of which are deployed by the superheroine, but it may very well be that this is what distinguishes a superheroine from the female martial artist. While both perfect the self in order to defend the self, the self is not the project of the martial artist in the same way it is of the superheroine, however similar their fighting styles.

The Melodrama of the Martial Actress

Less confined by codes for film realism, the martial fantasy film allows filmmakers and audiences to explore the limitations and possibilities of violence. Both *wuxia* and superhero films are about individual fighters, whatever social narrative they employ as a frame. I am more interested here in a set of ongoing exchanges between different film cultures around the image of fighting women. *Hero* and *Catwoman* look back at a history in which superhero and *wuxia* films interact and point to some emerging cross-cultural discourses on the reasons why and the styles in which women fight onscreen. Understanding these exchanges as hybridity renders the different histories and forces involved inert because it is superceded by the new and more resilient hybrid form and also imagines that there were, in the pre-hybrid past, coherently distinct and separate cinemas that can be absorbed into this hybridisation.[12] I want to set aside the hybridity model, therefore, in order to acknowledge ongoing history and ongoing exchanges between different but intersecting cinema histories.

Despite an all-star Hong Kong cast that overlaps in many respects with *Hero*, Ang Lee's *Crouching Tiger, Hidden Dragon* was not especially successful with Chinese-language audiences, although it was a singular success in the United States. In terms of box office results as well as awards and reviews, the Hollywood-centric cinematic schema leaves a space in the picture of Asian-ness where kung fu and swordplay are not only allowed and comprehensible but central. Although it is not the sole reason why women as martial artists are increasingly prominent amongst successful Chinese-language martial arts films, the impact of *Crouching Tiger* enabled the wider distribution and greater accessibility of Zhang's recent *wuxia* films. I want to suggest two reasons for this, both of which are evident in Ang Lee's film: first, because of their emphasis on crafting the body (and the embodied self) as a weapon and, second, because of the accessibility of their melodrama. That is, because of their common ground with the superheroine.

Among the elements of this film, identified as divergent from the traditions of *wuxia*, the most obvious is its emphasis on multiple roles for women martial artists that reflect on gender and other social hierarchies. The film compares women of three different generations and social situations in relation to both womanly destiny and the role of martial artist. These women represent specific possible responses to the woman's body as a weapon, all bound up in the question of love, and in each case the sword or the teaching of the hero is required in order for the woman as martial arts hero to master herself.[13] While the story is based on a serialised *wuxia* novel that includes both the young Jen's defiance and certain elements of her gender contestation, such as her cross-dressing, Jen struggles much more explicitly in the film with what is expected of her as a girl—should she be married by arrangement, should girls be allowed to learn Wutan, can she live the life she wants? Inflected as a quest for self-fulfilment rather than anything more spiritual or communal, Jen's dilemma comes closer to *Catwoman* than *Hero*.

Having fought herself into a frenzy, Jen has proven nothing but her own martial skill, which turns out to be rather unimportant, and everything begins to fall apart. The hero Li Mu-bai dies, declaring his love for Yu Shu-lien for the first time ever on his last breath; Shu-lien disappears and, despite her reunion with Lo, Jen throws herself off the mountain symbolising the martial code by which all the main characters define themselves. Melodrama is an emotional excess for its own sake. While it is always about the self, melodrama is so explicitly *not real* that it provides an outside to certain cultural standards; a reflection on the subject at the borders of cultural expectations in relation to which it is produced. The affective appeal of the martial actress in *Crouching Tiger*, as in *Hero*, may draw on an exotic Chineseness when sold in the US and an exotic feudal past when sold in China, but she is also beyond the experience of any audience member because of her melodramatic excess, and she shares this appeal as well as her fighting skills with the American superheroine. In both genres, the physical force of the woman who fights depends on her emotional investment and the investment of the audience in her motives and feelings rather than her spectacular skill.

Crouching Tiger was distributed in a climate much more familiar with martial arts genres than was *Enter the Dragon*, and itself provides new knowledge that helped popularise adaptations of Chinese martial arts genres such as the *Kill Bill* films.[14] The hero of Quentin Tarantino's *Kill Bill* (2003), who we eventually know as Beatrix, once belonged to a gang of female murderers, both American and Japanese.[15] Her violent soap-opera life is a much more graphic version of Catwoman's quest, with familiar weapons. Much of the plot draws directly on a set of precursor films, most notably *Lady Snowblood*, a *jidai geki* (Japanese period film) from the same year as *Enter the Dragon*, about another vengeful wounded female martial artist. Yuki's quest from *Lady Snowblood,* personified in O-Ren, battles it out with Li's quest from *Enter the Dragon*, symbolised in Lee's tracksuit from *Game of Death*. Despite its respect for the films it cites, *Kill Bill* is both orientalising and colonising. It deploys Asian martial arts cinema as a fascinating and eminently marketable exotica, occupying some of its precursor films in powerful ways that will take a long time to counter. Tarantino's films ignore the fact that Asian martial arts cinema is an ongoing history, not a closed archive of cult films to be mined for interesting retro pastiche and The Bride/Beatrix clearly transcends all her Asian martial arts reference points and sets them aside just as she defeats the less "hybridised" (and often Asian) martial artists around her.

In the context of this essay it is nevertheless significant that Jen, Shu-lien and Jade Fox from *Crouching Tiger,* and Beatrix and O-Ren from *Kill Bill*, are martial artists transformed into rather than using their bodies as weapons after the manner of superheroes; and in the case of Beatrix at least we already know we are in the middle of a series and that she cannot lose. Yet they are still not necessarily superheroines. That the superheroine also practices her martial arts with a melodramatic excess at the edge of cultural expectations about women is a more important similarity between these two films. It might be argued that *Kill Bill* makes a specific claim to realism foreign to most *wuxia* or superhero films because of its insistence on displaying bodily vulnerability. But the audience's suffering with Beatrix never falls back into bodily, at the expense of emotional, suffering. We suffer with Beatrix and O-Ren: we suffer their anger, fear, and emotional pain at a point of excess which is not measured in bodies, blood or even martial skill, but in the degree of attachment we are asked to have to their personal wounds.

The female martial artist may be at once the most gritty and the most accessible version of the female superhero precisely because even at her most magically inflected she is always a human mortal woman. While the martial artist is a product of training and technique, and a hero's "superpowers" are defined against what might be achieved by training or other ordinary forms of effort, in *wuxia* this line is not so clearcut and martial skill often has supernatural sources or reference points. The *wuxia* warrior's extraordinary power may be dependent in part on access to some magical weapon or mystical training or knowledge, but she perfects this as a mortal woman. While this is also true of Catwoman and Elektra, among other superheroines, this is because their own superheroism is expressed as martial artistry, as a mode of fighting which is accessible precisely because it is not dependent on Hollywood codes for masculine physical prowess. The female martial artist, like the superheroine, remains closely linked to a discourse on training the female embodied self in emotional as well as physical ways, rather than just being or using a weapon. While the melodrama of the female martial artist in recent films produced at the intersection of Hollywood and Chinese-language film cultures might thus keep the female martial artist attached to genres with apparently conservative relations to femininity, this is also, in fact, an element of their accessible (emotional) realism. However similar to the superheroine the female martial artist might be in her emotional intensity, and however significant the role of melodrama in communicating different modes of female heroism between cinema cultures, there are still some significant differences between these figures.

The girl heroines of recent Hollywood screen culture do not use martial arts styles with Asian origins for any reason of narrative convenience or for sheer visual spectacle. The superheroine has developed in relation to martial arts film genres, and particularly *wuxia* traditions, learning to fight from them, but they do not fight in the same way or for the same reasons or as the same embodiment of martial skill. The woman warrior of Chinese-language martial arts cinema has an overarching social commitment that frames any of her personal traumas and is restated in some way in all of her wounded violence. Despite her melodramatic intensity, the woman warrior of *wuxia* has a calling which articulates her personal wound as a wound to the community. In the superheroine such social commitment is only shadowy background. She is a fighter, and her skill rather than any social context remains pre-eminent.

Cinematographic, choreographic, and narrative strategies for depicting women who fight continue to be exchanged between Hollywood and Chinese-language cinemas across several genres, but the woman warrior's social cause is largely subsumed into the crafting of the superheroine's body. The superheroine is a different kind of technology of the body. This is not about skimpy, tight costumes, but rather describes the ways in which the superheroine's fighting skills are self-referentially about her body—she differs from other women primarily in being a physical force. Fighting is an art in *Hero*—a technology, like music or painting—but it is not proven by bodily strength or bodily weakness as much as by an attitude to the world instantiated in the face rather than the body. Unlike in the superheroine and other films centred on female martial artists who are fighters rather than warriors, like *Kill Bill*, there are no displays of muscular stomachs, straining thighs, or spectacular wounds amongst the women who fight in *Hero*. Instead the kung fu moves flow like the costumes, keeping pace with shifting colour schemes that frame the face and its changing character from scene to scene. In a superhero(ine) film only the techniques of the fight matter, because a superhero(ine) always wins; while in *wuxia pian* only the techniques of the fight matter because it is technique that articulates the justice of the hero's victory. The spectacular series of fight scenes in *Hero* are not pointless, but it is not any fight scene that resolves the drama and only the King as observer/victim/villain can make the social change that is necessary, outside the frame of the film.[16]

The movement of martial arts as a filmic practice between locations and historical trajectories cannot be summarised by post-colonial themes of orientalism, hybridity, or postmodernism. All of these are useful to considering the filmic forms in which the gendered practice of martial arts appear, but a preference for such binary markers of identity, location and belonging elides some of the historical exchanges between film cultures as fields of unevenly distributed but endlessly moving commodities to which we might pay attention. The figure of the martial actress is part of multiple ongoing histories, from which I have drawn two threads, that have learned from and indeed come to resemble one another in some important ways. We might see changing ideas about gender, and indeed its cultural location and reproduction, through the gendering of the woman who fights.

Notes

This essay is indebted to two very different friends: to Mark Mitchell, who taught me to respect comics, and to Auden Mikula, who helped me understand my own fascination with *wuxia pian*. For his Bruce Lee obsession, I am grateful to Peter Fuller; for producing images for the workshop, thanks to Morgan Howard; and for the workshop on "Women Willing to Fight" at the Australian National University, thanks to Ursula Frederick and Silke Andris.
1. Both "Chinese-language martial arts film" and "Hollywood film" are shorthands here. By the former I am referring to a changing set of film genres produced to the greatest commercial success in Hong Kong and, more recently, China, and by the latter I am

referring to mainstream film and television from the United States of America. Both terms, then, refer to tendencies and intensities rather than origins or absolute categories. This essay does not discuss female martial artists as they appear in Chinese-language film. Even films released in the same year, such as *House of Flying Daggers*, *Zatoichi* (remaking old martial arts classics), and *Silver Hawk* (a Chinese-language female superhero film), do not present the same display of fighting skills in relation to femininity and femaleness, or the same understandings of martial arts in terms of realism and social power.

2. The most recent bond film, *On Her Majesty's Secret Service* (1969) had starred George Lazenby as Bond. Lazenby was one of Lee's students and in fact took an uncredited role in Lee's next and final film, *Game of Death* (1978), which was being filmed when he died just before the release of *Enter the Dragon*.

3. Ien Ang, *Watching Dallas: Soap opera and the Melodramatic Imagination*, tr. Della Couling (London: Methuen, 1985).

4. As Hall has noted, *The Killer* is an important film for discussing cultural identity. Not only does it draw directly on Hollywood genres and images—Woo dedicated it to Martin Scorcese—it was successful in Western countries where Chinese-language films had been seen as exotic curiosities watched by audiences with special interest in martial arts. Stuart Hall, "Cultural identity and cinematic representation." *Framework*, 36, (1989).

5. *Catwoman* Website. http://pw2.netcom.com/~mwomack/

6. The now familiar catsuit was invented by the 1960s' TV series, and Catwoman appeared in the comics afterwards wearing a leotard and then a black catsuit in 1987, when she simultaneously received a new darker origin as an ex-prostitute (the suit is literally a dominatrix outfit). Ibid.

7. "Where Are They Now?" *TV Guide*, June 20, 2000. http://www.tvguide.com/ (accessed April 2005).

8. The 2004 film, however, offers Patience her costume ready-made—the mask is a gift and the tight pants and revealing leather top are a "dating emergency" outfit she has never worn.

9. On the small screen, variations on the superheroine have had some success, but the characteristics of the superheroine have also filtered through to supernatural and supernormal girls like Buffy in *Buffy the Vampire Slayer* and Sydney Bristow in *Alias*.

10. The kung fu-isation of Catwoman can be seen even more explicitly in Wonder Woman, the first female superhero, who had her mystical powers removed in order to be trained as a martial artist in the 1970s' series of the *Wonder Woman* comic.

11. Michel Foucault, "Technologies of the Self," in *Technologies of the Self: A Seminar with Michel Foucault*, ed. Luther Martin, et al (Amherst: University of Massachusetts Press, 1988).

12. Many critics use a hybridity model to explain "transnational" cinema. See, for example, Gina Marchetti, "Transnational Cinema, Hybrid Identities and the Films of Evans Chan." *Postmodern Culture* 8, no. 2 (1998), and Robert Stam and Ella Shohat, "Film Theory and Spectatorship in the Age of the 'Posts'", in *Reinventing Film Studies*, ed. Christine Gledhill and Linda Williams (London: Arnold, 2000), 383. It is indisputable perhaps that the economic flow of media and popular culture privileges some groups more than others so that, to quote Stam and Shohat, "even Third World airlines program

Hollywood suburban comedies as their idea of 'universal' fare'". More than economic flow matters, however, when talking about gender, the body, the self, society, all of which are involved in fighting, including on film. Although Stam and Shohat go on to qualify the "media imperalism" thesis, they remain dedicated to the distinction between global mass culture and local culture that allows "imported mass culture" to be "indigenised". Based on current discourses on Asian film and hybridity, it seems as if the new martial arts films coming out of Chinese-language cinema are simply nostalgic, feeding stereotypes about China to Chinese as well as foreign audiences. Any possible influence they have on US cinema would be as a field to be appropriated into a transnationally hybridised film.

13. With reference to the gossip over tea and the abortive declarations of love, William Leung claims that *Crouching Tiger, Hidden Dragon* is as influenced by Jane Austen, and Lee's experience of directing *Sense and Sensibility* (1995) as by *wuxia*.

14. Beyond the direct interactions between directors like Zhang Yimou, Ang Lee and Tarantino, there are many other production links between the films discussed here. Key actors and crew cross between Chinese-language and Hollywood films now, including *wuxia* fight choreographer Yuen Wo Ping, who had a spectacular return to prominence with *Once Upon a Time in China* (1991) and gained a new dimension of fame after being brought to work on first *The Matrix* (1999), and later *Kill Bill*, but in between these also *Crouching Tiger*.

15. This essay discusses *Kill Bill: Vol. 1*, although *Vol. 2*, which becomes a Western/action/thriller with a splice of *Kung Fu*-era television Chinese-ness, focuses more on the importation of martial arts cultures, even featuring the mythical heart punch that some fan conspiracy theories claim killed Bruce Lee. *Kill Bill: Vol. 1*, set partly in Japan, makes more explicit statements about the relation between American and Asian women as martial artists.

16. This outside is constituted by the audience's knowledge of a range of intersecting social fields, including state politics, transcultural commodity circulation, and residual, dominant and emerging gender norms. This point could be elaborated with reference to Raymond Williams' critique of "epochal analysis" *Marxism and Literature* (Oxford: Oxford University Press, 1977) and also Teresa De Lauretis' work on "The Technology of Gender" in *Technologies of Gender: Essays on Theory, Film and Fiction* (Bloomington: Indiana University Press, 1987).

BIBLIOGRAPHY

Affron, Charles, and Mirella Jona. *Sets in Motion: Art Direction and Film Narrative*. New Brunswick, New Jersey: Rutger University Press, 1995.

Anderson, Aaron. "Kinesthesia in Martial Arts Films: Action in Motion." *Jump Cut* 42, (December 1998), 1–11. Reprinted online *Jump Cut*, no. 48, (Winter 2006), http://www.ejumpcut.org/archive/onlinessays/JC42folder/anderson2/.

Andris, Silke. "On the Ropes: Gender Politics in the Boxing Movie." In *Visual Anthropology of Sport Films* (working title), edited by Peter Crawford, Denmark: Intervention Press (forthcoming).

Ang, Ien. "Melodramatic Identifications: Television Fiction and Women's Fantasy." In *Television and Women's Culture: The Politics of the Popular,* edited by Mary Ellen Brown, 75–88. London: Sage, 1990.

———. *Watching Dallas: Soap Opera and the Melodramatic Imagination*. Trans. Della Couling. London: Methuen, 1985.

"Army Lesbians Get Wed," *The Sun*, February 2, 2006.

Bakhtin, Mikhail. *Rabelais and His World*. Trans. Hélène Iswolsky. Bloomington: Indiana University Press, 1984.

Basinger, Jeanine. *The World War II Combat Film: Anatomy of a Genre*. New York: Columbia University Press, 1986.

Baudrillard, Jean. *Simulacra and Simulation*. Trans. Sheila Faria Glaser. Ann Arbor: The University of Michigan Press, 1994.

Baxter, Jane Eva. "Popular Images and Popular Stereotypes: Images of Archaeologists in Popular and Documentary Film," *The SAA Archaeological Record*, September (2002):16–17, 40.

Beale, Thomas, and Paul Healy. "Archaeological Films: The Past as Present." *American Anthropologist*, New Series 77, no. 4 (1975): 889–897.

Beebe, Roger Warren. "After Arnold." In *Meta-Morphing: Visual Transformation and the Culture of Quick-Change*, edited by Vivian Sobchack, 159–179. Minneapolis, London: University of Minnesota Press, 2000.

Bell-Metereau, Rebecca. "Woman: The Other Alien in *Alien*." In *Woman World Walkers*, edited by Jane B. Weedman, 9–24. Lubbock: Texas Tech Press, 1985.

Beltrán, Mary. "Más Macha: The New Latina Action Hero." In *Action and Adventure Cinema* edited by Yvonne Tasker, 186–201. London and New York, Routledge: 2004.

Bergan, Roland. *Sports in the Movies*. London and New York: Proteus Books, 1982.

Black, Daniel. "The Silicone Chick: Lara Croft and Sexy Technology," *Metro Magazine* 127/128, (Autumn/Winter 2001): 76–82.

Bolton, Christopher A., "From Wooden Cyborgs to Celluloid Souls: Mechanical Bodies in Anime and Japanese Puppet Theater." *Positions* 10, no.3 (2002): 729–71.

Bowman, James. "Pulp Garbage." *The American Spectator* 36, no.6 (Nov 2003): 5.

Bradshaw, Peter. "House of Flying Daggers", *The Guardian*, December 24, 2004. http://www.film.guardian.co.uk/News_Story/Critic_Reviews/Guardian_revie w/0,4267,1379290,00.html (accessed March 7, 2005).

Braidotti, Rosi. *Nomadic Subjects: Embodiment and Sexual Difference in Contemporary Feminist Theory*. New York: Columbia University Press, 1994.

Bren, Frank. "Fighting Women: Cheng Pei-pei (and King Hu Legacy)." *Metro* 113/114 (1998): 81–5.

Brody, Jennifer DeVere. "The Returns of *Cleopatra Jones*." *Signs: Journal of Women in Culture and Society* 25, no. 1 (Autumn 1999): 91–121.

Burke, Carol. *Camp All-American, Hanoi Jane, and the High-and-Tight: Gender, Folklore and Changing Military Culture*. Boston: Beacon Press, 2004.

Burrill, Derek Alexander. "Out of the Box: Performance, Drama and Interactive Software." *Modern Drama* 48, no. 3 (2005): 492–512.

Butler, Judith. "Athletic Genders: Hyperbolic Instance and/or the Overcoming of Sexual Binarism." *Stanford Electronic Humanities Review* 6, no. 2 (1998), http://www.stanford.edu./group/SHR/6-2/html/butler.html (accessed May 5, 2005).

———. *Bodies that Matter: On the Discursive Limits of "Sex"*. New York and London: Routledge, 1993.

Campbell, Joseph. *The Hero With A Thousand Faces*. London: Fontana Press, 1993.

Caputi, Jane. *Goddesses and Monsters: Women, Myth, Power, and Popular Culture*. Madison,WN: Popular Press, 2004.

Carr, Diane. "Playing with Lara." In *ScreenPlay: cinema/videogames/interfaces*, edited by Geoff King and Tanya Krzywinska, 171–180. London: Wallflower, 2002.

Chamberlin. James. "The Magic of Risking Everything for a Dream Nobody Sees: *Million Dollar Baby*: The Shadow Film." *Senses of Cinema* 2005, http://www.sensesofcinema.com/contents/05/35/ million_dollar_baby.html (accessed June 2006).

Chan, Felicia. "Crouching Tiger, Hidden Dragon: Cultural Migrancy and Translatability." In *Chinese Films in Focus: 25 New Takes*, edited by Chris Berry, 56–64. London: British Film Institute, 2003.

Chedgzoy, Kate. Impudent Women: Carnival and gender in early modern culture. http://www.arts.gla.ac.uk/SESLI/STELLA/COMET/glasgrev/issue1/chefgz. htm (accessed Oct 2005).

Chute, David, and Cheng-sim Lim, eds. *Heroic Grace: The Chinese Martial Arts Film.* Los Angeles: UCLA, 2003.

Clover, Carol. *Men, Women and Chain Saws: Gender in the Modern Horror Film.* Princeton: Princeton University Press, 1992.

Collins, Jim, Hilary Radner and Ava Preacher Collins. *Film Theory Goes to the Movies.* London: Routledge, 1993.

Courtney, Susan. "Looking for (Race and Gender) Trouble in Monument Valley." *Qui Parle* 6, no.2 (1993): 97–130.

Creed, Barbara. "Lesbian Bodies: Tribades, Tomboys and Tarts." In *Sexy Bodies: the strange carnalities of feminism*, edited by Elizabeth Grosz and Elspeth Probyn, 86–103. London: Routledge, 1995.

———. *The Monstrous Feminine: Film, Feminism, Psychoanalysis.* London and New York: Routledge, 1993.

———. *Phallic Panic. Film, Horror and the Primal Uncanny.* Melbourne: Melbourne University Press, 2005.

Creekmur, Corey. "Acting Like a Man: Masculine Performance in *My Darling Clementine.*" In *Out in Culture*, edited by Corey K. Creekmur and Alexander Doty, 167–82. London: Duke University Press, 1995.

Daly, Pierrette. *Heroic Tropes, Gender and Intertext.* Detroit: Wayne State University Press, 1993.

Davis, Natalie Zemon. "Women on Top." In *Society and Culture in Early Modern France*, Stanford: Stanford University Press, 1975: 124–151.

De Lauretis, Teresa. *Alice Doesn't: Feminism, Semiotics, Cinema.* Bloomington: Indiana University Press, 1984.

———. *Technologies of Gender: Essays on Theory, Film and Fiction.* Bloomington: Indiana University Press, 1987.

Doane, Mary Ann. *Femmes Fatales: Feminism, Film Theory, Psychoanalysis.* New York: Routledge, 1991.

Dominguez, Diana. "'It's Not So Easy Being A Cast Iron Bitch': Sexual Difference and the Female Action Hero." *Reconstruction* 5, no. 4 (Fall, 2005): 1–24.

Douglas, Mary. *Natural Symbols.* Middlesex: Penguin Books, 1970.

Eckstein, Arthur M., "After the Rescue: *The Searchers*, the Audience and *Prime Cut* (1972)." *Journal of Popular Culture* 28, no. 3 (1994): 33–53.

Edwards, Marlo. "The Blonde with the Guns: 'Barb Wire' and the 'Implausible' Female Action Hero." *Journal of Popular Film and Television* 32, no. 1 (2004): 39–47.

Ebert, Roger. "I Spit on Your Grave." (1980). http://rogerebert.suntimes.com/apps/pbcs.dll/article?AID=/19800716/REVIEWS/7160301/1023.

Emad, Mitra C. "Reading Wonder Woman's Body: Mythologies of Gender and Nation," *The Journal of Popular Culture* 39, no. 6 (2006) 954–984.

Enloe, Cynthia. *Maneuvers: The International Politics of Militarizing Women's Lives*. Berkeley: California University Press, 2000.

Evans, Peter William. "Westward the Women: Feminising the Wilderness." In *The Movie Book of the Western,* edited by Ian Cameron and Douglas Pye, 206–13. London: Studio Vista, 1996.

Fitzpatrick, Kathleen. "The Exhaustion of Literature: Novels, Computers, and the Threat of Obsolescence." *Contemporary Literature* 43, no.3 (2002): 518–19.

Foucault, Michel. "Technologies of the Self." In *Technologies of the Self: A Seminar with Michel Foucault*, edited by Luther Martin et al., 16–49. Amherst: University of Massachusetts Press, 1988.

Gamble, Sarah. "Postfeminism," In *The Icon Critical Dictionary of Feminism and Postfeminism*, edited by Sarah Gamble, 43–54. Cambridge: Icon Books, 1999.

Garber, Marjorie. *Vested Interests: Cross-Dressing and Cultural Anxiety*. London: Penguin, 1992.

Gleiberman, Owen. "Slay Anything." *Entertainment Weekly* 733, October 17, 2003, 57.

Gomes, Catherine. "Crouching Tiger, Hidden Genre: An Investigation into Western Film Criticism's Reading of Feminism in Ang Lee's *Crouching Tiger, Hidden Dragon*," *Limina* 11 (2005), http://www.limina.arts.uwa.edu.au/current_volume?f=79246 (accessed February 8, 2006).

Grieb, Margrit. "Run Lara Run." In *Screenplay: cinema/videogames/interfaces*, edited by Geoff King and Tanya Krzywinska, 157–70, London and New York: Wallflower Press, 2002.

Grig, Lucy. *Making Martyrs in Late Antiquity*. London: Duckworth, 2004.

Grosz, Elizabeth. *Volatile Bodies: Toward a Corporeal Feminism*. St Leonards, NSW: Allen & Unwin, 1994.

Hall, Ann M., *Feminism and Sporting Bodies: Essays on Theory and Practice*. Champaign, IL: Human Kinetics, 1996.

Hall, Stuart. "Cultural Identity and Cinematic Representation." *Framework* 36 (1989).

Haraway, Donna. "A Cyborg Manifesto: Science, Technology, and Socialist-Feminism in the Late Twentieth Century." In *Simians, Cyborgs and Women: The Reinvention of Nature,* 149-181. New York: Routledge, 1991.

Hargreaves, Jennifer. "Bruising Peg to Boxerobics: Gendered Boxing – Images and Meaning." In *Boxer: An Anthology of Writings on Boxing and Visual Culture,* edited by David Chandler, 121–131. London: Institute of International Visual Arts, 1996.

Hart, Claudia and Claudia Herbst, "Virtual Sex: The Female Body in Digital Art." *Bad Subjects* 72, (February 2005)
http://bad.eserver.org/issues/2005/72/hartherbst.html

Haskell, Molly. *From Reverence to Rape: Treatment of Women in the Movies.* Middlesex, England: Penguin, 1979.

Heywood, Leslie, and Shari L. Dworkin. *Built To Win: The Female Athlete as Cultural Icon.* Minneapolis, MN: University of Minnesota Press, 2003.

Hills, Elizabeth. "From 'Figurative Males' to Action Heroines: Further Thoughts on Active Women in the Cinema," *Screen* 40, no. 1 (Spring 1999): 38–51.

Ho, Sam. "From Page to Screen: A Brief History of *Wuxia* Fiction." In *Heroic Grace: The Chinese Martial Arts Film,* edited by David Chute and Cheng-sim Lim, 13–16. Los Angeles: UCLA, 2003.

Holtorf, Cornelius. *From Stonehenge to Las Vegas: Archaeology as Popular Culture.* Walnut Creek, CA.: Altamira Press, 2005.

Hong, Fan. *Footbinding, Feminism and Freedom: The Liberation of Women's Bodies in Modern China.* London and Portland: Frank Cass, 1997.

Hunt, Leon. *Kung Fu Cult Masters: From Bruce Lee to Crouching Tiger.* London: Wallflower Press, 2003.

Inness, Sherrie A., ed. *Action Chicks: New Images of Tough Women in Popular Culture.* New York: Palgrave Macmillan, 2004.

Izod, John, and Joanna Dovalis. "*Million Dollar Baby*: Boxing Grief," *Kinema,* (Fall 2005), http://www.kinema.uwaterloo.ca/izod052.htm (accessed 16 May 2006).

Jacobs, Lewis. *The Rise of the American Film: A Critical History.* New York: Teachers' College Press, 1969.

Jeffords, Susan. *Hard Bodies: Hollywood Masculinity in the Reagan Era.* New Brunswick: Rutgers University Press, 1994.

———. "Performative Masculinities, or, 'After a Few Times You Won't Be Afraid of Rape at All.'" *Discourse* 13, no. 2 (1991): 102–18.

Jennings, Ros. "Desire and Design: Ripley Undressed." In *Immortal/Invisible: Lesbians and the Moving Image*, edited by Tamsin Wilton, 193–206. London: Routledge, 1995.

Kane, Bob (cre.) *Batman*. New York: DC Comics. 1940–.

———. (cre.) *The Secret Life of Catwoman*. New York: DC Comics. 1951.

Kar, Law, and Frank Bren. *Hong Kong Cinema: A Cross-Cultural View*. Lanham, Maryland: Scarecrow Press, 2004.

Kennedy, Helen W. "Lara Croft: Feminist Icon or Cyberbimbo? On the Limits of Textual Analysis," *Game Studies* 2, no.2 (December 2002) http://www.gamestudies.org/0202/kennedy/.

King, Geoff, and Tanya Krzywinska. "Introduction." In *Screenplay: cinema/videogames/interfaces*, edited by Geoff King and Tanya Krzywinska, 1–32, London and New York: Wallflower Press, 2002.

King, Thomas F. "Preservation and Rescue." *Journal of Field Archaeology* 8, no.4 (Winter 1981): 505–9.

Kingston, Maxine Hong. *The Woman Warrior: Memoirs of a Girlhood Among Ghosts*. London: Picador, 1977.

Kirkham, Pay, and Janet Thumin, eds. *Me Jane: Masculinity, Movies and Women*. London: Lawrence & Wishart, 1995.

Ko, Andrew. "And then I saw her face... *Lara Croft: Tomb Raider* (review)." *Metro Magazine* 129/130 (2001): 212–5.

Kristeva, Julia. *Powers of Horror: an essay on abjection*. Translated by Leon S. Roudiez. New York: Columbia University Press, 1982.

Krutnik, Frank. *In a Lonely Street: Film Noir, Genre, Masculinity*. London: Routledge, 1991.

Kuni, Verena. "Cyborg configurations as formations of (self-)creation in the fantasy space of technological creation: Old and new mythologies of <artificial humans>," in *Mythical Bodies I*, http://www.medienkunstnetz.de/themes/ cyborg_bodies/mythical_bodies_I/. (accessed October 7, 2005).

Lehman, Peter. "Texas, 1868/America, 1956: *The Searchers*." In *Close Viewings: An Anthology of New Film Criticism*, edited by Peter Lehman, 387–415. Tallahassee: University of Florida Press, 1990.

———. "'Don't Blame this on a Girl': Female Rape-revenge Films." In *Screening the Male: Exploring Masculinities in Hollywood Cinema*, edited by Steven Cohan and Ina Rae Hark, 103–117. London and New York: Routledge, 1993.

Leung, William. "Crouching Sensibility, Hidden Sense." *Film Criticism* 26, no. 1 (2001): 42–57.

Liu, James J. Y., *The Chinese Knight-errant*. Chicago: University of Chicago Press, 1967.

Lo, Kwai-cheung. *Chinese Face-Off: The Transnational Popular Culture of Hong Kong*. Urbana and Chicago: University of Illinois Press, 2005.

Maaskant-Kleibrink, Marianne. "Nymphomania." In *Sexual Asymmetry: Studies in Ancient Society,* edited by Josine Block and Peter Mason, 275–297. Amsterdam: J.C.Gleiben, 1987.

Mace, Nancy, and Mary Jane Ross. *In the Company of Men: A Woman at the Citadel*. New York: Simon & Schuster, 2001.

McCaughey, Martha and Neal King (eds) *Reel Knockouts:Violent Women in the Movies*. Austin, TX: The University of Texas Press, 2001.

McGee, Patrick. *From Shane to Kill Bill: Rethinking the Western*. Oxford: Blackwell, 2006.

McKinney, Devin. "Violence: The Strong and the Weak." 1993. In *Screening Violence*, edited by Stephen Prince, 99–109. New Brunswick: Rutgers University Press, 2000.

McRobbie, Angela. "Post-feminism and Popular Culture." *Feminist Media Studies* 4, no. 3 (2004): 255–264.

Magoulick, Mary. "Frustrating Female Heroism: Mixed Messages in *Xena, Nikita*, and *Buffy*." *The Journal of Popular Culture* 39, no. 5 (2006): 729–755.

Marchetti, Gina. "Transnational Cinema, Hybrid Identities and the Films of Evans Chan." *Postmodern Culture* 8, no. 2 (1998).

Mathieu, James R. "Time Travel, Trebuchets, and Atlatls," *science & archaeology* 45, no. 3: 6–7.

Meltzer, Françoise. "Joan of Arc in America." *Substance* 100, 31, no. 1 (2003): 90–9.

Mikula, Maja. "Gender and Videogames: the political valency of Lara Croft." *Continuum: Journal of Media & Cultural Studies* 17, no. 1 (2003): 79–87.

Mile, Siân. "Roseanne Barr: Canned Laughter–Containing the Subject." In *New Perspectives on Women and Comed,* edited by Regina Barecca, Amsterdam: OPA, 1992.

Mitchell, Lee Clark. "Violence in the American Western." In *Violence and American Cinema*, edited by David Slocum, 176–91. London: Routledge 2001.

Mitchell, Mark R., "Rethinking the Funnybook." Honours thesis, University of Adelaide, 2001.

Mizejewski, Linda. *Hardboiled & High Heeled: The Woman Detective in Popular Culture*. New York: Routledge, 2004.

Modleski, Tania. "Million Dollar Baby: A Split Decision." *Cineast* 30, no. 3 (Summer 2005): 11.

Moulton, Charles (cre.) *Wonder Woman*. New York: DC Comics. 1940—.

Mulvey, Laura. *Visual and Other Pleasures*. Bloomington : Indiana University, 1989.

Neale, Steve. "Action Adventure as Hollywood Genre." In *Action and Adventure Cinema*, edited by Yvonne Tasker, 71–83. London: Routledge, 2004.

———. "Masculinity as Spectacle." In *Screening the Male*, edited by Steven Cohen and Ina Rae Hark, 9–20. London: Routledge, 1993.

Neroni, Hilary. *The Violent Woman: Femininity, Narrative, and Violence in Contemporary American Cinema*. Albany: State University of New York Press, 2005.

Oates, Joyce Carol. *On Boxing*. London and New York: Routledge, 1987.

O'Day, Marc. "Beauty in Motion: Gender, Spectacle and Action Babe Cinema." In *Action and Adventure Cinema*, edited by Yvonne Tasker, 201–18. London and New York: Routledge, 2004.

Palmer, Jerry. *The Logic of the Absurd:On film and television comedy*. London: BFI, 1987.

Palmer, Augusta Lee, and Jenny Kwok Wah Lau. "Of Executioners and Courtesans: The Performance of Gender in Hong Kong Cinema of the 1990s." In *Multiple Modernities: Cinemas and Popular Media in Transcultural East Asia*, edited by Jenny Kwok Wah Lau, Philadelphia: Temple University Press, 2003.

Polsky, Allyson D. "Skins, Patches, and Plug-ins: Becoming Woman in the New Gaming Culture" *Genders* 34 (2001) http://www.genders.org/g34/g34_polsky.html (accessed October 6, 2005)

Pomeroy, Sarah B. *Goddesses, Whores, Wives and Slaves: Women in Classical Antiquity*. New York: Schocken Books, 1976.

Pumphrey, Martin. "Why Do Cowboys Wear Hats in the Bath?: Style Politics for the Older Man." In *The Movie Book of the Western*, edited by Ian Cameron and Douglas Pye, 50–62. London: Studio Vista, 1996.

Pyle, Forest. "Making Cyborgs, Making Humans: Of Terminators and Blade Runners." In *Film Theory Goes to the Movies*, edited by Jim Collins, Hilary Radner and Ava Preacher Collins, New York and London: Routledge, 1993.

Rappaport, Mark. "I, Jean Seberg." *Film Quarterly* 55, no.1 (Fall 2001): 2–13.

Reynaud, Berenice. "Gong Li and the Glamour of the Chinese Star." *Sight and Sound* 3, no. 8 (1993): 12–15.

———. "The Book, the Goddess and the Hero: Sexual Politics in the Chinese Martial Arts Film," *Senses of Cinema* 26, (2003), http://www.sensesofcinema.com/contents/03/26/sexual_politics_chinese_martial_arts.html (accessed February 16, 2006).

Rose, Mark. "Excavating with Bullets (review)," *Archaeology,* June 14, 2001. http://www.archaeology.org/online/reviews/tombraider/movie.html

Sabin, Roger. *Comics, Comix & Graphic Novels: A History Of Comic Art.* London: Phaidon Press, 1996.

Schleiner, Anne Marie. "Does Lara Croft Wear Fake Polygons? Gender Analysis of the '3rd Person Shooter/adventure Game with Female Heroine' and Gender Role Subversion in the Game Patch." *Leonardo/The International Society for the Arts, Sciences and Technology* 34, no. 3: 221–6.

Seno, Alexandra. "Lights, Camera - Tourists!" *AsiaWeek.com* 27 no. 8, March 2, 2001, http://www.asiaweek.com/asiaweek/magazine/nations/0,8782,100229,00.ht ml

Singer, Ben. "Female Power in the Serial-Queen Melodrama: The Etiology of an Anomaly," [1990] In *Silent Film*, edited by Richard Abel, 163–194, New Brunswick & New Jersey: Rutgers University Press, 1996.

Smith, Gavin. "Quentin Tarantino." *Film Comment* 30, no. 4 (July 1994): 33.

Stam, Robert, and Ella Shohat. "Film Theory and Spectatorship in the Age of the 'Posts'." In *Reinventing Film Studies*, edited by Christine Gledhill and Linda Williams, 381–401. London: Arnold, 2000.

Stephens, Chuck. 'The Whole Shebang.' *Film Comment* 40, no. 4 (July/August 2004): 46.

Streible, Dan. "A History of the Boxing Film, 1894-1915: Social Control and Social Reform in the Progressive Era." *Film History* 3, no. 3 (1989): 235–57.

Studlar, Gaylyn. "What Would Martha Want? Captivity, Purity and Feminine Values in *The Searchers*." In *The Searchers: Essays and Reflections on John Ford's Classic Western*, edited by Arthur M. Eckstein and Peter Lehman, 171–96. Detroit: Wayne State University Press, 2004.

Tasker, Yvonne. "Cowgirl Tales." In *Genre, Gender, Race and World Cinema: An Anthology,* edited by Julie F. Codell, 195–221. Oxford: Blackwell, 2006.

———. "Fantasizing Gender and Race: Women in Contemporary US Action Cinema." In *Contemporary Hollywood Cinema,* edited by Michael Hammond and Linda Ruth Williams, 410–28. London: McGraw Hill, 2006.

———. *Soldiers Stories: Military Women in Cinema and Television Since WWII.* Durham: Duke University Press (forthcoming).

———. "Soldiers' Stories: Women and Military Masculinities in *Courage Under Fire*." *Quarterly Journal of Film and Video* 19, no.3 (2002): 209–22.

———. *Spectacular Bodies. Gender, Genre and the Action Cinema.* London and New York: Routledge, 1993.

———. *Working Girls: Gender and Sexuality in Popular Cinema.* London and New York: Routledge, 1996.

Tasker, Yvonne, and Diane Negra, eds. *Interrogating Postfeminism: Gender and the Politics of Popular Culture.* Durham: Duke University Press, 2007 (forthcoming).

Taubin, Amy. "Invading Bodies: *Alien 3* and the Trilogy." *Sight & Sound* (July 1992): 8–12.

Taylor, Charles. "The Missing (review)," 2003, http://dir.salon.com/story/ent/movies/review/2003/11/26/missing/index.html (accessed October 13, 2006).

Teo, Stephen. "*Crouching Tiger, Hidden Dragon*–Passing Fad or Global Phenomenon?" In *Heroic Grace: The Chinese Martial Arts Film,* edited by David Chute and Cheng-sim Lim, 23–26. Los Angeles: UCLA, 2003.

Thomson, David. "The Last Frontier." *Sight and Sound* 14, no.2, n.s., (2004): 12–15.

Toole, F.X., *Rope Burns: Stories from the Corner.* New York: Ecco Press, 2000.

Turkle, Sherry. "Cyborg Babies and Cy-Dough-Plasm: Ideas about Life in the Culture of Simulation." In *Cyborg Babies: From Technosex to Technotots,* edited by Robbie Davis-Floyd and Joseph Dumit, 317–329. New York: Routledge, 1998.

Udovitch, Mim. "Quentin Tarantino's Girlfights; [Interview]." *New York Times,* October 5, 2003, 2, late edition East Coast.

Unknown Author. "Come Drink with Me." *Southern Screen* 96 (1966): 77–81.

Vogler, Christopher. *The Writer's Journey: Mythic Structure for Storytellers and Screenwriters.* London: Pan Books, 1998.

Walters, Ben. "*The Missing* (review)" *Sight and Sound* 14, no.3, n.s., (2004): 50.

Walton, Saige. "Showcasing the Spectacular." *Metro Magazine* 134, (2002): 234–9.

Warner, Marina. *Joan of Arc: The Image of Female Heroism.* New York: Vintage Books, 1981.

Warshow, Robert. "Movie Chronicle: The Westerner." In *Film Theory and Criticism: Fifth Edition*, edited by Leo Braudy and Marshall Cohen, 654–67. Oxford: Oxford University Press, 1999.

Weaver, David. "The Narrative of Alienation: Martin Scorsese's *Taxi Driver*." *Cine-Action*, (Summer/Fall 1986): 12–16.

Weinstock, Laura. "*Miss Congeniality* directed by Donald Petrie. Starring and Produced by Sandra Bullock. A Must-See. Funny, irreverent, feminist." *Feminist Filmtakes* 2001, http://www.awakenedwoman.com/filmtakes7.htm (accessed December 7, 2005).

Wheelwright, Julie. *The Fatal Lover: Mata Hari and the Myth of Women in Espionage.* Vermont, USA: Trafalgar Square, 1993.

Williams, Linda Ruth. "Film Bodies: Gender, Genre and Excess." In *Feminist Film Theory: A Reader*, edited by Sue Thornham, 268–69. Edinburgh: Edinburgh University Press, 1999.

————. "Ready for Action: *G.I. Jane,* Demi Moore's body and the female combat movie." In *Action and Adventure Cinema,* edited by Yvonne Tasker, 169–85. London, Routledge: 2004.

Williams, Raymond. *Marxism and Literature.* Oxford: Oxford University Press, 1977.

Wilson, Eric. *The Melancholy Android: On the Psychology of Sacred Machines.* Albany: State University of New York Press, 2006.

Zhang, Zhen. "The 'Rice Bowl of Youth' in Fin de Siècle Urban China." In *Globalization,* edited by Arjun Appadurai, 131–54. Durham and London: Duke University Press, 2003.

Websites

Catwoman website, http://pw2.netcom.com/~mwomack/ (accessed March 2005).

"Where Are They Now?" *TV Guide,* June 20, 2000. http://www.tvguide.com/ (accessed April 2005).

Miss America, http://www.missamerica.org/competition-info/become-a-contestant.asp (accessed December 16, 2005).

Miss Congeniality, http://miss-congeniality.warnerbros.co.uk (accessed December 17, 2005).

Miss Earth, http://www.missearth.tv/

Miss International, http://www.miss-international.org/

Miss Universe, http://www.missuniverse.com/index2.html

Miss World, http://www.missworld.tv/

Planet Lara, http://www.planetlara.com

FILMOGRAPHY

A Touch of Zen/Hsia Nu (1969) King Hu, Taiwan.
A League of Their Own (1992) Penny Marshall, USA.
A Town Like Alice (1956) Jack Lee, UK.
A Question of Silence (1982) Marleen Gorris, Netherlands.
Abbott and Costello Meet the Mummy (1955) Charles Lamont, USA.
Adam's Rib (1949) George Cukor, USA.
Aeon Flux (2005) Karen Kusama, USA.
Alien (1979) Ridley Scott, USA.
Aliens (1986) James Cameron, USA.
Alien³ (1992) David Fincher, USA.
Alien Resurrection (1997) Jean-Pierre Jeunet, USA.
Allan Quatermain and the Lost City of Gold (1987) Gary Nelson, USA.
All the Pretty Horses (2000) Billy Bob Thornton, USA.
American Outlaws (2001) Les Mayfield, USA.
Ancient Evil: Scream of the Mummy (2000) David DeCoteau, USA.
Attack of the Mayan Mummy (1963) Rafael Lopez Portillo, Jerry Warren, Mexico/USA.
Bad Girls (1994) Jonathan Kaplan, USA.
Baise-Moi (2000) Virginie Despentes, France.
Basic (2003) John McTiernan, USA/Germany.
Batman (1989) Tim Burton, USA/UK.
Batman Returns (1992) Tim Burton, USA/UK.
Batman Begins (2005) Christopher Nolan, USA.
Ben Hur (1959) William Wyler, USA.
Betrayed (1988) Costa-Gavras, USA/Japan.
Beyond the Forest (1949) King Vidor, USA.
Black Cat (1991) Stephen Shin, Hong Kong.
Black Widow (1987). Bob Rafelson, USA.
Blade Runner (1982) Ridley Scott, USA.
Blonde Venus (1932) Josef von Sternberg, USA.
Blood From the Mummy's Tomb (1971) Michael Carreras, Seth Holt, UK.
*Blue Steel (*1990) Kathryn Bigelow, USA.
Blue Velvet (1986) David Lynch, USA.
Bodily Harm (1995) James Lemmo, USA.
Body and Soul (1947) Robert Rossen, USA.
Body and Soul (1981) Lawrence Kasdan, USA.
Boys Don't Cry (1999) Kimberly Peirce, USA.

Brokeback Mountain (2005) Ang Lee, USA.
Calamity Jane (1953) David Butler, USA.
Camille (1936) George Cukor, USA.
Carve Her Name with Pride (1958) Lewis Gilbert, UK.
Catwoman (2004) Pitof, USA.
Chambers of Shaolin/Shao Lin San Shi Liu Fang (1978) Chia-Liang Liu, Hong
    Kong.
Charlie's Angels (2000) McG, USA/Germany.
Charlie's Angels: Full Throttle (2003), McG, USA.
Charlotte Gray (2001) Gillian Armstrong, UK/Australia/Germany.
Chinatown (1974) Roman Polanski, USA.
Cleopatra (1973) Jack Starrett, USA.
Cleopatra Jones and the Casino of Gold (1975) Chick Bail, Hong Kong/USA.
Come Drink With Me/Da Zui Xia (1966) King Hu, Hong Kong.
Copycat (1995) Jon Amiel, USA.
Courage Under Fire (1996) Edward Zwick, USA.
Crouching Tiger, Hidden Dragon/Wo Hu Cang Long (2000) Ang Lee,
    Taiwan/Hong Kong/USA/China.
Dances With Wolves (1990) Kevin Costner, USA.
Dark Victory (1939) Edmund Goulding, USA.
Desert Hearts (1985) Donna Deitch, USA.
Dirty Harry (1971) Don Siegel, USA.
Disclosure (1994) Barry Levinson, USA.
Dishonoured (1931) Josef von Sternberg, USA.
Double Indemnity (1944) Billy Wilder, USA.
Duel in the Sun (1946) King Vidor, USA.
Dr. No (1962) Terence Young, UK.
Dragon Swamp/Du Long Tan (1969) Wei Lo, Hong Kong.
Elektra (2005) Rob Bowman, USA.
Enter the Dragon (1973) Robert Clouse, Hong Kong/USA.
Erin Brockovich (2000) Steven Soderbergh, USA.
Executioners from Shaolin/Hung His-Kuan (1976) Chia-Liang Liu, Hong Kong.
Fantastic Four (2005) Tim Story, USA/Germany.
Far From Heaven (2002) Todd Haynes, France/USA.
Fargo (1996) Joel Coen, UK/USA.
Fat City (1972) John Houston, USA.
Fatal Beauty (1987) Tom Holland, USA/Japan.
From Here to Eternity (1953) Fred Zinnemann, USA.
Game of Death/So Wang You Ju (1978) Robert Clouse, Hong Kong/USA.
Germany Pale Mother/Deutschland Bleiche Mutter (1980) Helma Sanders-
    Brahms, West Germany.

Gorillas in the Mist (1988) Michael Apted, USA.
G.I. Jane (1997) Ridley Scott, USA.
Gilda (1946) Charles Vidor, USA.
Girlfight (2000) Karyn Kusama, USA.
Hero/Ying Xiong (2002) Yimou Zhang, Hong Kong/China.
House of Flying Daggers/Shi Mian Mai Fu (2004) Yimou Zangh, China/Hong Kong.
Humoresque (1946) Jean Negulesco, USA.
I Spit on Your Grave (1978) Meir Zarchi, USA.
In the Cut (2003) Jean Campion, Asutralia, USA/UK.
Indiana Jones and the Last Crusade (1989) Steven Spielberg, USA.
Indiana Jones and the Temple of Doom (1984) Steven Spielberg, USA.
Impulse (1990) Sondra Locke, USA.
It's My Life: My Life to Live/ Vivre Sa Vie (1962) Jean Luc Godard, France.
Jean at the Stake/Giovanna d'Arco al Rogo (1954) Roberto Rossellini, Italy/France.
Joan of Arc (1948) Victor Fleming, USA.
Johnny Guitar (1954) Nicholas Ray, USA.
Ju Dou (1989) Fengliang Yang and Yimou Zangh, Japan/China.
Kid Galahad (1937) Michael Curtiz, USA.
Kill Bill: Vol. 1 (2003) Quentin Tarantino, USA.
Kill Bill: Vol. 2 (2004) Quentin Tarantino, USA.
King Solomon's Mines (1985) J. Lee Thompson, USA.
King Solomon's Mines (2004) (TV) Steve Boyum, USA.
Klute (1971) Alan J. Paluka, USA.
Keep Your Powder Dry (1945) Edward Buzzell, USA.
La Jetée (1962) Chris Marker, France.
Lady from Shanghai (1948) Orson Welles, USA.
Lady Snowblood/Shurayukihime (1973) Toshiya Fujita, Japan.
La femme Nikita/ Nikita (1990) Luc Besson, France/Italy.
La Passion de Jeanne d'Arc (1928) Carl Dreyer, France.
Lara Croft: Tomb Raider (2001), Simon West, UK/Germany/USA/Japan.
Lara Croft Tomb Raider: The Cradle of Life (2003) Jan de Bont, USA/Germany/Japan/UK/Netherlands.
Lipstick (1976) Lamont Johnson, USA.
Magnum Force (1973) Ted Post, USA.
Mare Nostrum (1926) Rex Ingram, USA.
Mata Hari (1985) Curtis Harrington, USA.
Marnie (1964) Alfred Hitchcock, USA.
Memoirs of a Geisha (2005) Rob Marshall, USA.
Metropolis (1927) Fritz Lang, Germany.

Mildred Pierce (1945) Michael Curtis, USA.

Million Dollar Baby (2004) Clint Eastwood, USA.

Miss Congeniality (2000) Donald Petrie, USA.

Miss Congeniality 2: Armed and Fabulous (2005) John Pasquin, USA.

Monster (2003) Patty Jenkins, USA/Germany.

Mulholland Dr. (2001) David Lynch, France, USA.

My Brilliant Career (1979) Gillian Armstrong, Australia.

My Darling Clementine (1946) John Ford, USA.

Nancy Drew–Detective (1938) William B. Clemes and John Langan, USA.

Nancy Drew, Reporter (1939) William B. Clemes and John Langan, USA.

Nancy Drew, Trouble Shooter (1939) William B. Clemes, USA.

Nancy Drew and the Hidden Staircase (1939) William B. Clemes, USA.

National Treasure (2004) Jon Turteltaub, USA.

Norma Rae (1979) Martin Ritt, USA.

North Country (2005) Niki Caro, USA.

November Moon/Novembermond (1984) Alexandra von Grote, West Germany/France.

Now Voyager (1942) Irving Rapper, USA.

Odette (1950) Herbert Wilcox, UK.

Once Upon a Time in China/Wong Fei Hung (1991) Tsui Hark, Hong Kong.

Once Upon a Time in the West/C'era Una Volta Il West (1968) Sergio Leone, Italy/USA.

On Her Majesty's Secret Service (1969) Peter Hunt, UK.

On The Waterfront (1954) Elia Kazan, USA.

Open Range (2003) Kevin Costner, USA.

Out of Sight (1998) Steven Soderbergh, USA.

Plenty (1985) Fred Schepisi, UK/USA.

Point of no Return (1993) John Badham, USA.

Portrait of a Lady (1996) Jane Campion, UK/USA.

Pretty Woman (1990) Garry Marshall, USA.

Private Benjamin (1980) Howard Zieff, USA.

Pumping Iron II: The Women (1985) Georg Butler, USA.

Raiders of the Lost Ark (1981) Steven Spielberg, USA.

Raise the Red Latern/Da Hong Deng Long Gao Gao Gua (1991) Yimou Zangh, China/Hong Kong/Taiwan.

Raging Bull (1980) Martin Scorsese, USA.

Rebecca (1940) Alfred Hitchcock, USA.

Red Heroine/Hong Xia (1929) Zimin Wen, China.

Robin Hood (1922) Alan Dwan, USA.

Rocky (1976) John G. Avildsen, USA.

Rocky II (1979) Sylvester Stallone, USA.

Romance (1999), Catherine Breillat, France.
Run, Lola, Run/Lola Rennt (1998) Tom Tykwer, Germany.
Rush Hour 2 (2001) Bret Ratner, USA.
Sahara (2005) Breck Eisner, UK/Spain/Germany/USA.
Saint Joan (1957) Otto Preminger, USA.
Sense and Sensibility (1995) Ang Lee, UK/USA.
Serenity (2004) Joss Whedon, USA.
Serial Killer (1995) Pierre David, Canada/USA.
Shane (1953) George Stevens, USA.
Shanghai Noon (2000) Tom Dey, USA.
She (1965) Robert Day, UK.
Sheba, Baby (1975) William Girdler, USA.
Silence of the Lambs (1991) Johnatan Demme, USA.
Silkwood (1983) Mike Nichols, USA.
Silver Hawk/Fei Ying (2004) Jingle Ma, Hong Kong.
Six-Fingered Lord of the Lute/Liu Zhi Qin Mo (1965) Lipin Chen, Hong Kong.
Somebody Up There Likes Me (1956) Robert Wise, USA.
Spartacus (1961) Stanley Kubrick, USA.
Spider-Man (2002), Sam Raimi, USA.
Spider-Man 2 (2004) Sam Raimi, USA.
Sphinx (1981) Franklin J. Schaffner, USA.
Stagecoach (1939) John Ford, USA.
Stargate/Stargate, La Porte Des Étoiles (1994) Roland Emmerich, France/USA.
Starship Troopers (1997) Paul Verhoeven, USA.
Stealth (2005) Rob Cohen, USA.
Stella (1990) John Erman, USA.
Swordman II/Xiao Ao Jjiang Hu Zhi Dong Fang Bu Bai (1991) Siu-Tung Ching and Stanley Tong, Hong Kong.
Talos the Mummy/Tale of the Mummy (1998) Russell Mulcahy, UK/USA.
Tank Girl (1995) Rachel Talalay, USA.
Terminator 2: Judgement Day (1991) James Cameron, France/USA.
Terminator 3: The Rise of the Machines (2003) John Mostow, USA/Germany/UK.
Texas Rangers (2001) Steve Miner, USA.
The Awakening (1980) Mike Newell, UK/USA.
The Ballad of Little Jo (1993) Maggie Greenwald, USA.
The Bone Collector (1999) Phillip Noyce, USA.
The Champ (1931) King Vidor, USA.
The Children's Hour (1961) William Wyler, USA.
The Constant Gardener (2005) Fernando Meirelles, Germany/UK.
The Deaf and Mute Heroine/Long E Jian (1971) Ma Wu, Hong Kong.

The Emperor and the Assassin/Jing Ke Ci Qin Wang (1999) Keige Chen, France/Japan/China.

The Fate of Lee Kahn/Ying Chung Ge Zhi Fengbo (1974) King Hu, Hong Kong/Taiwan.

The Fifth Element/Cinquième Element (1997) Luc Besson, France/USA.

The Fox (1968) Mark Rydell, USA.

The General's Daughter (1999) Simon West, Germany/USA.

The German Sisters/Die Bleierne Zeit (1981) Margarethe von Trotta, West Germany.

The Ghost in the Shel/Kôkaku Kidôtai (1995) Mamoru Oshii, Japan/UK.

The Harder They Fall (1956) Mark Robson, USA.

The Heroic Trio/Dung Fong Saam Hap (1990) Jonny To, Hong Kong.

The Heroic Trio II: Executioners/Dai Hao Xia Zuhan (1993) Siu-Tung Ching, Jonnz To, Hong Kong.

The Hours (2002) Stephen Daldry, USA/ UK.

The Incredibles (2004) Brad Bird, USA.

The Killer/Dip Hyut Shueng Hung (1989) John Woo, Hong Kong.

The Killing of Sister George (1968) Robert Aldrich, USA.

The Lair of the White Worm (1988) Ken Russell, UK/USA.

The Last Seduction (1994) John Dahl, USA.

The Legend of Zu/Shu Shan Zheng Zuhan (2001) Hark Tsui, Hong Kong/China.

The Long Kiss Goodnight (1996) Renny Harlin, USA.

The Matrix (1999) Andy Wachowski and Larry Wachowski, USA.

The Messenger: The Story of Jean of Arc/Jeanne d'Arc (1999) Luc Besson, France.

The Missing (2003) Ron Howard, USA.

The Mummy (1932) Karl Freund, USA.

The Mummy/Terror of the Mummy (1959) Terence Fisher, USA/UK.

The Mummy (1999) Stephen Sommers, USA.

The Mummy Lives (1993) Gerry O'Hara, USA.

The Mummy Returns (2001) Stephen Sommers, USA.

The Mummy's Shroud (1967) John Gilling, UK.

The Naked Killer/Chiklo Gouzeung (1992) Clarence Fok Ziu-Leung, Hong Kong.

The Night Porter/Il Portiere Di Notte (1974) Lilana Cavani, Italy/USA.

The Old Maid (1939) Edmund Goulding, USA.

The Piano (1993) Jane Campion, Australia/New Zealand/France.

The Postman Always Rings Twice (1946) Taz Garnett, USA.

The Quick and the Dead (1995) Sam Raimi, USA/Japan.

The Red Shoes (1948) Michael Powell and Emeric Pressburger, USA.

The Road Home/Wo De Fu Qin Mu Qin (1999) Yimou Zangh, China.

The Sands of Iwo Jima (1949) Allan Dwan, USA.
The Set Up (1949) Robert Wise, USA.
*The Searchers (*1956) John Ford, USA.
The Story of the Kelly Gang (1906) Charles Tait, Australia.
The Terminator (1984) James Cameron, USA.
The Thief of Bagdad (1924) Raoul Walsh, USA.
The 36th *Chamber of Shaolin/Shaolin Sanshiliu Fang* (1978) Chia-Liang Liu, Hong Kong.
The X-Men (2000) Bryan Singer, USA.
Thelma and Louise (1991) Ridley Scott, USA.
Thirteen (2003) Catherine Hardwicke, USA.
Timeline (2003) Richard Donner, USA.
Top Gun (1986) Tony Scott, USA.
Trial of Jean Arc//Le Procès de Jeanne d'Arc (1962) Robert Bresson, France.
Sin City (2005) Robert Rodriguez and Frank Miller, USA.
Starship Troopers (1997) Paul Verhoeven, USA.
Unforgiven (1992) Clint Eastwood, USA.
Ultraviolet (2006) Kurt Wimmer, USA.
Ulzana's Raid (1972) Robert Aldrich, USA.
Vera Drake (2004) Mike Leigh, UK/ France/New Zealand.
Veronica Guerin (1998) Joel Schumacher, USA/Ireland/UK.
Violated (1984) Richard Cannistraro, USA.
Wonder Woman (1974) Vincent McEveety, USA.
Wrestling Women vs. the Aztec Mummy/Las Luchadoras Contra La Momia (1964) René Cardona, Mexico/USA.
X-2: X-Men United (2003) Brian Singer, USA.
Zatoichi (2003) Takeshi Kitano, Japan.
Zero Woman: Red Handcuffs/Zeroka No Onna: akai Wappa (1974) Yukio Noda, Japan.
Zero Woman 2 (1995) Daisuke Gotoh, Japan.
Zero Woman: Final Mission/Keishichô O-ka No Onna (1995) Koji Enokido, Japan.
Zero Woman: Assassin Lovers/Keishichô O-ka No Onna (1996) Masahide Kuwabara, Japan.
Zero Woman: The Hunted/Kesenai Kioku (1997) Norihisa Yoshimura, Japan.
Zero Woman: The Accused/Namae No Nai Onna (1997) Daisuke Gotoh, Japan.
Zero Woman: Dangerous Game/Abunai Yûgi (1998) Hidekazu Takahara, Japan.
Zero Woman Returns/Saigo No Shirei (1999) Yasushi Saisyu, Japan.

Television Movies and Series

Alias (2001–) Ken Olin, USA.
Batman (1966–8) Robert Butler, USA.
Buffy the Vampire Slayer (1997–2003) Joss Whedon, USA.
Cagney and Lacey (1982–8) Ted Post, USA.
Charlie's Angels (1976–81) Bill Bixby and Ivan Goff, USA.
Cold Case (2003–) Meredith Stiehm, USA.
Crossing Jordan (2001–) Tim Kring, USA.
Deadwood (2004–) David Milch, USA.
Firefly (2002–03) Joss Whedon, USA.
Joan of Arc (1999) Christian Duguay, Canada.
Kung Fu (1972–5) Jerry Thorpe, USA.
Marple: The Body in the Library (2004) Andy Wilson, UK.
Marple: 4.50 from Paddington (2004) Andy Wilson, UK.
Marple: The Murder in the Vicarage (2004) Charles Palmer, UK.
Marple: A Murder is Announced (2005) John Strickland, UK.
Nikita (1997-2001), Joel Surnow, Canada.
Over There (2005) Chris Gerolmo, USA.
Profiler (1996–2000) Ian Toynton, USA.
Red Heroine/HongXia (1929) Yinin Wen, China.
Sex and the City (1998–2004) Susan Seidelman, USA.
Star Trek (1966–9) Walter Jefferies, USA.
Stargate SG-I (1997–) William Gereghty, USA/Canada.
The Burning Bed (1984) Robert Greenwald, USA.
The Closer (2005–) Michael Robin, USA.
The Hardy Boys/Nancy Drew Mysteries (1977–9) John Dumas, USA.
The Librarian: Quest for the Spear (2004) Peter Winther, USA.
The Librarian II: Return to King Solomon's Mines (2006) Jonathan Frakes, USA.
The X-Files (1993–2002) Rob Bowman, USA.
Veronica Mars (2004–) Nick Mark, USA.
Wonder Woman (1975–9) Barry Crane, USA.

CONTRIBUTORS

Silke Andris is a visual anthropologist and filmmaker. Her research focuses on film studies, urban anthropology, youth culture and sports. She recently completed her PhD at the Centre for Cross-Cultural Research, Australian National University. Her thesis explores the embodied experiences of women in the full-contact sport of boxing. She has written and produced a documentary on women's boxing, called *Erin: Make Me or Break Me* (2006). She is currently researching the representations of gender in sports movies, which will be published in a forthcoming essay *On the Ropes: Gender Politics in the Boxing* published by Intervention Press.

Barbara Creed is Professor of Cinema Studies at the University of Melbourne. She is author of a number of books on the cinema including *The Monstrous-feminine: film, feminism and psychoanalysis*, *Pandora's Box: essays in film theory* and *Phallic Panic: film, horror and the primal uncanny*. She is currently researching the impact of Darwinian theory on the cinema which will be published in her forthcoming book, *The Darwinian Screen*.

Catherine Driscoll is Chair of Gender and Cultural Studies at the University of Sydney. Her research and teaching engages widely with cultural theory, popular culture, modernism, and youth studies and she has published in all those areas. Her first book, *Girls: Feminine Adolescence in Popular Culture and Cultural Theory*, was published by Columbia University Press in 2002.

Martin Flanagan is Senior Lecturer in Film and Media Studies at the University of Bolton, in the North West of England. He has recently published on issues around authorship, the blockbuster and cinematic adaptations of comics, and his work has appeared in the *New Review of Film and Television Studies* as well as in a number of edited collections. He is currently exploring the notion of the 'progressive violent movie' in relation to the film *V for Vendetta* (2006). He is also preparing a full-length study of the cinematic application of the theories of Mikhail Bakhtin, which was the focus of his doctoral thesis.

Ursula Frederick is an archaeologist and scholar of visual arts and material culture. Her particular research interests include the archaeology of contact and cross-cultural exchange, popular representations of archaeology, contemporary archaeologies, cultures of mobility, and the visual culture of mark-making behaviours. Ursula has published papers on art and archaeology. As well as undertaking doctoral research she coordinates a range of scholarly activities at the Centre for Cross-Cultural Research, The Australian National University in Canberra, Australia.

Leon Hunt is a Senior Lecturer in Film and TV Studies at Brunel University. He is the author of *British Low Culture: From Safari Suits to Sexploitation* (1998) and *Kung Fu Cult Masters: From Bruce Lee to Crouching Tiger* (2003). He has published widely on martial arts cinema, and contributed to *Framework, New Cinemas: Journal of Contemporary Film*, *British Crime Cinema* (1999), *British Horror Cinema* (2002), *Action TV* (2002), *Screenplay: Cinema/Videogames/Interfaces* (2002), and *Defining Cult Movies* (2003), amongst others. He is currently co-editing an anthology on transnational East Asian cinema and writing a book on the cult comedy *The League of Gentlemen* for the BFI's TV Classics series.

Catherine Summerhayes is a lecturer at the Film Studies and the Centre for New Media Arts, Australian National University (ANU). She is currently writing a monograph on the films of the internationally renowned Australian indigenous artist, Tracey Moffatt. *The Moving Images of Tracey Moffatt* will be published by Charta in Milan in 2008. Her major research areas are in documentary film studies and new media theory and performance. In 2004, she convened and directed *AD—Art of the Documentary*: a combined international conference, film competition for emerging filmmakers and film festival hosted by the National Institute of the Humanities & Creative Arts at ANU. Her work has been published in national and international journals and anthologies.

Polona Petek has recently completed her PhD in the Cinema Studies program at the University of Melbourne, Australia. She has been teaching in the program of Cinema Studies and has published articles on the psychoanalytic interpretations of the double in cinema, the prominence of the myth of Narcissus and Echo in spectatorship theories, and the Lacanian notion of the gaze in the films of David Cronenberg. Her current research focuses on the ongoing transformations of the public spheres as they pertain to cinema. Polona is working on a project involving diasporic, transnational and cosmopolitan modes of film representation, reception and circulation. She is particularly interested in these processes as they transpire in the cinemas of Europe's southern and eastern regions.

Yvonne Tasker teaches Film and Television Studies at the University of East Anglia, UK. She is the author and editor of a number of books including *Action and Adventure Cinema* (Routledge, 2004), *Working Girls: Gender and Sexuality in Popular Cinema* (Routledge, 1998) and *Spectacular Bodies: Gender, Genre and Action Cinema* (Routledge, 1993). She is currently researching representations of the military woman in different media which will be published in her forthcoming book, *Soldiers Stories: Military Women in Cinema and Television Since WWII* (Durham: Duke University Press).

INDEX

A League of Their Own, 20
A Question of Silence, 24
A Touch of Zen, 152
ability, 82
absence, 79–80, 114
action babe cinema, 57, 59, 155
action heroine, 22–23, 92, 129
Adam's Rib, 25
adventurer, 58
Aeon Flux, 5, 9, 12–13, 189
aesthetics of movement, 166
African-American woman, 134
agency, 5, 39–40, 42, 45–46, 49, 51, 71, 73, 100, 112, 115
agent, 101
Alien, 2, 21, 24–25, 28, 132
Alien Resurrection, 30
Alien³, 28, 30, 107
Aliens, 21, 78
All the Pretty Horses, 113
ambiguity, 66
American Dream, 102
American Outlaws, 113
Americanisation, 155
androgyny, 8, 27, 28, 42, 48, 156
android, 39, 57
anti-heroine, 22, 145, 150
anxieties, 81
appearance, 33–34, 57, 69
archaeologist, 56, 58
archaeology, 57, 70
armoury, 67
artefact, 56, 59, 61–62, 64
Asian cinema, 133
assassin, 132–33, 162, 170
athlete, 52, 88, 98, 101, 153
athleticism, 107
authority, 40, 84, 121, 136, 146
Bad Girls, 113
Base-Moi, 24
Basic, 79

Basinger, Jeanine, 83, 93
Batgirl, 168
Batman, 166, 168
Batman Returns, 168–69
Baudrillard, Jean, 50, 54
beauty, 154
beauty contest, 130
Beebe, Roger Warren, 48, 53
Beijing Opera, 152
Bergan, Roland, 96, 102, 110, 179
Beyond the Forest, 25
Black Cat, 133
Blade Runner, 44, 51, 189
blaxploitation, 7, 129, 131, 142
Blonde Venus, 21–22
Blood from the Mummy's Tomb, 61
Blue Steel, 21, 24, 129, 131, 140
Blue Velvet, 21
body, 8, 45, 81, 96–98, 168, 170, 172, 175
Body and Soul, 96
body armour, 46
Body Heat, 24
Bond girls, 165
boots, 168
boxing, 96–108
Boys Don't Cry, 22, 25
bravery, 34
Brokeback Mountain, 114
Butler, Judith, 100, 107
C'era una volta il West, 113
Calamity Jane, 113
Camille, 25
Campbell, Joseph, 19, 26, 35
career, 85
carnival, 136
Carr, Diane, 74, 77
catsuit, 169
Catwoman, 135, 142, 162, 166–74, 176, 183
Chamberlain, James, 104

Chan, Felicia, 154
Charlie's Angels, 79, 102, 155, 168
Charlie's Angles: Full Throttle, 7, 90
Chinatown, 21, 25
choice, 5, 42, 69, 79, 84–85, 90
class, 70, 85, 101
Cleopatra Jones, 7, 131, 135, 141, 179
clothing, 9, 32–33, 118, 163
coach, 98
colonial displacement, 122
Come Drink with Me, 147, 151, 156, 159, 187
comedy, 117, 135–36
comic book, 135, 170
conflict, 24, 28
    with authority, 22
    with patriarchal order, 24
    with patriarchy, 23
Confucian, 153–54
consumption, 100, 154
contagion, 116, 118
Copycat, 129
corporeality, 10, 103, 148
corruption, 25, 62, 92, 102, 137, 151, 156
costume, 66, 167, 169. *See* clothing, uniform, dress
costumes, 58, 175
courage, 28, 34
Courage Under Fire, 79, 86, 90, 94, 186
cowgirl, 116
Creed, Barbara, 47, 53, 94, 110, 134
criminal, 25, 167
cross-dressing, 152, 172
Crouching Tiger, Hidden Dragon, 2, 144–51, 153–56, 158, 160, 172, 177, 180, 198
cyborg, 31, 51, 38–54, 73
Dances With Wolves, 113
Daoism, 146
Daoist *fantastique*, 147
Dark Victory, 25
Darley, Andrew, 11
Deadwood, 114
death, 25, 27, 33, 104, 107, 157

as symbolic act, 25
decorative femininity, 139
Desert Hearts, 22
design intensity, 145
desire, 146
detective, 129
determination, 81
Dietrich, Marlene, 32–34
difference, 120
Dirty Harry, 131
disability, 104
Dishonoured, 19, 25, 32
disruption, 60, 64
Dominguez, Diana, 30, 36
Double Indemnity, 25
Douglas, Mary, 103
dress, 33–34. *See* clothing, costume, uniform.
Duel in the Sun, 113
duplicitous appearance. *See* appearance
duty, 59, 83
Elektra, 5, 9, 13, 170, 174
Ellen Ripley, 2, 16, 20, 22–31, 35, 132
embodiment, 87
emotion, 163–64
emotional excess, 172
empowered object, 61. *See* artefact
empowerment, 8, 100, 134, 138, 147, 154
Enter the Dragon, 165, 170, 173
equality, 85
espionage, 32
euthanasia, 105
evolution, 96
exceptional, 87
excess, 104, 164
Executioners from Shaolin, 151
exoticism, 118. *See* orientalism
failure, 6, 25, 83, 101, 120, 134, 150, 164
fantasy, 80, 135, 162, 164
Far From Heaven, 21, 25
Fat City, 102
fate, 5, 16, 39, 49–50, 101, 108, 122, 157

federal agent, 130
female masculinity, 80–81
female-centred narratives, 154
feminine, 39
feminine appearance, 87
feminine desire, 124
femininity, 30, 34, 99, 124, 139, 152, 163–64, 168–69, 174
feminism, 19, 57, 82, 90, 100, 121, 129, 131, 137, 146, 170
femme fatale, 7, 13, 16–17, 22, 32–33, 57, 156, 167, 168
fetishism, 80
fighting style, 147, 150, 163, 168–69, 171
film noir, 22, 25, 167
final fight, 96
final girl, 7
Firefly, 114
Fitzpatrick, Kathleen, 45
Five-point Exploding Heart Technique, 149
Foucault, Michel, 172
freedom, 146, 151, 153
friendship, 134
From Here to Eternity, 96
G.I.Jane, 2, 3, 7, 21, 78–93, 94, 99, 109
Game of Death, 173
gaming, 57–58, 64, 68, 71
gay, 134
gaze, 11, 27, 30, 47, 70
gender, 3, 27, 42, 45, 70, 85, 87, 97, 99, 106, 113, 117, 119, 122, 124, 131, 135, 146, 152, 156, 175
gender norms, 84, 107
gender paradigm, 163
gender play, 152
gender roles, 171
gender stereotypes, 47
gender traditionalism, 124
genre, 3, 4, 9, 23, 58, 67, 70, 79, 83, 102, 113, 115, 120, 131, 135, 148, 162, 164
Gilda, 21, 24
girl power, 169
Girlfight, 20, 101, 107

goddess, 52, 65, 68–69, 71–72, 150, 169
Gomes, Catherine, 154
gongfu, 148–49
gongfu pian, 146, 152, 158
Gorillas in the Mist, 21
Gracie Hart, 129–39
Grosz, Elizabeth, 103
guise, 2, 27, 32, 86, 147, 151–52, 156
guns, 69. *See* weapon
hair, 28, 34, 46, 87, 88
Haraway, Donna, 43–44, 51, 182
heretic, 26
Hero, 145, 152, 161–64, 166, 171, 175
heroine, 2, 4, 6, 8, 19, 20, 57, 102, 138, 145, 152, 154, 170
heroism, 45, 84, 97, 108, 158, 174
heterosexuality, 89
hierarchies, 172
high heels, 130, 133, 168
Hollywood, 2–3, 5, 18, 58, 78, 166, 172, 174
Hong Kong action cinema, 133
Hong, Fan, 153
House of Flying Daggers, 2, 144–46, 148, 150–59,165, 176, 179
human, 2, 39, 52
human resistance, 40
humanism, 45
humanity, 30, 39, 42, 118
humankind, 5
Humoresque, 25
humour, 136
hybridity, 118, 171, 175
hysteric, 26
I Spit on Your Grave, 7, 24, 181
iconic status, 81
identification, 165
identity, 4, 16, 19, 24, 26, 27–28, 31, 45, 58, 69, 71, 82, 88, 115, 118, 124, 134, 152, 175
In the Cut, 24
independence, 117, 124
Indiana Jones, 56–59, 66, 70, 73–74, 76–77
individualism, 8, 57, 84, 134

invincibility, 102
irony, 131
Jacobs, Lewis, 139
James Bond, 131, 165, 168
Jean at the Stake, 26
Jeffords, Susan, 91, 94
jianghu, 146, 151–54, 156–58
Joan of Arc, 15–16, 21, 26, 87
Johnny Guitar, 113, 124
Journey, 20, 124
Ju Dou, 145
Kennedy, Helen, 57, 73, 76
Kill Bill, 20, 21, 24, 79, 90, 114, 133, 149–50, 170, 173
Klute, 25
Krutnik, Frank, 97
kung fu, 164–65, 168
Kwok Wah Lau, Jenny, 156
La femme Nikita, 129, 132–33
La Jetée, 49
La Passion de Jeanne d'Arc, 15, 26
Lady from Shanghai, 25
Lady Snowblood, 173
Lair of the White Worm, 60, 66, 74, 194
landscape, 116
Lara Croft, 55–72
  Tomb Raider, 55–72, 102, 155
law enforcement, 132
Le Procès de Jeanne d'Arc, 26
Lee Palmer, Augusta, 156
Lehman, Peter, 115–16
lesbian, 25, 89, 116, 134
Lipstick, 24
Lo, Kwai-cheung, 155
Maggie Fitzgerald, 96–108
Maggie Gilkeson, 114–24
magic, 5, 147, 164, 170, 174
Magnum Force, 131
makeover, 87, 135, 137, 139
male attire, 27–28, 152. *See* guise
male order, 22, 33. *See* conflict with authority
manhood, 30
Mare Nostrum, 32
marginalisation, 115

Marnie, 21
Martial Arthouse, 4, 144–47, 152, 154–55, 157–58
martial artist, 162
martial arts cinema, 133, 161–62
masculinity, 30, 34, 79, 87, 89–90, 97, 99, 106–07, 116
masochism, 82
master, 147–48, 151
Mata Hari, 22, 25, 32
maternal, 5, 27, 48, 116, 119, 124, 130, 137
maternal instincts, 42
matriarch, 150
McGee, Patrick 124
melodrama, 138, 164, 171–72
melodramatic excess, 174. *See* excess
Memoirs of a Geisha, 145
Mildred Pierce, 21
Mile, Siân, 137
militarism, 32, 44
military, 32, 34, 44, 46
military woman, 78–80, 82–83, 85–88, 90–94
Million Dollar Baby, 2, 21, 25, 95–110, 179, 182, 184
miscegenation, 122
mise-en-scene, 32, 163
misogyny, 86
Miss Congeniality, 2, 9, 128–39, 140, 142, 187–88
*Miss Congeniality 2
  Armed and Fabulous*, 130
Mizejewski, Linda, 130–37, 139, 140–41, 143
mobility, 153
modernity, 78, 117–18, 120, 122, 146, 153, 157
monomyth, 18
Monster, 25, 31
monsterous-feminine, 68–69
morphing, 47
mortality, 5, 22, 66, 146–47, 174
mother, 34, 39, 114
movement-narrative, 100
Mulholland Dr., 21, 24

Mulvey, Laura, 11, 13, 132
murder, 91
muscle, 46, 87, 90
musculinity, 45, 53, 138
My Brilliant Career, 20, 22, 25
My Darling Clementine, 113
myth, 19, 118, 130
mythology, 164
narcissism, 139
narrative, 11, 17–18, 20, 43, 50, 60–61, 67, 79–80, 96, 114, 121, 148
narratives, 92
nationalism, 32–33
nature, 60
neomyth, 19, 30, 33
New Hollywood, 2, 4, 39, 108, 121, 133
newcomer, 131
Nikita, 133
November Moon, 21
Now Voyager, 20–21
nurses, 114
nuxia, 2, 145–48, 151–57
O'Day, Marc, 59, 93, 155, 160
Oates, Joyce Carol, 107
objectification, 170
On The Waterfront, 96
Once Upon a Time in the West, 113
Open Range, 114
orientalism, 146, 156–57, 168, 173, 175
other, 17, 23, 25, 34, 63, 69, 115, 118–19
otherness, 118, 121, 124
outlaw, 132
outsider, 25–26, 146
Over There, 92
pacifism, 82
Pale Mother, 24
Palm Power, 147, 149, 177
Palmer, Jerry, 136
patriarchal, 44, 48, 84, 124, 137
patriarchal oppression, 155
patriarchy, 91, 120, 129, 132, 149, 153–54
patriot, 26

patriotism, 33, 83
performance, 116
personal struggle, 164
phallic identity, 115
phallocentric, 17, 20, 22–23, 26, 28, 35
phallus, 69
physical combat, 23
physical prowess, 135
physical transformation, 79
Point of No Return, 133
police, 23, 101
political agenda, 82
Portrait of a Lady, 21
poster, 99
posthumanism. *See* humanism
postmodernism, 175
power, 33, 45, 150, 162
power reversal, 106
preparation, 99
Pretty Woman, 20, 22, 25
profession, 58–60, 83, 96–97, 101, 129–31
prostitute, 16, 19, 23, 25–26, 31–35, 114, 176
pseudo male, 25, 27, 30
Pumping Iron II: The Women, 107
punishment, 91
qingcheng qingguo, 156
race, 43, 85, 119
racial difference, 134
racial hierarchies, 83
racial representation, 118
racism, 119
Raging Bull, 96, 102, 107
Raiders of the Lost Ark, 59
Raise the Red Lantern, 145
rape, 7, 24, 90–92, 94, 127, 156, 165
realism, 173
Rebecca, 21
rebel, 156
Rebirth, 25, 33
Red Heroine, 147–48
reenactment, 71
revenge, 169
revenge narrative, 168

Reynaud, Berenice, 145, 148, 152, 158–59, 185
rite of passage, 86–87
Rocky, 96, 99, 102, 110
Romance, 24
routine, 100
Rowe, Kathleen, 136
Run Lola Run, 12, 74
Rush Hour 2, 144
saint, 6, 15–16, 26–27, 34
Sarah Connor, 2, 6, 16, 19, 24, 30, 38–53, 132
scars, 90
schizophrenic, 26
science-fiction, 9, 78, 138, 162
sci-fi Western, 114
scopophilia, 97
segregation, 85, 88
self-awareness, 40
self-care, 171
self-creation, 100
self-destruction, 105
self-discovery, 20, 24, 33, 71. *See* identity
self-fulfilment, 172
selfhood, 106
selfishness, 157
self-production, 100
self-sacrifice, 45, 152, 169
Serenity, 114
serial, 114, 138, 147, 164, 172
serial-queen, 138
sex, 122–23
Sex and the City, 24
sexual ambivalence, 168
sexual relations, 123
sexual struggle, 99
sexual violence, 91
sexualisation, 157
sexuality, 33, 134
Shane, 116
Shanghai Noon, 113
shenguai, 147
shifu, 147, 150
showgirl, 116
Silence of the Lambs, 24, 129, 131, 141

simulacra, 50
singularity, 7, 57, 68
sisterhood, 157
Six-Fingered Lord of the Lute, 152
social struggle, 164
soldier, 19, 22–23, 26–27, 33–34, 42, 78, 80, 83, 85, 89, 92, 99, 101
Somebody Up There Likes Me, 96
spectacle, 11, 79, 88, 116, 148, 174
Spider-Man, 166
spirituality, 164
sport, 96, 98, 102
spy, 32–33
star persona, 90
Star Trek, 78
Stargate, 62, 66, 74, 78, 196
Stargate SG-I, 78
Starship Troopers, 78
Stella, 21
subterranean, 64
success, 164
suffering, 27–28, 107, 124, 157, 173
suicide, 98, 157, 163, 165
superhero, 147, 162, 166, 168, 170
superheroine, 69, 129, 135, 162, 168, 170–71, 173–74
superhuman figures, 169
supernatural, 120–21
supernatural weapon, 170
superpower, 135
Swordsman II, 147
symbolic order, 21, 23, 25, 27–28, 31, 35, 103
Talos the Mummy, 61
Tank Girl, 56, 137, 142
Tarantino, Quentin, 114, 133, 149, 173
Tasker, Yvonne, 12, 13, 42, 46–47, 73, 94, 102, 108–10, 116, 126, 133–34, 137, 141, 143, 186, 188
Taylor, Charles, 121
technique, 175
technological reproduction, 120
technologies of the self, 171
technology of the body. *See* body
Terminator 2, 21, 38, 53
    Judgement Day, 19, 38–53, 132

Terminator 3, 39

test, 87, 99, 124

Texas Rangers, 113

The 36th Chamber of Shaolin, 149

The Awakening, 61

The Ballad of Little Jo, 22, 113

The Burning Bed, 21

The Champ, 96

The Children's Hour, 25

The Constant Gardener, 21

The Deaf and Mute Heroine, 151

The Emperor and the Assassin, 163

The Fate of Lee Khan, 156

The Fox, 25

The General's Daughter, 79, 91

The German Sisters, 21

The Ghost in the Shell, 51

The Harder They Fall, 102

The Heroic Trio, 133

*The Heroic Trio II
    Executioners*, 133

The Hours, 21

The Incredibles, 5, 194

The Journey, 20

The Killer, 165–66

The Killing of Sister George, 22

The Last Seduction, 24

*The Librarian II: Return to King
    Solomon's Mines*, 62

The Long Kiss Goodnight, 24

The Matrix, 90, 156, 177

*The Messenger: The Story of Jean of
    Arc*, 12, 26

The Missing, 2, 112–28, 187

The Mummy, 60

The Naked Killer, 133

The Night Porter, 24

The Old Maid, 21

The Perils of Pauline, 138

The Piano, 21, 24

The Postman Always Rings Twice, 25

The Quick and the Dead, 113–14, 124

The Red Shoes, 20

The Searchers, 3, 112–27, 181, 183,
    186

The Set Up, 102

The Terminator, 2, 19, 21, 24, 39

The Threshold, 20–21, 24–25, 33

The X-Men, 155, 170

Thelma and Louise, 24–25, 107, 129,
    132

Thirteen, 123

Thomson, David, 122

time, 61, 64

Timeline, 62, 65, 71

time-travel, 39, 42, 59, 62–64

time-zone, 39, 43

tomboy, 113, 118, 126, 136

Toole, F.X., 107

tradition, 86, 157

training, 81, 87, 102, 135, 147–48, 164

transformation, 17, 19, 22, 31, 47, 67,
    79–82, 87, 89–90, 97, 98, 100–01,
    136–37, 142, 155, 168

transgression, 60, 64, 71, 88, 96, 103,
    107, 110, 136, 152, 157

transnational action heroine, 146

transnationality, 153

transvestite theatre, 152

treachery, 163

trial, 96

triumph, 87

Ulzana's Raid, 121

unfeminine, 138

Unforgiven, 113

uniform, 23. *See* clothing, costume

vengeance, 121, 124, 163

Vera Drake, 21, 24

Veronica Guerin, 24

victimisation, 101

victory, 99. *See* success

video game, 135

viewer, 27

vigilante, 132, 137

Violated, 24

violence, 10, 90, 166

virgin, 26, 34

visibility, 79

Vivre Sa Vie, 15, 20, 22, 25, 35

vulnerability, 90, 102, 117, 173

wanderlust, 121

war, 40, 49

war film, 99
wardrobe, 168
warrior woman, 2, 22–23, 25–26, 28, 31–33, 35, 65, 69, 153, 157, 162, 174
weakness, 175
weapon, 9, 23, 150, 163, 169–70, 172, 174. *See* guns
Western, 112–24
wife, 34
wilderness, 116, 122
Williams, Linda Ruth, 86–87, 93, 99, 176
willingness, 82. *See* choice
willpower, 107
winning, 101, 107
witch, 26, 119
woman as hero, 17

woman warrior, 36. *See* warrior woman
womanhood, 30, 139
woman-on-top, 56, 64
wound, 9, 44, 46, 169, 174
wounded girl, 168
Wudang, 147–51
wuxia, 4, 8, 145–51, 154, 157, 159, 164–66, 168, 171–74, 177
wuxia pian, 145–46, 148, 152, 158, 160, 162, 163–65, 175
xia, 146–47, 151, 157
Yimou, Zhang, 144–46, 158–60, 162, 177
youth, 154
Zemon-Davis, Natalie, 64
Zero Woman: Red Handcuffs, 133
Zhang, Ziyi, 151, 154, 158
Zhen, Zhang, 154, 157